2

Revise
PE
for Edexcel

second edition

by

Dennis Roscoe
Jan Roscoe

A2 Revise PE for Edexcel
second edition

by
Dennis Roscoe
Jan Roscoe

Jan Roscoe Publications Ltd
An imprint of Heath Books Ltd

First edition published in 2010 by Jan Roscoe Publications.
Second edition September 2017.

Heath Books Ltd
Willow House, Willow Walk
Sutton
Surrey
SM3 9QQ
United Kingdom

tel: 020 8644 7788
fax: 020 8641 3377
email: orders@heathbooks.co.uk

A Catalogue record for this book is available from the British Library.

ISBN 978-1-911-24103-4.

Cover designs by Roscoe Rutter.

Published via Adobe InDesign, CorelDraw 10.410, Adobe Illustrator 9.0, Smartdraw 6.0, laid out and typeset by Dennis Roscoe

Printed and bound by

Hobbs the Printers Limited
Brunel Road
Totton
Hampshire
SO40 3WX
United Kingdom

tel: 023 8066 4800
fax: 023 8066 4801

email: estimating@hobbs.uk.com

INTRODUCTION

This 'A' level PE book has been written to address the changes in content and style of the Edexcel Level 3 Advanced Year 2 GCE Physical Education (9PE0) syllabus which commences in September 2017.

These Physical Education syllabuses are multi-disciplinary in nature, covering applied anatomy and exercise physiology, skill acquisition and sports psychology, and historical and contemporary studies. These subject areas have generated a substantial quantity of specialist literature each with its own specific language. At times you may be overwhelmed by the amount of material covered, however this book addresses the problem of dealing with copious notes by summarising the content of the subject matter and attempting to explain in simple language what are sometimes complicated concepts or issues.

Practice questions are provided at the end of each chapter, and answers can be downloaded by going to the following link: http://www.jroscoe.co.uk/downloads/a2_revise_pe_edexcel/ on the JRP website. The answers will amplify the subject matter and provide clues as to how the exam itself should be approached. A continuing feature is that there will be a number of multiple choice questions on each exam paper, and we include a small number of such questions at the end of each chapter along with the practice questions. There is also a requirement that the final exam questions on each section of the syllabus shall include an essay type answer worth 15 marks. This allows students to express their ability and knowledge in the context of properly written language (prose) with attention to grammar and punctuation. Question assessment guidelines and use of terminology are included immediately before the index section in this book.

Materials are presented in a concise and visual approach for effective and efficient revision. Modern terminology, nomenclature and units have been used wherever possible. At the end of the book there is a comprehensive index for easy reference.

Please note that students are recommended to have a clear understanding of the content as outlined in the Edexcel (Pearson) specification and not rely solely on this guide.

HOW TO USE THIS REVISION GUIDE

The ideal use of this Revision Guide would be to purchase it at the start of the course and relate each of the summary pages to the specific areas of the syllabus as an aide memoire. The inclusion of specific questions and full answers (to be found on the following link: http://www.jroscoe.co.uk/downloads/a2_revise_pe_edexcel/) provide a means of self-testing. Each chapter has its own link specified on the questions pages. Don't be tempted to find out the answers before attempting a question.

In reality, whole examination questions contain a much broader content than those given in this guide. Examiners will attempt to examine more than one small area of the syllabus within the context of one full question and therefore it is important that you revise all aspects of your syllabus. You are advised to print off your Edexcel (Pearson) syllabus specification for a clear understanding of the syllabus content and not rely solely on this revision guide.

The main use of the Revision Guide should be during the final revision period leading up to your examinations, as it should help you to understand and apply concepts i.e. link summary content with examination question.

The aim of this book is to provide an aid that enhances syllabus analysis, and to raise your level of success in examinations.

THE QUALITY OF AUTHORS

The authors are experts in the physical education field and have considerable experience in teaching 'A' Level Physical Education. They have written examination syllabuses, and have set and marked examination questions within this subject area and taught at revision workshops throughout the UK. Much of the material within this book has been thoroughly student tested.

The authors hope that this Revision Guide will prove useful to staff and students. Jan Roscoe Publications will welcome any comments you would wish to make about the book's utility or layout. Thank you for using this work.

Dennis Roscoe
Jan Roscoe

ACKNOWLEDGMENTS

The authors wish to thank Bob Davis for his contribution in the Historical and Contemporary Issues elements of this book. Thanks are also due to Helen Roscoe-Rutter and David Roscoe-Rutter for their contributions as cover designers and photographers, Debbie Francis of Heath Books and Gary Dobson as proof readers, and Lois Cresswell, Jenny Pacey, Helen Roscoe-Rutter and Osian Jones for their patience as photographic models. The authors wish to thank members of the Belgian Olympic Athletics Squad for permission to use their images. **Dennis Roscoe -** *Editor*

ACKNOWLEDGMENTS FOR GRAPHICS

p. 14 figure 1.5 Caterine Ibarguen Rio Olympics 2016, Erik Van Leewen/Wikipedia.org,

p. 18 figure 1.11 S.Kuvona/Shutterstock.com, p. 19 figure 1.13 Maxipsort/ Shutterstock.com,

p. 24 figure 1.21 Chuck Wagner/ Shutterstock.com, p. 30 figure 2.2 Praissaeng/ Shutterstock.com,

p. 32 figure 2.4 Singaporeoesteopathy/Pinterest.com, p. 40 figure 2.12 Aircast ankle brace,

p. 41 figure 2.13 Loughborough University Sport Technology Institute,

p. 43 figure 2.17 PhysioRoom.com, p. 44 figure 2.19 well photo/Shutterstock.com,

p. 45 figure 2.21 sylv1rob1/Shutterstock.com, p. 47 figure 2.25 fibromyjianewtoday.com,

p. 58 figure 3.9 Sergey Nivens/Shutterstock.com, p. 66 figure 4.2 Biles Rio Olympics 2016, A. Richardo/Shutterstock.com,

p. 68 figure 4.5 Dmitry Morgan/Shutterstock.com, p. 72 figure 4.17 Loughborough University Sport Technology Institute,

p. 74 figure 4.22 Wth/Shutterstock.com, p. 75 figure 4.26 Wikipedia Commons.org,

p. 82 figure 5.1 Avevizavi/Shutterstock.com, p. 84 figure 5.6 Snap2Art/Shutterstock.com,

p. 85 figure 5.7 Mitch Gunn/Shutterstock.com, p. 87 figure 5.11 Chris Van Lennep/Shutterstock.com,

p. 93 figure 5.22 Physical Education and the Study of Sport 5e, ISBN 978072343750,

p. 94 figure 5.26 Sergey Nivens/Shutterstock.com, p. 97 figure 6.3 Leonard Zhukovsky/Shutterstock.com,

p. 99 figure 6.7 Ligfo/Shutterstock.com, figure 6.8 maradon333/Shutterstock.com,

p. 100 figure 6.11 Dame Jessica Ennis-Hill Anton Ivanov/Shutterstock, p. 101 figure 6.12 Shahjehan/Shutterstock.com,

p. 103 figure 6.15 Johanna Konta, Jimmy48 photography/Shutterstock.com,

p. 104 figure 6.17 K Richardson-Walsh @katewalsh11, p. 106 figure 6.20 David Rogers/Getty images,

p. 112 figure 7.2 mmichaelangelo/Shutterstock.com, figure 7.3 Miche+alpuche/Shutterstock.com,

p. 113 figure 7.5 Leonard Zhukovsky/Shutterstock.com, p. 119 figure 7.11 Sue Barker Wimbledon2017 On the box,

p. 120 figure 7.13 Nicola Adams Wikipedia Commons.org, p. 121 figure 7.16 Wikipedia Commons.org,

p. 122 figure 7.17 IOC Sport for Hope programme, figure 7.18 Hatters/flickr.com,

p. 123 figure 7.19 singularityhub.com, p. 129 figure 7.25 Wikipedia Commons.org,

p. 132 figure 7.31 Chris Froome flickr.com, p. 138 figure 8.2 Wikipedia Commons.org,

p. 139 figure 8.5 webphotographer/istockphoto.com, p. 142 figure 8.11 Vlad/Shutterstock.com,

p. 143 figure 8.12 UEFA 2016 Alberto Girotto/ Shutterstock.com,

p. 147 figure 8.15 Maria Sharapova Leonard Zhukovsky/Shutterstock.com,

p. 147 figure 8.16 Marcos Mesa Sam Worldey/Shutterstock.com,

p. 148 figure 8.17 Sir Bradley Wiggins Yoann Morin/Shutterstock.com,

p. 150 figure 8.20 Andrew Safonov/Shutterstock.com, p. 151 figure 8.21 Diane Modahl Wikimedia Commons.org,

p. 153 figure 8.22 Club betting/flickr.com, p. 156 figure 8.24 Dwain Chambers Maxisport/Shutterstock.com,

p. 157 figure 8.25 Hillsborough Kenny1/Shutterstock.com,

p. 165 figure 9.5 Air images/Shutterstock.com , figure 9.6 Sport England, figure 9.7 StreetGames.org,

p. 166 figure 9.8 David Beckham Everett Collection/Shutterstock.com,

p. 172 figure 9.18 GB Women's hockey team Rio Olympics 2016, BOA/Andy Ryan,

p. 173 figure 9.20 well photo/Shutterstock.com, p. 177 figure 9.24 pinterest.com,

p. 144 figure 9.24 domhnall doda/Shutterstock.com

All other photographs or graphics are by Helen Roscoe-Rutter, David Roscoe-Rutter, Jan Roscoe, Dennis Roscoe, Bob Davis or other free sources.

We have made every effort to trace all copyright holders, but if any have been inadvertently overlooked, the publishers will be pleased to make the necessary arrangements as soon as possible. We have also used current website and other URL information which is accurate at the date of going to press, but may be subject to changes made by owners and authors.

HIGH QUALITY PHOTOS

QUALITY GRAPHS

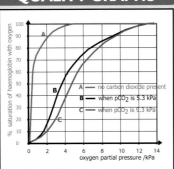

REVISION SUMMARY NOTES

Disadvantages of the part method
- Transfer from part to whole may be ineffective.
- Highly organised skills are very difficult to break down.
- Difficult to create kinaesthetic feel/sense of skill.
- Can be **demotivating** for performer.
- Can be **time consuming**.

REVISION SUMMARY CHARTS

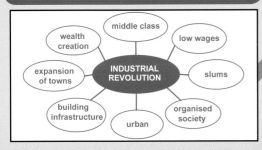

ANSWERS TO QUESTIONS are found on the JRP Website

20) With reference to sporting performance, explain how cognitive and somatic anxiety differ.   5 marks
Answer:
You must use a sporting example in your answer.
- *Cognitive anxiety is a psychological response consisting of:*
- *Worry.*
- *Inability to concentrate.*
- *Loss of attention.*
- *Fear of failure.*
- *For example, worry that a tennis opponent is a much better player than you.*

For **full listings** see the
JRP Catalogue or visit
www.jroscoe.co.uk

ROSCOE et al
AS/A1 Revise PE for Edexcel
ISBN 978-1-901-42488-1

Our Revise Series covers all aspects of the examinable AS and 'A' Level year 1 Edexcel syllabus which commenced in September 2016. The book consists of student notes, full colour illustrations, photographs and exam questions. Key concepts are clearly defined with examples that can be used in answers to exam questions, enabling the student to self-test. Answers are provided via a link to the JRP Website. This student revision guide supports a comprehensive revision plan and will enhance student grades.

HOW TO ORDER

tel **+44(0)208 644 7788**
(open 9am-5.30pm)

fax **+44(0)208 641 3377**
(open 24 hours a day)

email **orders@heathbooks.co.uk**

by post to: **Heath Educational Books,
Willow House, Willow Walk, Off Whittaker Rd,
Sutton, Surrey, SM3 9QQ**

CONTENTS

A2 Revise PE for Edexcel

Endorsement Statement

In order to ensure that this resource offers high-quality support for the associated Pearson qualification, it has been through a review process by the awarding body. This process confirms that this resource fully covers the teaching and learning content of the specification or part of a specification at which it is aimed. It also confirms that it demonstrates an appropriate balance between the development of subject skills, knowledge and understanding, in addition to preparation for assessment.

Endorsement does not cover any guidance on assessment activities or processes (e.g. practice questions or advice on how to answer assessment questions), included in the resource nor does it prescribe any particular approach to the teaching or delivery of a related course.

While the publishers have made every attempt to ensure that advice on the qualification and its assessment is accurate, the official specification and associated assessment guidance materials are the only authoritative source of information and should always be referred to for definitive guidance.

Pearson examiners have not contributed to any sections in this resource relevant to examination papers for which they have responsibility.

Examiners will not use endorsed resources as a source of material for any assessment set by Pearson.
Endorsement of a resource does not mean that the resource is required to achieve this Pearson qualification, nor does it mean that it is the only suitable material available to support the qualification, and any resource lists produced by the awarding body shall include this and other appropriate resources.

1
APPLIED ANATOMY AND PHYSIOLOGY

CHAPTER 1
ENERGY SYSTEMS, FATIGUE and RECOVERY

CHAPTER 1: *Energy systems, fatigue and recovery*

Energy definitions

Energy is the capacity to do work, and work has a mechanical definition,
namely **work = force x distance** moved in the direction of the force.
Energy and work are measured in joules (J).

Chemical energy is energy that is produced by a complex series of chemical reactions,
which can then be made available as **kinetic energy** and **potential energy**.
Chemical energy in the form of ATP is the most useful form of energy in living systems
because it is used to run almost all functional processes.

figure 1.1 – kinetic
energy in motion

All chemical reactions either give out energy (**exothermic reaction**) or take in energy
(**endothermic reaction**). The clever way that the biological system works is to **take in**
energy (endothermic) with a series of chemical reactions from food and fuel, and **give
out** the same energy (exothermic) with a **different** series of chemical reactions in order
to provide energy for muscular contractions and other bodily functions. In muscle tissue,
chemical energy is converted into **mechanical energy** when the muscle contracts.

Kinetic energy is energy due to the movement or motion of an object, observed by the
constant moving of an object or living thing, for example, a person running (figure 1.1) or
walking and a bouncing ball.

Potential energy is stored energy that has the potential or capacity to do work but is not
presently doing so. For example, your leg muscles have potential energy when you sit still
in a chair. When potential energy is released it is converted into kinetic energy.

Mechanical energy is energy directly produced by forces which do work in moving
matter. For example, when you ride a bike, your legs provide the mechanical energy
for moving the pedals and propelling the bike (figure 1.2).

figure 1.2 – mechanical energy
converting to kinetic energy

Electrical energy results from the movement of charged particles. In the human
body, electrical currents are generated when charged particles called ions move along
and across cell membranes. The nervous system uses electrical currents called nerve
impulses to transmit messages from one part of the body to another.

STUDENT NOTE

Refresh your memory on the transmission of an action potential down an axon of
a motor neurone, by referring to AS/A1 Revise PE for Edexcel A Student Revision
Guide ISBN 9781901424881, Chapter 5 page 68.

Power is the **rate** at which energy is used, or the energy used per second which is measured in
watts (W). Power can be calculated using the formula:

$$\text{power} = \frac{\textbf{energy (in joules)}}{\textbf{time (in seconds)}} \quad \text{(answer in watts)}$$

Energy transfer in the body

We derive our energy from food, namely carbohydrates (CHO), fats, and to a lesser
extent proteins.

The energy derived from carbohydrates, fats and proteins is stored in bodily tissues in the
form of a high energy compound called **adenosine triphosphate** (ATP), which can be
generated via three different processes:

• **ATP-PC** system (also called the alactic anaerobic system).

• **Anaerobic glycolytic** system also known as the **lactic acid** system (which is also anaerobic).

• **Aerobic** system.

ATP - adenosine triphosphate

ATP is the compound which stores energy and is therefore the energy currency linked to **intensity** and **duration** of physical activity. ATP exists in every living tissue and its breakdown gives energy for all life functions - this includes the action of the liver and the brain for example, as well as the contraction of muscle tissue. All muscular activity requires the availability and breakdown of ATP (figure 1.3).

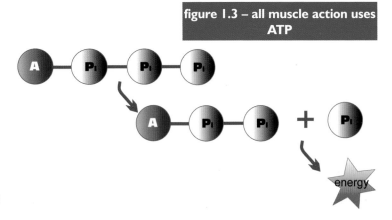

figure 1.3 – all muscle action uses ATP

The energy released during tissue respiration is stored in the chemical bonds in ATP, and this energy is released (an exothermic reaction) during the reaction:

$$\text{ATP} \rightarrow \text{ADP} + P_i + \text{energy}$$

Resynthesis of ATP from ADP (**adenosine diphosphate)** uses the reaction:

$$\text{energy} + \text{ADP} + P_i \rightarrow \text{ATP}$$

This is an **endothermic** reaction since energy is **given** to the molecule to enable the reaction to happen. This energy will be derived from **food fuels**.

The enzymatic catabolism (breakdown) of fat within the muscle cell mitochondria is termed **beta-oxidation**. Energy derived from the breakdown of **free fatty acids** (FFAs) is the preferred fuel food for long duration, low intensity exercise. The fatty acid molecule transforms into **acetyl-CoA** in the mitochondria. This reaction involves the successive splitting of 2-carbon acyl fragments from the long chain of the fatty acid.

Anaerobic energy systems

The ATP-PC system

This system of replenishing of ATP from ADP is the predominant one for activity which lasts between 3 and 10 seconds, which means for high intensity maximum work, for example, flat out sprinting - the 100m sprint.

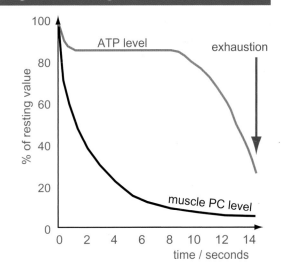

figure 1.4 – changes in muscle ATP and PC

No oxygen is needed - the process is **anaerobic**. The chemical reactions within this system are a **coupled reaction** in which ATP is resynthesised via **phosphocreatine** (PC) stored in muscle cell sarcoplasm.

The following reactions take place:

$$\text{PC} \rightarrow P_i + C + \text{energy}$$
$$\text{energy} + \text{ADP} + P_i \rightarrow \text{ATP}$$

The two reactions together are called a **coupled reaction** and are facilitated by the enzyme **creatine kinase** (CK).

The net effect of these two coupled reactions is:

$$\text{PC} + \text{ADP} \rightarrow \text{ATP} + C$$

PC is re-created in muscle cells during the recovery process, which requires energy and is an **endothermic** reaction.

During intense exercise, peak anaerobic power is attained within the first 5 seconds, and depletion of PC occurs between 7 and 9 seconds (figure 1.5, page 14).

Look at the graph in figure 1.4 showing changes in muscle ATP and PC. After an initial small fall, the ATP level is maintained, then falls as the PC is used up because the energy from PC is being used to resynthesise ATP.

The ATP-PC system

This causes PC levels to fall rapidly to zero after about 10 seconds. The capacity to maintain ATP production at this point depends on the anaerobic glycolytic or lactic acid system.

> **STUDENT NOTE**
>
> This process does not directly require glucose as an energy source - but the re-creation of PC during recovery will do so.

Anaerobic glycolytic system or the lactic acid system

Glycolysis (figure 1.6) is anaerobic (without the presence of oxygen) and takes place in the muscle cell sarcoplasm.

- Carbohydrate, from the food we eat, is stored as glycogen in and liver tissues.

- Glycogen is converted into **glucose** by the hormone glucagon, released when blood glucose levels fall (when glucose is used during tissue respiration).

- The breakdown of glucose provides the energy to rebuild ATP from ADP.

- This is facilitated by enzymes such as **glycogen phosphorylase** (GPP) and **phosphofructokinase** (PFK).

- The whole process produces **pyruvic acid**.

- Pyruvic acid is then converted to **lactic acid** by the enzyme **lactate dehydrogenase** (LDH).

- Rapid glycolysis allows ATP to form quickly without oxygen, generating **2 ATPs** per molecule of glucose.

As work intensity increases, lactic acid starts to accumulate above resting values, which produces **muscle fatigue** and pain. The resultant low pH inhibits enzyme action and cross-bridge formation, hence muscle action is inhibited and physical performance deteriorates.

The lactic acid system is the predominant one used to resynthesise ATP in sport or activities in which the flat-out effort lasts up to 30-60 seconds. For example, a 400m run or a 100m swim.

After exercise stops, extra oxygen is taken up to remove lactic acid by changing it back into pyruvic acid - this is the **EPOC** (**Excess Post-exercise Oxygen Consumption**, sometimes called the oxygen debt), see page 19 for the details of EPOC.

Aerobic energy system

The aerobic energy system releases stored energy from muscle glycogen, fats and proteins.

The aerobic system (figure 1.7, page 15) relies on the presence of oxygen to completely break down stored energy (from muscle glycogen, fats and proteins) into carbon dioxide, water and energy.

The energy yield is high – one molecule of glucose yields 36 molecules of ATP (note that in the lactic acid process the yield is two molecules of ATP). This process will continue indefinitely until energy stores run out.

figure 1.5 – triple jump - under 7 seconds to complete

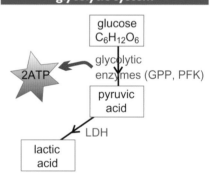

figure 1.6 – anaerobic glycolytic system

glucose $C_6H_{12}O_6$

glycolytic enzymes (GPP, PFK)

2ATP

pyruvic acid

LDH

lactic acid

Stage one - glycolysis

The first stage of the aerobic process is the same as that in the anaerobic glycolytic system namely glycolysis, i.e. the conversion of glycogen into two molecules of pyruvic acid (page 14), two ATP molecules and a number of hydrogen atoms. This process occurs via a series of 10 chemical reactions within the cell sarcoplasm.

From this point on, all chemical reactions involved in the aerobic system take place within the muscle cell mitochondria. The mitochondrion is often referred to as the power house of the cell, since it is the site of most energy production.

ATP regenerated = 2 ATP per molecule of glucose.

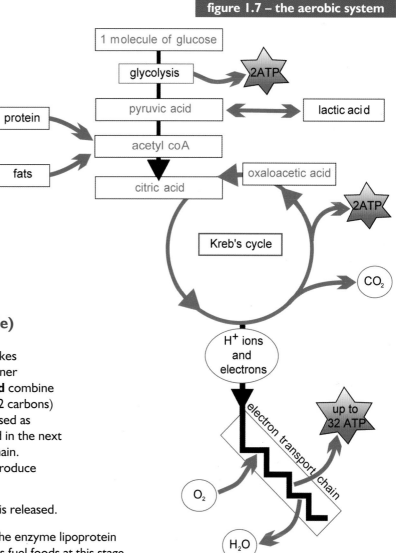

figure 1.7 – the aerobic system

Stage two - Kreb's cycle (citric acid cycle)

This stage occurs in the **presence of oxygen**, and takes place in the **muscle cell mitochondria** within the inner **fluid filled** matrix. Here, 2 molecules of **pyruvic acid** combine with **oxaloacetic acid** (4 carbons) and **acetyl coA** (2 carbons) to form citric acid (6 carbons). The citric acid is oxidised as hydrogen is removed from this compound to be used in the next stage of energy production, the electron transport chain. Carbon and oxygen are left behind and combine to produce carbon dioxide which is eliminated via the lungs.

In addition, energy sufficient to resynthesise **2 ATPs** is released.

Free fatty acids (FFA) from body fat, facilitated by the enzyme lipoprotein lipase, and protein (keto acids from muscle) can act as fuel foods at this stage, as indicated in figure 1.7 as exercise duration increases. Stored fat represents the body's most plentiful energy source.

Protein also serves as a potentially important energy substrate for long duration, endurance-type activities. The protein-to-energy pathways occur at two sites, acetyl-CoA and directly into Kreb's cycle. After nitrogen removal from the amino acid molecule during **deamination**, the remaining carbon skeleton enters the metabolic pathway to produce ATP aerobically or is converted to fat for further future energy needs.

Stage three - the electron transport chain

The **electron transport chain** occurs in the presence of oxygen within the **cristae** (inner part of the muscle cell mitochondria). The hydrogen given off at Krebs cycle is carried to the electron transport chain by **hydrogen carriers** (NADs and FADs). The hydrogen is split into hydrogen ions (H^+) and electrons (e^-). During a step-by-step chemical reaction, the hydrogen ions are oxidised to produce water (H_2O) and the electrons provide the energy to resynthesise ATP.

Aerobic respiration

In summary, the total effect of aerobic respiration is that it is an **endothermic** reaction:

$$\text{glucose} + \textbf{36ADP} + \textbf{36P}_i + \textbf{6O}_2 \rightarrow \textbf{6CO}_2 + \textbf{36ATP} + \textbf{6H}_2\textbf{O}$$

Fat fuels produce 2 ATPs less per molecule than glucose.

Energy transfer during long duration/lower activity exercise

The aerobic system requires carbohydrate in the form of **glucose** which is **derived from glycogen** stored in muscle cells (mostly slow twitch - SO type I) or in the liver.

The graph in figure 1.8 shows how the rate of usage of muscle glycogen is high during the first 30 minutes of steady exercise - which has to be replaced if a sportsperson is to continue at the same rate. Hence consumption of energy drinks and bananas during a long tennis match.

After the first 30 minutes of exercise, the body runs out of its glycogen stores and then turns mainly to what is left of the glucose in the blood and then finally to fatty acids and amino acids (derived from muscle protein).

By far the largest energy reserve in the human body is adipose tissue **triglycerides**, and these reserves are an important source of fuel during prolonged endurance exercise. As exercise progresses from low to moderate intensity, for example, 25-65% $\dot{V}O_{2max}$, the rate of total fat oxidation increases due to a relatively large use of intramuscular triglycerides.

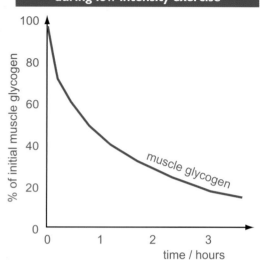

figure 1.8 – change in muscle glycogen during low intensity exercise

STUDENT NOTE

The abbreviation $\dot{V}O_2$ indicates oxygen uptake or consumption where the VO_2 denotes the volume consumed and the dot placed above the V expresses oxygen uptake as per minute.

Endurance athletes can utilise **free fatty acids** (FFAs) during prolonged exercise sooner than untrained people. This training adaptation enables the trained athlete to not use glycogen up immediately, but save it for later on in an exercise effort, or when the intensity of exercise increases. This is called **glycogen sparing**.

During exercise, the human body consumes large amounts of oxygen. The characteristics of oxygen uptake ($\dot{V}O_2$) kinetics differ with exercise intensity. When exercise is performed at a given work rate which is below lactate threshold (LT), $\dot{V}O_2$ increases exponentially to a **steady-state level**.

Figure 1.9 illustrates oxygen consumption during a 20 minute slow jog at a steady pace. At rest oxygen consumption is low, followed by a rapid increase during the first minute of the jog, to reach a relative plateau or steady state of aerobic metabolism between 4-6 minutes. This steady state represents a balance between energy required by the body and rate of aerobic ATP production.

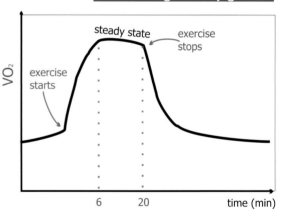

figure 1.9 – oxygen uptake during a slow jog

$\dot{V}O_{2max}$ is therefore a key component of aerobic endurance and is called **aerobic power** or **maximum oxygen uptake**, and so represents an accurate indicator of an athlete's fitness.

Energy continuum of physical activity

This describes the process by which ATP is regenerated via the different energy systems depending on the **intensity** and **duration** of exercise. Although **all** the systems contribute to ATP regeneration during any activity, one or other of the energy systems usually provides the major contribution for a given activity. Table 1.1 shows approximate proportions of ATP resynthesised via aerobic and anaerobic pathways for some sporting activities.

Table 1.1 – **percentage contribution of the aerobic and anaerobic energy systems to different sports**

sport or event	aerobic %	anaerobic (all) %
100m sprint	0	100
200m sprint	10	90
100m swim	20	80
boxing	30	70
800m run	40	60
hockey	50	50
2000m rowing	60	40
4000m cycle pursuit	70	30
3000m run	80	20
cross country run	90	10
marathon	100	0

figure 1.10 – variation in contribution of energy systems

% of maximum rate of energy production

overall performance

ATP store

ATP-PC system

lactic acid system

aerobic system

base rate

2s 10s 60s 2hrs time

T = threshold point

The graph in figure 1.10 shows how the different energy systems contribute resynthesis of ATP during flat-out exercise. Obviously, at reduced intensity of exercise, the contributions will be slightly different. But note that **all systems** are contributing from the start of exercise, only it takes some time for the lactic acid and aerobic systems to get going.

Short-term responses - thresholds

The concept of a **threshold** applies to the time at which one particular system of ATP regeneration takes over from another as the major regenerator of ATP during flat out exercise - marked as **T** in figure 1.10.

- For example, **ATP muscle stores** are depleted **within 2 seconds**, and towards the end of this period the ATP-PC system has risen enough to be able to provide the ATP necessary for the exercise.
- **Peak anaerobic power** is attained within the first 5 seconds of flat-out exercise, but depletion of PC occurs between 7 and 9 seconds.
- At this point, the lactic acid system has risen enough to be able to provide the ATP required for the next 40 seconds or so.

Hence the **threshold** between **ATP-PC and lactic acid** systems occurs between 7 and 9 seconds after the start of an exercise period. The lactate threshold occurs at the highest oxygen uptake or exercise intensity achieved with less than 1.0 mmol increase in blood lactate level concentration above the pre-exercise level.

Long-term training effects - thresholds

It is found that thresholds are **delayed** by training, so that the trained individual has a greater capacity for ATP-PC, has a greater lactic acid toleration, and more efficient ATP regeneration than the untrained person.

Other factors affecting the proportions of energy systems

- The **level of fitness** (whether adaptations to training have included enhancement of relevant enzymes - which would for example postpone levels of lactate accumulation).
- The **availability of O$_2$ and food fuels**. For example, a high CHO diet (figure 1.11) would assist replenishment of glycogen stores which would then be available for glycolysis.

figure 1.11 – CHO

Differences in ATP generation in muscle fibres

Intensity and **duration** determine the energy system and hence metabolic mixture and muscle fibre type activation.

High powered activities, such as a 60m sprint, and other forceful muscular actions and stop and go activities or change of pace in sports such as basketball, netball, soccer and field hockey depend almost entirely on anaerobic metabolism for high energy release needed to activate the **fast twitch fibres**.

- High energy release is mainly due to **high glycolytic enzyme activity** and **myosin ATPase activity** within the anaerobic glycolytic system.
- Since only **2 ATPs** are produced per molecule of glucose, high powered exercise can only continue for a few seconds before fatigue sets in.
- **Fast twitch muscle fibre type 11b** have a **low aerobic capacity** and therefore quickly **fatigue** during maximal activity.
- **Fast twitch fibres type 11a** possess a relatively **higher aerobic capacity** when compared with type 11b, and so support **increased force** when needed, for example, when running up hills whilst maintaining a constant speed.

- **Slow twitch muscle fibres** generate energy for ATP resynthesis, predominantly by aerobic energy transfer, producing up to **36 ATPs** per molecule of glucose.
- High concentration of **mitochondrial enzymes** and **capillary density** support this fibre's aerobic capacity to **resist fatigue** and power-prolonged aerobic exercise.

- Activities at near maximum aerobic and anaerobic levels, like middle distance running, swimming or multiple sprint sports such as field hockey, soccer basketball and netball, activate both fast twitch and slow muscle fibre types and their relative energy production via both the anaerobic and aerobic pathways.
- Specific exercise training improves the energy-generating capacity of each fibre type.

> ### STUDENT NOTE
>
> Information on the classification and characteristics of muscle fibres types are located in the Edexcel AS/A1 Student Revision Guide ISBN 9781901424881, Chapter 4 page 65.

Fatigue

Effects of fatigue on performance

Performance can be affected by muscle fatigue, the depletion of energy stores in muscle (and the liver). Various factors contribute to this.

Muscle fatigue

Muscle fatigue can be described as a reduction of muscular performance, and an inability to maintain expected power output. Performance can often be continued at quite a high level in spite of fatigue, but the outcome of 'jelly legs' or 'jelly shoulders' will be well known to all sportspeople after an exhausting performance has been completed.

figure 1.12 – fatigued athlete

Depletion of energy stores

- Depletion of **PC** (phosphocreatine) and muscle and liver **glycogen** stores will be the major cause of fatigue.
- Fatigue in marathon runners is due to depletion of **muscle glycogen** in both ST and FT muscle fibres.
- **FT muscle fibres** have low aerobic capacity and therefore **quickly fatigue** during maximal activity. This is because stored ATP and PC are quickly used up (in under 7 seconds) during this sort of activity (weight training, sprinting for example).

Metabolic accumulation

During intense exercise lasting longer than 7 seconds and under 45 seconds, **accumulation of lactic acid** and CO_2 in muscle cells causes extreme fatigue and complete loss of muscle function. This is because increase in H^+ ions (decrease in pH due to the lactic acid acidity) inhibits both aerobic and anaerobic enzyme activity required for ATP regeneration.

Body fluid balance and dehydration

- Fluid loss **decreases plasma volume** which reduces blood pressure and hence produces a reduction in blood flow to skin and muscles.
- This means that the heart has to work harder, body temperature rises, and **fatigue** occurs.
- Hence **fluid intake is important** during endurance activities (figure 1.13).

figure 1.13 – taking in water throughout a marathon

Stages of recovery

- **Structured rest** is essential to any intense training programme.
- **Sleep**, since all athletes need good quality sleep, since running a constant sleep debt can impair both workout intensity and recovery.
- **Hydrate**, since after a workout it is very important to replace the fluids lost during exercise.
- **Stretching** before and after a workout can help facilitate muscle recovery by reducing lactic acid and improving circulation.
- **Cryotherapy** methods such as Ice baths are used by many professional athletes for recovery benefits.
- Proper **nutrition** is about eating the right nutritional diet. For example, not enough protein can lead to loss of muscle mass.
- **Massage**, by a good sports massage therapist, will be able to help the athlete to relieve tension in muscles, flush toxins from the body and put the athlete in an all around relaxed state.
- Mind power or **positive self-talk** can help stimulate the sub-conscious to aid performance and recovery.

Oxygen consumption during recovery

Bodily processes do not immediately return to resting levels after exercise ceases. The time taken for this to occur is called the **recovery period**. The recovery period is dependent on the intensity and duration of the exercise.

Excess post-exercise oxygen consumption (EPOC)

After every strenuous exercise (figure 1.14), there are **four** tasks that need to be completed before the exhausted muscle can operate at full efficiency again.
- **Replacement of ATP and phosphocreatine** (fast replenishment component).
- **Removal of lactic acid** (slow replenishment component).
- **Replenishment of myoglobin** with oxygen.
- **Replacement of glycogen**.

The first three require oxygen in substantial quantities, hence the need for rapid breathing and a high pulse rate to carry oxygen to the muscle cells.

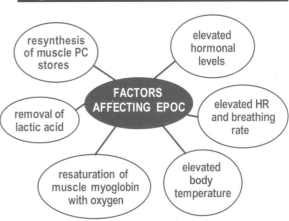

figure 1.14 – factors contributing to EPOC

resynthesis of muscle PC stores

elevated hormonal levels

removal of lactic acid

FACTORS AFFECTING EPOC

elevated HR and breathing rate

resaturation of muscle myoglobin with oxygen

elevated body temperature

The need for oxygen

The need for oxygen to rapidly replace ATP and remove lactic acid is known as the oxygen debt. The more modern term for oxygen debt is **excess post-exercise oxygen consumption** (EPOC) or oxygen recovery. This represents the elevation of the metabolic rate above resting values which occurs after exercise during the recovery period.

EPOC is the excess O_2 consumed following exercise needed to provide the energy required to resynthesise ATP used and remove lactic acid created during previous exercise. EPOC has **two** components (figure 1.15):
* **Alactic or alactacid**.
* **Lactic or lactacid**.

The **oxygen deficit** is the difference between the oxygen required during exercise and the oxygen actually consumed during the activity. The graph in figure 1.15 shows the relationship between oxygen consumption and the time before, during and after exercise.

As an athlete works from light to moderate to high intensities the oxygen deficit will increase. All-out physical effort demands a larger energy requirement than the aerobic processes can supply. Consequently anaerobic energy transfer increases and blood lactate accumulates, with considerable time required to achieve complete recovery to resting values.

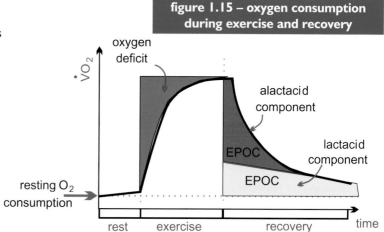

figure 1.15 – oxygen consumption during exercise and recovery

The alactacid component (without lactate build-up)

Figure 1.15 follows a single-component exponential curve termed the fast component of recovery oxygen uptake. This component involves the **conversion of ADP back into PC and ATP**, and is known as **restoration of muscle phosphagen**. This is a very rapid process (120 seconds to full restoration - see figure 1.16) and is of size 2 to 3.5 litres of O_2.

Phosphagen recovery

Phosphagen recovery (figure 1.16) is achieved via **three** mechanisms:
* There is **aerobic** conversion of carbohydrates into CO_2 and H_2O to resynthesise ATP from ADP and P_i.
* Some of the ATP is immediately utilised **to create PC** using the coupled reaction: **ATP + C → ADP + PC**.
* A small amount of ATP is **resynthesised via glycogen,** producing small amounts of lactic acid.

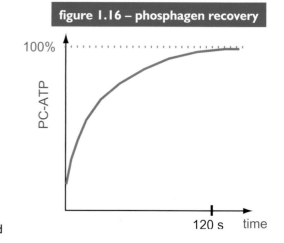

figure 1.16 – phosphagen recovery

Recovery oxygen uptake

During the **post-exercise period**, oxygen recovery is continuous. This is because:
* Muscle myoglobin recovers.
* Temperature falls.
* Hormone levels fall.

During the **recovery period**, temperature and hormone levels are higher than normal (although falling), which increases **EPOC** and:
* Keeps metabolic rate high.
* Keeps respiratory rate high.
* Keeps heart rate high.
* Requires more oxygen than normal.

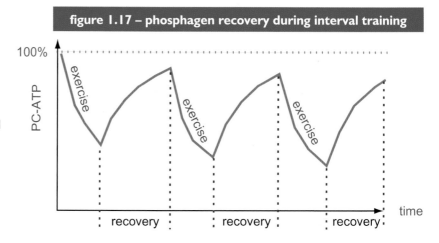

figure 1.17 – phosphagen recovery during interval training

The implications for interval training

- If there is only a short interval between bouts of exercise, the level of phosphagen stores gradually reduces (figure 1.17, page 20) thereby reducing the energy available for the later bouts.
- This stresses the ATP and PC storage and forces the muscle cells to adapt by storing more of these quantities.
- Also, cells will adapt by improving their ability to provide O_2, and hence increase the possible size of the alactic component.
- Anaerobic interval training studies have shown that 30 second bouts of exercise increase the activities of **glycolytic enzymes**, such as phosphorylase, phosphofructokinase and lactate dehydrogenase, from around 10% to 25%.
- This increase in **glycolytic capacity** will allow the muscle to develop greater tension for a longer period of time as the muscle tissue increases its **tolerance to lactate**.

OBLA (Onset of Blood Lactate Accumulation)

As discussed on page 13 and 14, the anaerobic energy systems have a limited capacity of ATP production. As **work intensity** increases, **lactic acid** starts to **accumulate** above resting values. At a certain point (called the OBLA point) this produces muscle fatigue and pain, since the resultant low pH (high acidity) inhibits enzyme action and cross-bridge formation during muscle contraction. This means in turn that muscle action is inhibited and **physical performance deteriorates**.

The exact cause of OBLA remains controversial:

- It could be due to the point of **muscle hypoxia** or inadequate oxygen.
- It could be due to **muscle lactate accumulation** even in the presence of adequate muscle oxygenation.
- It could be due to **decreased total lactate clearance** or increased lactate production only in specific muscle fibres.

OBLA can be expressed as a percentage of $\dot{V}O_{2max}$ as shown in figure 1.18.

This point governs the **lactic aerobic threshold**.

- In the graph (figure 1.18), as exercise intensity increases and $\dot{V}O_2$ increases, untrained people have blood lactate which increases sharply at about 50% of $\dot{V}O_{2max}$.
- But trained athletes can exercise up to 70% of $\dot{V}O_{2max}$ before lactate concentration in the blood increases markedly.
- Hence **trained athletes** begin **OBLA at higher work intensities** - especially since trained athletes have higher values of $\dot{V}O_{2max}$ than untrained people in the first place.
- All this means that the **lactic aerobic threshold** moves to **higher values of $\dot{V}O_{2max}$**.
- Training adaptations that facilitate a rapid achievement of steady state oxygen uptake also facilitate a rapid recovery process.

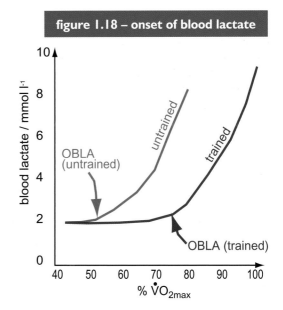

figure 1.18 – onset of blood lactate

Hence OBLA effectively predicts endurance performance.

Summary of factors affecting OBLA

- **Rate of blood lactate removal**: when removal and production are roughly equal, then blood lactate concentrations should stay constant. Only when production exceeds removal will lactic acid levels rise.

- **Exercise intensity**: as a performer works towards a higher intensity workload it is less likely to be performed aerobically and more likely to be performed **anaerobically** thereby producing lactic acid. Regular anaerobic physical activity increases the ability of the performer to tolerate higher levels of lactate and is able to remove lactic acid more quickly through a process called buffering (a chemical process that converts a strong acid to a weaker acid).

Summary of factors affecting OBLA

- **Muscle fibre type recruited**: slow twitch muscle fibres produce less lactic acid at the same intensity as fast twitch fibres due to increased mitochondria density.

- **Type of fuel being used**: RER (page 29) the closer the value is to 1, the more glycogen is being used and the more likely lactic acid is to be produced.

- **Training status of muscles**: trained muscles will have adaptive responses including more mitochondria, greater capillary density, improved used of FFAs as fuel, and higher myoglobin content, increasing aerobic capacity of muscle and reducing lactic acid production.

Lactacid oxygen recovery

High intensity exercise up to about 60 seconds creates **lactic acid**, and **oxygen is needed** to remove this lactic acid. This process begins to restore muscle and liver glycogen, and is relatively slow with **full recovery** taking up to 1 hour (figure 1.19).

Relatively large amounts of lactic acid (15 to 20 times the resting value of 1 to 2 mmol litre^{-1}) are produced during high intensity exercise, which is removed according to the proportions listed in table 1.2..

A small proportion of EPOC resynthesises lactate to glycogen. This **gluconeogenic** mechanism would probably progress faster during activity in trained individuals, for example an elite 400 m athlete.

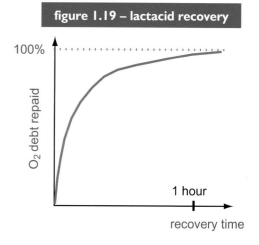

figure 1.19 – lactacid recovery

Removal of the lactic acid

Table 1.2 – **removal of the lactic acid**

oxidation into CO$_2$ + H$_2$O	65%
conversion into glycogen then stored in muscle and liver (Cori cycle)	20%
conversion into protein	10%
conversion into glucose	5%

The lactate shuttle

During the recovery process after intense exercise, a small proportion of the lactic acid produced is recycled back into glucose in the muscle cell. This is the reverse process to glycolysis and requires energy from ATP breakdown.

Buffering

A **blood buffer** is a chemical substance which resists abrupt changes in **hydrogen ion** (H$^+$) concentration. For example, when H$^+$ concentration increases as a result of intense exercise, H$^+$ reacts with oxyhaemoglobin (buffer) to form haemoglobinic acid. These ions are released when H$^+$ concentration falls. So this is a temporary solution to rapid changes in acidity or alkalinity which would otherwise cause rapid fatigue symptoms.

Implications of EPOC for physical activity and recovery

Understanding EPOC dynamics provides a basis for structuring activity intervals to optimise recovery during training sessions and competitions.

No appreciable lactate accumulates either in **steady-state aerobic activity** (for example, a 5 k run) or with 5 to 10 second bouts of all-out effort powered by the **intramuscular high-energy phosphates** (figure 1.17 page 20, for example, a long jump, 60 m sprint and gymnastic vault).

Implications of EPOC for physical activity and recovery

Recovery progresses rapidly and activity can begin again with only a short rest period, with recommended **passive recovery** whereby the athlete rests, thus reducing the **resting energy requirements** and freeing up more oxygen for fuel recovery.

For example, a **trained sprinter** can perform many sprint starts over 30 m with a 3 minute recovery period. An **endurance-based athlete**, such as a 10,000 m runner, a work relief ratio of 1:1 will provide aerobic physiological adaptations, such as an increase in $\dot{V}O_{2max}$, delay in OBLA, and muscle fatigue increase.

Work relief ratio represents the ratio of the work and relief intervals, for example, 6 x 1000 m each timed at 3 minutes with 3 minutes recovery.

In contrast, **anaerobic efforts** (from 10 s +, for example, 400/800 m training, a set of 4 x 500 m all out-efforts or a series of races) produce considerable lactate build-up in active muscle and blood, with disruption in most physiological support systems. As such, recovery $\dot{V}O_2$ often requires additional time to return to pre-activity baseline levels.

For example, where athletes are predominantly working with the **anaerobic glycolytic energy source** a work relief ratio of 1:2+ is recommended, alongside an **active recovery**. In active recovery the individual performs light exercise to facilitate lactate removal. This gives sufficient time for the athlete to recover before the next repetition and at the same time helps build up lactate tolerance levels.

Prolonged recovery between activity intervals would impair performance in sports such as basketball, hockey, soccer, tennis and badminton. In a practical sense, an athlete pushed to a high level of anaerobic metabolism may not fully recover during brief time-out periods or intermittent intervals of less physical activity. Hence, in these games the effects of fatigue are often apparent towards the end of a match.

Elite athletes and their coaches need to understand the significance of the effects of light to hard physical activity on the human body and the required work relief ratios, in order to achieve optimal fitness/recovery and performance in their chosen sport.

Cool-down following exercise

Cool-down (the process of continuing low level exercise immediately after the end of a high intensity exercise bout) **continues to provide oxygen** to skeletal muscle. This therefore **enhances oxidation of lactic acid** and ensures that less lactic acid remains in tissue. Hence there is less muscle soreness (**less DOMS**).

Figure 1.20 shows how **blood lactate** falls after exercise, and that when an active cool-down is undertaken less lactate remains in muscle tissue.

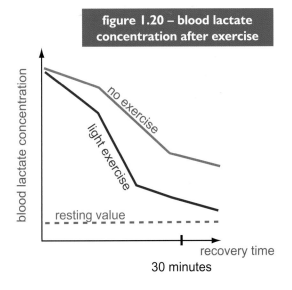

figure 1.20 – blood lactate concentration after exercise

blood lactate concentration

no exercise

light exercise

resting value

recovery time

30 minutes

Restoration of muscle glycogen stores post-exercise and nutrition

- During short duration high intensity exercise, restoration of glycogen takes up to 2 hours, and after prolonged low intensity aerobic exercise, restoration can take days.

Restoration of muscle glycogen stores post exercise and nutrition

When an athlete completes a hard training session, **glycogen depletion** will have taken place. It is essential that a **restoration** of energy stores is completed for recovery of the athlete prior to the next session or competition.

Post-competition or **training nutrition** should consist of:
- **Hypertonic** sports drink immediately after exercise has finished.
- This begins **replenishment of blood glucose** and **glycogen** stores.
- A **high CHO** meal within 15 minutes of exercise ending (or as soon as possible) continues glycogen replenishment.
- For optimal recovery, carbohydrate mixed with protein enhances all-round recovery due to an increase in **protein synthesis** post-exercise.
- Many athletes regularly consume sports drinks (figure 1.21) that are designed to supplement the **energy**, **fluid** and **protein** needs of the athlete.
- **Protein supplements**, such as whey protein, enable muscle hypertrophy and muscle repair following hard training.
- This particularly applies to sports requiring large muscle mass, as in weight lifting.

figure 1.21 – sports drinks

Restoration of myoglobin

Muscle myoglobin (an iron protein molecule located in skeletal muscle similar to haemoglobin) serves as a storage site for O_2, and has a temporary but greater affinity for O_2 than haemoglobin. Hence it acts as a **carrier of O_2** from HbO_2 (in blood) to mitochondria (in a muscle cell). Myoglobin is reoxygenated within 2 minutes.

Restoration of muscle myoglobin is important for recovery from high intensity exercise.

During high intensity exercise an increase in the recruitment of low-efficiency type IIb fibres (the fibres involved in the slow component) can cause an increase in the oxygen cost of exercise. A change in the pattern of motor unit recruitment, and thus less activation of type IIb fibres, may also account for a large part of the reduction in the slow component of $\dot{V}O_2$ observed after physical training.

Thermoregulation following exercise

The **thermoregulatory system** is situated in the **hypothalamus** in the brain. Changes in **body temperature** are sensed by central and peripheral **receptors**. Body temperature is maintained by balancing **heat input** and **heat loss**. Figure 1.22 lists the heat energy transfer methods into and out of the human body.

Blood acts as the major means of transferring heat energy between the **core** and body **shell**. During recovery from exercise, heat must be removed from the body through **radiation**, **conduction** and **convection** and **evaporation** (i.e. vasodilation of blood vessels beneath the skin results in sweating). Profuse **sweating** can lead to heat exhaustion or a heat stroke, indicated by a rise in blood pressure, dehydration and collapse. This condition is more likely when exercising and recovering in **hot humid conditions**.

When runners cross the finishing line of an endurance event, such as a marathon, their internal receptors tell their bodies to keep shedding

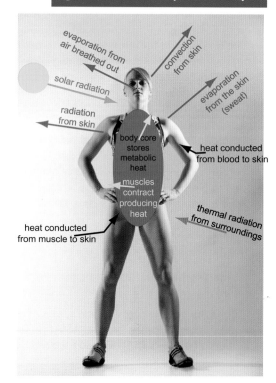

figure 1.22 – heat input and output

evaporation from air breathed out

convection from skin

solar radiation

evaporation from the skin (sweat)

radiation from skin

body core stores metabolic heat

heat conducted from blood to skin

muscles contract producing heat

thermal radiation from surroundings

heat conducted from muscle to skin

heat. In the meantime, when external temperatures are cool, runners will lose body heat rapidly because their heads, legs, and arms are exposed. Under these conditions, runners completing an endurance event can run the risk of venting off too much heat and becoming **hypothermic**. Silver foil aluminium blankets (figure 1.23) help the athletes regulate their body temperatures. The heat the athletes are giving out is held inside the blanket allowing them to regulate their temperature as their body heat drops.

Exercise induced muscle damage

During a hard training session, such as eccentric to concentric **plyometric training** (figure 1.24), sarcomeres can be stretched beyond their optimum functional length thus creating muscle tissue instability, weakness, and micro tears that can cause local inflammation.

Protein enzymes such as **creatine kinase** (CK), and **myoglobin** may leak from damaged membranes into the blood circulation causing potential pain and inflammation. This acute inflammation is known as **exercise induced muscle damage** (EIMD). The prominent symptoms of **EIMD** are pain, swelling, stiffness, reduced strength and fatigue. Most of these symptoms are related to the **delayed onset of muscle soreness** (DOMS).

Treatments include cold therapies, massage, anti-inflammatory medication, and sufficient rest between hard training sessions.

figure 1.23 – foil blankets prevent heat loss

figure 1.24 – plyometrics can damage muscle tissue

Recovery

There is improved oxygen recovery as a result of long-term aerobic training because of **better muscle capillarisation**. If an efficient cool-down is used, **lactic acid removal** is improved, hence there is a reduction in **DOMS** (delayed onset muscle soreness).

Table 1.3 summarises the probable six phases in DOMS development that ultimately lead to an inflammatory process and subsequent recuperation. The soreness usually disappears within about 72 hours after appearing.

If treatment is desired, any measure that increases blood flow to the muscle, such as low-intensity activity, massage and hot baths may help to relieve the symptoms.

Table 1.3 - **the six-phase sequence for DOMS following unaccustomed exercise**

phase	
1	unaccustomed exercise using eccentric muscle actions (downhill running, slowly lowering weights)
2	high muscle force damage sarcolemma causing release of protein enzymes, such as creatine kinase and myoglobin
3	damage to muscle contractile myofibrils and noncontractile structures
4	metabolites (e.g. calcium) accumulate to abnormal levels in the muscle tissue to produce more cell damage and reduce force capacity
5	DOMS considered to result from inflammation, tenderness and pain, the inflammation process begins, the muscle cell heals
6	the adaptive process makes the muscle more resistant to damage from subsequent bouts of the same exercises

Warm-up and its role in improving recovery

As discussed on page 12, **all three energy systems** contribute to ATP regeneration during an activity.

A **warm-up** (figure 1.25) is intended to raise the **body temperature** and prepare an athlete **physiologically** and **psychologically** to train or compete in a competitive situation. The **intensity** and **duration** of warm-up determine which fuel source is the predominant energy supplier.

A warm-up progresses from a light jog and general stretching into a sport specific section (providing skill rehearsal for the activity). This will be from low to moderate intensity, and can increase muscle and core temperature without inducing fatigue or reducing immediate energy stores. During the **sport specific** part of a warm-up, short, dynamic skill drills are often rehearsed and energy for this work will be provided via the ATP-PC system and regulated by blood serum creatine kinase (CK) levels (the primary enzyme responsible for regulating anaerobic metabolism).

Priming exercise

Priming exercise is a way of manipulating a warm-up to speed up how quickly the aerobic system starts at the onset of exercise by changing the intensity of the 'pulse raiser' element of the warm-up. Physiologists refer to this as O_2 **uptake kinetics** (kinetics is the measuring and studying of the rates of reactions), which has recently shown to have predictable positive consequences for performance. There are three factors that are important in priming exercise:

The intensity of the priming exercise

There is some debate about the optimum intensity. Research showing positive benefits from priming has generally shown to be just below or just above the maximum steady state, provided there is a long enough gap between the end of the priming exercise and the start of the performance.

Maximal steady state is defined as the highest blood lactate concentration and work load that can be maintained over time without a continual blood lactate accumulation (figure 1.18, page 21). For priming exercise to improve performance, there is a balance between the effect of priming on the O_2 uptake kinetics. On the one hand this would be due to the predominance of energy supplied via the **aerobic** system, and on the other hand, the extent to which the anaerobic capacity has been depleted without the athlete experiencing **muscle fatigue**.

The intensity of the performance

Priming exercise is of most **benefit** to **anaerobic** activities since the increased oxygen delivery to active tissue cells will delay the onset of OBLA.

For example, a **traditional** track cyclist's warm-up may be anything up to an hour with intense efforts which can result in **significant fatigue** and impair the performance. Switching on the aerobic energy system to just below maximum steady state (that monitors the intensity in relation to O_2 uptake kinetics by using a shorter and more controlled warm-up) will limit muscular fatigue by reducing the amount of energy sourced from the glycolytic system. Heart rate and breathing rates will increase progressively, enabling more oxygen to be transported through the blood and used within the working muscles. With increased body temperature, the range of motion around joints will also improve and will get close to the athletes' optimal efficiency very quickly.

For **aerobic** activities, a less intense and shorter warm-up is recommended to prepare the body for steady state performance.

The gap between the end of the priming exercise and the start of the performance

Optimally, a competitive event or activity should begin within several minutes after the end of a warm-up to conserve energy stores and at the same time maintain the physiological benefits of the warm up. Somewhere **between 6 and 20 minutes** has been shown to be effective. Less than six minutes and performers seem to have some residual fatigue. The upper limit is more difficult to gauge but higher intensity priming exercise is still effective with a long break.

In global sporting events, athletes are often required to go to the call room anytime between **20-30 minutes prior** to their events. In this situation, athletes must attempt to **maintain** the effects of the warm-up, often in cramped spaces.

Practice questions

1) Explain the differences between chemical, potential and kinetic energy. **3 marks**

2) During any event of low or high intensity, all three energy systems are used. However the physical demands of the event will determine the relative proportions of the energy system(s) being used. Complete the gaps in table 1.4 identifying the major energy systems and examples in sporting activities in relation to performance time. **8 marks**

Table 1.4

Area	Performance time	Major energy systems related to performance time	Examples of type of activity
1	Less than 10 s	ATP –PC	100m sprint / gymnastics vault / discus throw
2	10 –30 s		
3	20 s to 1.5 minutes		
4	1.5 –3 minutes		
5	greater than 3 minutes		

3) An elite swimmer performs a flat-out 100 metre freestyle swim in 50 seconds. Describe how most of the ATP is regenerated during the swim. Sketch a graph which shows the use of the appropriate energy systems against time during the swim. **8 marks**

4) a) Taking part in a triathlon involved swimming, cycling and running. Briefly describe how the aerobic energy system within the cell mitochondria supports this endurance event. **6 marks**

   b) Construct a graph which illustrates the food fuel usage against time during a triathlon race lasting 2 hours. **3 marks**

5) Compare the relative efficiency of ATP production via the aerobic and anaerobic routes. Explain your answer. **3 marks**

6) Identify the predominant energy system being used in the following activities: shot put, 200 metres breaststroke, a game of hockey, 100 metres hurdles race, gymnastics vault and modern pentathlon. **6 marks**

7) Figure 1.26 illustrates the contribution of the anaerobic and aerobic energy systems to the total energy requirements for four different track events: 200 m, 400 m, 800 m and 1500 m.

   a) Which column, grey or pink, represents the contribution from the anaerobic system? **1 mark**

   b) With reference to the data provided, justify your answer. **3 marks**

   c) What is the role of the anaerobic systems in the 1500 m event? In your response, refer to the data provided. **2 marks**

8) Elite games players require high levels of fitness and psychological preparation, therefore regular fitness testing and after-match performance analysis are common. Using your knowledge of energy systems, outline and explain the relationship between energy sources and intensity of exercise. **15 marks**

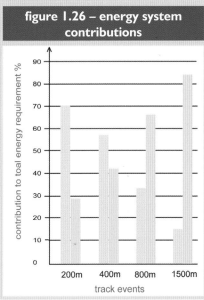

figure 1.26 – energy system contributions

contribution to toal energy requirement %

track events

Practice questions

9) The diagram in figure 1.27 is an energy continuum in relation to a variety of sports activities.

   a)   Explain the concept 'the energy continuum'.   2 marks

   b)   At each end of the continuum examples of sporting activities have been omitted. Give one example of a sporting activity that is predominantly anaerobic and one example of a sporting activity that is predominantly aerobic.   2 marks

   c)   Suggest two factors that need to be considered in evaluating sports activities on the basis of their relative position on the energy continuum.   2 marks

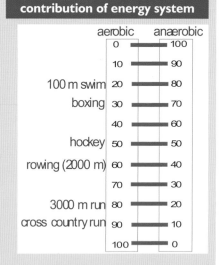

figure 1.27 – variation in contribution of energy system

10) Competitive swimmers will often compete in several events and suffer from fatigue due to limited recovery time. Explain the possible causes of fatigue during a race.   6 marks

11) Figure 1.28 shows oxygen uptake of an elite games player undertaking exercise followed by a recovery period.

   a)   Using the appropriate letters, identify the oxygen deficit and Excess Post Oxygen Consumption (EPOC).   3 marks

   b)   Why does the elite player incur an oxygen deficit during exercise?   2 marks

   c)   Excess Post Oxygen Consumption (EPOC) is considered to have two components. State two aims of the first component and explain how this component is achieved.   4 marks

   d)   Describe the process of ATP production that restores the oxygen debt or EPOC.   6 marks

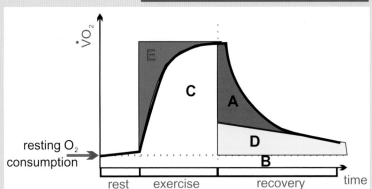

figure 1.28 – oxygen consumption during exercise and recovery

12) A high anaerobic capacity is important to any team player. Outline the physiological processes that will happen during a 5 minute recovery phase following an intense period of anaerobic exercise.   8 marks

13) How could information on oxygen debt recovery (EPOC) be of use to an athlete and coach in designing training sessions?   5 marks

14) A high anaerobic capacity is important to any team player. Outline the physiological processes that will happen during a 30 minute recovery phase following an intense period of anaerobic exercise and discuss their implications when planning anaerobic interval training sessions.   15 marks

15) A friend comments 'I workout with free weights and swim regularly, yet on the odd occasion when I do some hill running, my leg muscles are sore a day or two after the event'. Explain why this is so.   4 marks

16) How can priming for exercise assist an athlete in the planning of a warm-up routine?   6 marks

Answers link: http://www.jroscoe.co.uk/downloads/a2_revise_pe_edexcel/EdexcelA2_ch1_answers.pdf

CHAPTER 2: *Injury prevention and the rehabilitation of injury*

Types of injury

A **sports injury** is any kind of injury, pain or physical damage that occurs as a result of sport, exercise or physical activity.

Sports injuries are unfortunately inevitable, and are dependent on a performer's intensity of training, the preparation he or she makes to avoid injury, and the ways in which rest and recovery are planned into a training and competitive programme. Figure 2.1 outlines the factors influencing how injuries are caused and can be dealt with.

Sports injuries are:
* Most commonly associated with the musculo-skeletal system, which includes muscles, joints and their associated tissues such as ligaments and tendons.
* Commonly classified as **acute** or **chronic**.
* Mild, moderate or severe.
* Characterised by pain, swelling, tenderness, weakness and the inability to use or place weight on the injured area.
* **Acute** injuries refer to sports injuries that happen in a moment.
* **Chronic** injuries are characterised by a slow, sustained development of symptoms, that culminate in a painful inflammatory condition.

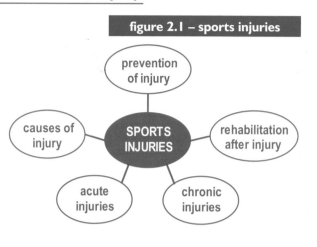

figure 2.1 – sports injuries

Acute injuries

Common symptoms associated with acute sports injuries:
* Acute injuries require **immediate first aid treatment** at the scene of the injury.
* Sudden severe **pain**.
* **Stretching painful** in the case of a muscle strain.
* Swelling, **inflammation**, bruising or tenderness over injured area.
* **Restricted mobility** above and below injured area.
* Loss of **stability** in the case of leg injuries.
* Loss of **function** in the injured area.
* **Protruding bone** from the skin in the case of a compound fracture.
* **Deformity** around injured area.
* Cold **purple colouration** of skin indicating a lack of proper blood circulation in that injured part.

Fractures

A bone fracture is a break in the bone and is caused by excessive external forces and so is classified as traumatic fracture. There are two major classes:
* **Simple fractures** (figure 2.2) are broken bones that remain within the body and do not penetrate the skin.
* **Compound fractures** are broken bones that penetrate through the skin and expose the bone and deep tissues to the exterior environment, creating an open wound with a risk of infection.

Dislocations

A dislocation occurs when the **bones which meet at a joint, are separated by a violent action so that the joint no longer functions**.
* For example, a shoulder dislocation occurs when a player's arm is forced outwards and upwards by a tackle or heavy landing and the shoulder joint pops out.
* Injuries can occur quite **easily** because the shoulder joint is a shallow ball and socket when compared to the hip joint.
* A dislocation is usually accompanied by a **sprain** (page 31).
* **Repeat dislocations** of the same joint are common because the initial dislocation stretches the joint capsule and ligaments, and results in joint hypermobility.

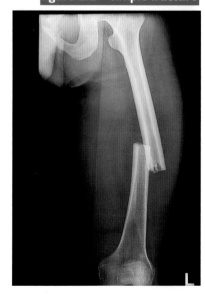

figure 2.2 – simple fracture

Common soft tissue injuries

A soft tissue injury occurs when **muscles**, **ligaments** and **tendons** are damaged. Common soft tissue injuries usually occur from a sprain, a strain or a one off blow resulting in a contusion or bruise (caused when blood vessels are damaged or broken as the result of a blow to the skin). Contusions are common in contact sports such as rugby and boxing. Soft tissue injuries can result in pain, swelling, bruising and loss of function.

Strains

- Muscles can be damaged both by **direct** trauma (impact) or **indirect** trauma (overloading).
- A strain (pull or tear) refers to **damage to muscle fibres** or its attaching tendons caused by a sudden stretching force or a very forceful contraction of the muscle.
- The tearing of the muscle can also damage small blood vessels, causing local bleeding, or **bruising** (known as a **haematoma**), and pain caused by **irritation of the nerve endings** in the area.
- The most common muscle injuries occur in **high speed activities** such as sprinting and weight lifting, which load muscles such as the hamstrings, quadriceps, calf, back and biceps.
- Muscle tears range from a mild to moderate to severe strains or complete rupture.

Sprains and tears of ligaments

- A **ligament** is an extension of a joint capsule consisting of tough, fibrous connective tissue that provides stability by joining bone to bone positioned inside a joint (intrascapular) and outside of a joint (extracapsular).
- In a sprain, **ligaments** reinforcing a joint are **stretched** or torn.
- One of the most common knee injuries is an **anterior cruciate ligament** (ACL) sprain or rupture. The ACL runs diagonally across the middle of the knee and prevents the tibia from sliding out in front of the femur, as well as providing rotational stability to the knee.
- Athletes who participate in high demand sports like soccer and basketball, are more likely to injure their ACLs.
- About half of all injuries to the ACL occur along with damage to other structures in the knee, such as articular cartilage, meniscus or other ligaments.

Ligament injuries

There are three graded categories for all ligament injuries:

Grade 1 sprain: the ligament is mildly damaged as it has been slightly stretched, but is still able to help keep the knee joint stable.
Grade 2 sprain: the ligament is stretched to a point where it becomes loose, and is commonly known as a partial tear of the ligament.
Grade 3 sprain: a complete tear of the ligament into two pieces. For example, a complete tear of the ACL creating an unstable knee joint (figure 2.3).

A complete rupture leads to mechanical instability, whilst tearing may damage the proprioceptive feedbak mechanism.

The ACL can be injured in several ways:
- Changing direction rapidly.
- Stopping suddenly.
- Slowing down while running.
- Landing from a jump incorrectly.
- Direct contact or collision, such as a football tackle.

figure 2.3 – a complete ACL tear

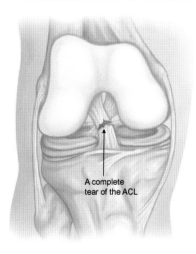

A complete tear of the ACL

Symptoms of cruciate ligament injuries

- A '**popping**' noise is associated with a ruptured ACL.
- The knee gives way and becomes **unstable**.
- Causing further damage to the cushioning cartilage (meniscus) of the knee.
- **Pain** and **swelling** within 24 hours.
- Loss of full range of motion.
- Tenderness along the joint line.
- Discomfort whilst walking.

- When a ligament is torn completely, it can be replaced with a **graft**, for example, the anterior cruciate ligament of the knee joint can be replaced using a hamstring tendon graft (page 43).

Achilles tendon injuries

- A tendon is a tough cord or band of dense white fibrous connective tissue which contacts a muscle to a bone and transmits the force which the muscle exerts.
- The Achilles tendon is located at the back of the ankle and connects the powerful calf muscles to the heel bone (calcaneus).
  - When the calf muscles contract, the Achilles tendon is tightened, pulling the heel.
  - This allows the foot to point and stand on tiptoe, vital to such activities as walking, running, and jumping.

- Tears of the Achilles tendon can be tiny (**microtears**), or large (**macrotears**), causing pain, swelling, and impaired movement.
  - Tears may occur suddenly (**acute**), during activity or gradually over time (**chronic**).
  - A complete tear through the tendon, which usually occurs about 2 inches above the heel bone, is called an Achilles tendon **rupture**.
  - A rupture can occur when a significant load has been applied quickly and sustained without adequate warm-up.
- An Achilles tendon rupture is more common in those with pre-existing tendinitis of the Achilles tendon.
- By the age of thirty, tendons begin to lose their elasticity with increasing degenerative changes, but the process can be delayed by regular exercise.

- **Total tendon ruptures** often occur in a degenerated tendon and is especially common in older athletes who return to sport after some years' absence from training, and middle-aged men and women participating in recreational sports that require bursts of jumping, pivoting, and running. Most often these are in sports such as tennis, squash, basketball, and badminton.

- A rupture is most likely to occur when an individual makes a **forceful push-off** by the thigh muscles whilst the knee is extended. One example might be preparing for a overhead shot during a badminton rally.
- Other common causes for a rupture can occur as a result of a sudden **trip** or **stumble** when the foot is thrust in front to break a fall, forcefully overstretching the tendon, or abruptly stepping into a hole.
- A complete rupture of the Achilles tendon may make a 'popping' sound, followed by pain and swelling of the lower leg.
- Figure 2.4 compares a ruptured and normal Achilles tendon.
- Treating an Achilles tendon rupture requires surgery or long-term immobilisation of the ankle.

figure 2.4 – a ruptured and normal achilles tenndon

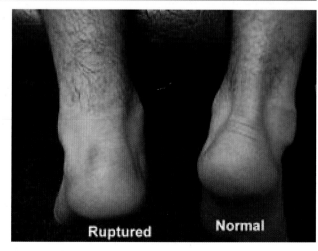

Ruptured   Normal

Sprains and tears within joints

- Common sites of sprains are the ankle, knee and thumb joints.
- Sprains happen most often in the **ankle** (figure 2.5) in sports that involve twisting and turning movements, such as in netball.
- Knee sprains are common football injuries.
- Thumb sprains are common in skiing and contact sports such as judo.

figure 2.5 – a sprained ankle

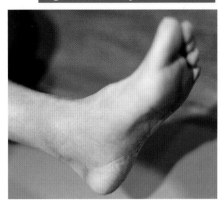

Ice therapy is a common method used for acute joint and muscle injuries and is part of the **RICE** First Aid procedure as follows:

- **Rest** - stop the activity as soon as the injury occurs to prevent making it any worse.
- **Ice** - apply to injured area for 10-15 minutes then remove for 20 minutes (and repeat) to reduce internal bleeding and swelling.
- **Compression** - reduces swelling, supports soft tissues, minimising further damage, and so speeds recovery.
- **Elevation** - elevating the injured area above the heart aids the drainage of any liquid/leakage caused by the injury thereby reducing swelling and inflammation.

Chronic or overuse injuries

Common symptoms associated with chronic overuse sports injuries:

- Chronic injuries start off with **mild symptoms** that enable performer to ignore the injury and carry on with his or her activities.
- Followed by a gradual **increase of pain** and inflammation over a period of time resulting from continued **overuse**.
- Increase in pain during sporting activity.
- Mild swelling after completion of sporting activity.
- Constant **aching** at rest.
- Chronic injuries are also associated with fatigue.

Shin splints (periostitis)

Shin splints are a type of **soft tissue injury** due to **inflammation** of the **periosteum** (a layer of connective tissue that surrounds bone), usually caused by repeated stress on the tibia. Shin splints are common in people who do a lot of running or other activities that involve repeatedly putting weight on the legs, such as tennis or basketball.

Shin splints can usually be treated at home as follows:

- **Rest**: stop the activity that causes shin splints for at least two to three weeks, then gradually resume normal activities
- **Ice**: for around 10 minutes every few hours for the first few days. This helps to relieve pain and swelling
- **Pain relief**: such as paracetamol and ibuprofen help to relieve the pain.
- **Switch to low-impact activities**: such as cycling, swimming and yoga.

Tendinopathy

Tendinopathy refers to a disease of a tendon including tenderness on palpation and pain, often felt when exercising. Tendonitis is an acute tendon injury accompanied by swelling ('itis'), resulting from **excessive overuse**, and describes common elbow injuries, experienced by tennis players, golfers and throwers.

The elbow joint

The **elbow joint** is surrounded by muscles that move the elbow, wrist and fingers. The tendons in the elbow join the bones and muscles together, and control the muscles of the forearm. **Golfer's elbow** is not as well known as its cousin, **tennis elbow**. Both are forms of tendinopathy. The difference is that **tennis elbow** stems from overusing tendon attachments to the **outside** of the elbow, while **golfer's elbow** is caused by overusing tendons on the **inside** of the elbow.

Elbow

Golfer's elbow is a common overuse injury associated with playing golf and throwing activities such as javelin and bowling in cricket. It is caused by **overusing** the muscles in the **forearm** that allow the individual to grip, rotate the arm, and flex the wrist.

Repetitive flexing, gripping, or swinging can cause irritations to the tendons creating pronounced tenderness and pain when the medial epicondyle is subjected to pressure, and when the hand is flexed downwards (**palmer flexion**) at the wrist joint against a resistance.

Tennis elbow is a common overuse injury associated with racket sports such as squash, badminton and tennis. For example, in tennis it can be caused by repetitive faulty stroke technique, such as hitting backhand balls by using wrist movements instead of hitting backhand balls with a firm wrist and a movement of the whole arm and shoulder.

figure 2.6 – wrist supination can cause elbow tondonitis

Top level tennis players (figure 2.6) may develop **lateral epicondylitis** despite having good playing technique and is usually caused by the serving action during which the wrist is bent at the same time as the forearm is turned inwards.

Those who hit an exaggerated 'top spin' and in so doing rotate the forearm vigorously inwards (excessive pronation) can also be affected. This was the injury sustained by Andy Murray at the beginning of the 2017 tennis season. The flexor muscles, that are principally responsible for these movements, have their origins at the medial epicondyle of the elbow.

The **symptoms** are similar to those of golfer's elbow, but are located on the **outer aspect** of the **elbow joint**. If the muscles and tendons are irritated, it can cause thickening of the tendon and pain near the bony lump (the lateral epicondyle) on the outside of the joint.

General **tendonitis symptoms** include:
*   **Pain** which mainly affects the outside aspect of the elbow (tennis elbow) or inside of the elbow (golfer's elbow) that can radiate along the upper and lower arm.
*   **Weakness** in the wrist.
*   A **tender local hot** spot over the epicondyle.

Stress fractures

A **stress fracture** is a small crack in a bone resulting from **overuse**. There are two theories about the origin of stress fractures:

*   The **fatigue theory** states that during repeated protracted effort, such as running, the muscles pass their peak of endurance and are no longer able to support the skeleton during impact applied as the foot strikes the ground. The **load** is therefore transferred **directly to the skeleton**. Its tolerance is eventually exceeded causing a tiny crack or stress fracture.

*   The **overload theory** is based on the fact that certain muscle groups contract in such a way that they cause the **bones** to which they are attached, to **bend**. For example, the contraction of the calf muscles causes the tibia to bend forward like a drawn bow. After repeated contractions the innate strength of the tibia is exceeded and it cracks.

More than 50 percent of all **stress fractures** occur in the weight-bearing bones of the foot and lower leg because of the repetitive forces they must absorb. Typically, runners sustain stress fractures of the lower third of the fibula and high jumpers of the upper third of the fibula.

Symptoms and diagnosis

- **Pain** is felt during training as intensity increase and eventually a dull ache which persists after the exercise period.
- Local **swelling** and **tenderness** can be felt over the fracture area.
- Stress fractures affect people of **all ages** who participate in repetitive sporting activities and are especially common in tennis players, runners, gymnasts and basketball players.
- Repeated use of **X-ray** examination is used to check the **process of healing**, whilst the athlete is resting and using prescribed crutches to relieve the injured part.
- If stress fractures are to be avoided, the athlete should pay particular attention to selecting appropriate **footwear**, **equipment** (page 40) and periodisation of training or load.

Overuse or chronic injuries are particularly difficult to diagnose and treat.
Recovery from chronic injuries takes time and needs careful programming to restore the individual back to pre-injury levels using many of the rehabilitation methods discussed on page 42 onwards.

Prevention of injuries

Extrinsic and intrinsic risk factors affecting sports injuries

Table 2.1 outlines the intrinsic and extrinsic risk factors which affect sport injury. Intrinsic risk factors are those within the performer, and extrinsic risk factors are those derived outside the performer.

Table 2.1 – **intrinsic and extrinsic risk factors in sport injuries**

intrinsic risk factors	extrinsic risk factors
gender	training volume, overtraining
age increases injury risk as bone tissue loses strength	sport technique
body mass and body composition	playing surfaces
muscle balance/imbalance	equipment difficulties, eg selecting the perfect ski boots, skis and poles
joint flexibility (or lack of it)	clothing/footwear/equipment
orthopaedic and skeletal features	environmental conditions
conditioning	

Although the **chances of injury** in sport can never be fully eradicated, preventative measures and procedures can be put into place to minimise the risk of getting injured, as discussed in managing risks (page 41).

Intrinsic risk factor variables

Conditioning

Regardless of the sport involved, most athletes need **general muscle fitness** to reduce the risk of injury to the muscle-tendon unit itself and to the joints protected by muscle activity. **Weight training** and **circuit training** are common training methods that are used improve the general **strength and conditioning** of muscles.

Athletes must be fit enough to be able to perform the skills needed to compete in their sport and so long-term preparation is needed in training for many activities, for example, running a marathon for which preparation can take several months.

When athletes become tired, performance levels can drop and injuries are more likely to occur due to fatigue.

Conditioning

A **core stability** conditioning programme benefits good **muscle balance** and **coordination** (figure 2.7). Good core stability involves the effective recruitment of the muscles that **stabilise** the **lumbo-pelvic-hip complex**, together with those that stabilise the shoulder girdle. Many athletes attend **pilates**, a body-conditioning technique that concentrates on strengthening the core postural muscles needed by all active sportspersons.

figure 2.7 – the plank

Variance in training avoids the overuse injuries associated with using the same exercises and movements year round, and builds the right foundation for achieving peak performance at the right time.

All training/competitive activities should begin with a **warm-up**. A warm-up takes the body from a non-active state to one ready for exercise. The absence of a warm-up or an inadequate warm-up is a common cause of injury.

Lack of flexibility can limit **range of movement** (ROM) and lead to sprain and strain injuries. **Hyper-mobility** enables joints to move beyond the normal range expected for that particular joint and can lead to poor joint stability and dislocations.

A **cool-down** gradually returns the body to its former resting state with reduced injury risk. A major physiological value of an active cool-down is to **flush out lactic acid** thereby preventing muscle soreness (**DOMS**).

Sport performers require **sports specific** training programmes aimed at developing those muscle fibres which are used most intensively in competition. These programmes should include a variety of skills, drills and techniques that should mimic the desired sporting action as closely as possible.

STUDENT NOTE

For reviews of antagonistic muscle action, warm-up, cool-down and preparation and training methods refer to AS/A1 Edexcel ISBN 978190142488, Chapter 1, page 25, Chapter 2, page 32, Chapter 8, page 121 and Chapter 7, page 87 respectively.

Muscle balance

Human movement and function requires a **balance** of muscle **length** and **strength** between opposing muscles surrounding a joint. Normal amounts of opposing force between muscles are necessary to keep the bones centred in the joint during motion, to create muscle balance.

Muscle imbalance occurs when opposing muscles provide different **directions of tension** due to tightness and/or weakness. When a muscle is too tight, the joint tends to move in that direction and is limited in the opposite direction since this is typically the path of least resistance.

There are also two recognised causes of **muscle imbalance**:
*   **Neuromuscular imbalance** due to the predisposition of certain muscle groups to be either tight or weak.
*   **Biomechanical imbalance** resulting from poor technique.

Muscle imbalances can be characterised by either **side-to-side** (right versus left) or **front-to-back** (agonist versus antagonist) differences in muscle length or strength. Most musculoskeletal pain syndromes are caused by front-to-back differences, or imbalances of muscles surrounding a joint, rather than side-to-side differences (in the frontal plane).

For example, the quadriceps and hamstrings of the knee joint perform opposite motion (antagonistic pairing), and so an imbalance between the two could put undue stress on the knee joint. A tight hamstring would not allow the joint to glide normally or fully extend, which could put extra stress on the quadriceps muscle and patella (knee cap) tendon.

Muscle balance

Muscle imbalance can be the result of poor weight training techniques, or playing intense sports where one side of the body is used slightly more than the other as in the repetitive action of kicking in football.

When muscles are balanced the human body moves efficiently, requiring less energy and preventing unnecessary stress on the muscles, nerves, ligaments and joints. This synergy is known as **neuromuscular efficiency**, requiring the interaction of the neuromuscular systems.

It is important to know which muscles need to be **strengthened** and which muscles need to be **stretched** in order to create good muscle balance.

Good posture ensures that movements can be performed with minimal strain. For example, when the body leans slightly to one side, the nerves associated with the muscles and ligaments send messages to other muscles to help correct this movement by telling muscles to contract to regain muscle balance. If there are imbalances within this unit, problems can occur, such as **decreased performance**, muscle trauma and injury.

Running posture is an important technical aspect for both enhancing performance and minimising injury risk. Runners who lean forward (figure 2.8) to a greater extent are more economical (run faster for a given oxygen uptake) and less likely to suffer from knee injuries, the most common of which occurs at the **patellofemoral joint** (PFJ) - a joint between the patella and femur).

PFJ pain syndrome is often caused by imbalances in the muscles surrounding the knee, which affect the kneecap (patella) and cartilage within the joint. Symptoms include a **scratching**, **grinding** or **clicking** sensation in the knee, and non-specific knee pain.

Maintaining a **forward lean** without losing straight alignment over long distances requires certain level of **torso strength**, which is why **strength** and **mobility** exercises are fundamental in improving running performance and reducing injury risk.

Muscle balance assessment

A muscle balance assessment is a series of tests and observations that evaluate joint ROM, strength and coordination, and muscle flexibility. Such assessments can establish what is working well or not so well.

For example, an **isokinetic lido leg strength test** can assess the strength ratio between the quadriceps and hamstring muscle groups. For good muscle balance the ideal ratio should be 2:1. If it is greater that this value, the hamstring muscle group becomes susceptible to injury.

STUDENT NOTE

Proprioceptors, such as Golgi tendon organs and muscle spindles, are specialised sensory receptors sensitive to stretch, tension and pressure located in tendon, joints and muscles. They relay information about muscular dynamics, limb position and kinaesthesia (movement sense) to conscious and subconscious portions of the CNS.

Proprioceptive training methods

Proprioceptive training methods can improve muscle balance, as is the case with **plyometric** training. The emphasis is placed on making the ROM more stable, in particular in single limb tasks.

Proprioceptive training methods

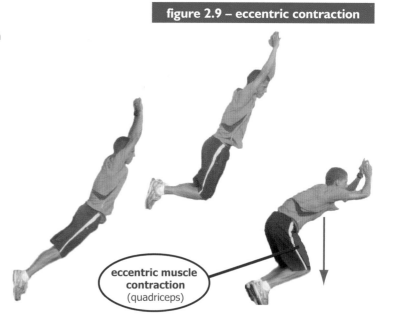

figure 2.9 – eccentric contraction

eccentric muscle
contraction
(quadriceps)

Proprioception is the ability to sense stimuli arising within
the body regarding position, motion, and equilibrium.

For example, in an ideal **long-term athlete
development** plan (LTAD) a coach could teach a young
athlete to land bilaterally off low level drops, from
horizontal jumps/bounding (figure 2.9) and jumps using
a multi-directional approach.

To achieve a **softer landing**, the coach could tell the
athlete that they need to land on the front of the foot,
and then flex the knees into a squat position in order
to dissipate the ground reaction force effectively.

This would **avoid** such **high peak forces** in shorter time
frames on landing, which has been demonstrated as a
most likely cause of knee and muscle/tendon injuries.

The aim is to be able to absorb and handle the impact
of **eccentric loads** on landing and ground stroke in high
velocity running.

The progression within single leg landings would ensure the athlete can land softly
to begin with, promoting good landing mechanics of holding and maintaining good
postural balance by controlling the alignment of the knee and effective position
of the trunk in a neutral position.

The proprioceptors therefore have to **adapt** to control these movements and
keep a balanced athletic position on landing. Once achieved, the young athlete
is ready to progress from low level muscle balance work through to **greater
training loads**, thereby increasing the muscular strength and balance.

By improving an athlete's proprioceptive ability, he or she can gain the balance
skills necessary to maintain stability for their sporting needs.

Muscle balance is enhanced by having a **strong core** as discussed above.

Extrinsic risk factor variables

Technique

If an athlete does not have a good technique he or she is more likely to sustain a
sports injury. **Poor technique** can expose players to the risk of acute injury.
For example, rugby tackling with the head in front of the ball carrier's leg
rather than behind it.

Injuries are not the only by-product of poor technique, **performance levels**
will also be decreased by **poor technique** as this will prevent optimum strength,
power and speed in the particular movement or shot.

In injury prevention, **good technique training** from a **coach** is vital and
should start when athletes are young. **Movement patterns** in technique
training must be performed correctly right from the start as it can be difficult to
correct a faulty pattern later (as illustrated in the example within the
proprioceptive training methods).

Achieving optimal coordination requires **constant repetition** of the
various elements of the movement. This is achieved by establishing good
interaction between the muscles and the nervous system to produce
good **muscular coordination**.

Technique

Technique training should be assigned to the **beginning** of the training session when it is easier to concentrate and the body is well-rested.
All athletes should have a **solid technical foundation** before taking part in competition.

The coach is responsible for **planning** appropriate levels of **intensity**, **duration**, **frequency** and **variance** within a training programme to prevent **overtraining**.

Overuse injuries refer to injuries sustained from repeated action. For example, **repetitive**, **excessive overload** can cause microscopic injuries, leading to inflammation, which is the body's response to injury.

Repeated low level impacts can cause chronic injury, for example, Achilles tendinopathy if long-term measures, such as rest and strengthening are not taken.

Protective equipment and clothing

For some sports, protective equipment is important to prevent damage to participants.
This is particularly relevant when the sport or activity involves physical contact with other players.

Equipment in any sport may be inadequate, poorly designed or ineffective and not suitable for age, stature or ability. For example, generic trainers (footwear) will not provide the support and grip needed for throwing events.

Protective clothing can be faulty or insufficient to meet the needs of the sporting activity. Specialised protective clothing (figure 2.10) has been developed for many sports with well known examples from fencing, field hockey, cricket, baseball, American football and equestrianism.

figure 2.10 – specialist equipment for injury prevention

Boxing and other **martial arts** require **helmets** (with or without face guards), padding, boxes, strapping, gloves, mouth guards and so on, depending on the rules of the sport, and the damage allowed to be inflicted within the rules of the sport. All these pieces of equipment are designed to prevent injury to **vulnerable** parts of the body.

Specialist clothing is also required for **low and high temperatures** to maintain body temperature within a safe range.

Wicking fabrics (a mixture of cotton and man-made light and stretchy fibres) are used in a range of sports clothing. The wicking properties have the ability to soak up sweat then move it away from the body, thus saving energy on maintaining skin temperature, and **preventing hyperthermia** (heat exhaustion). In cold conditions such fabrics insulate the body thereby reducing hypothermia.

Energy absorbing plastics (also known as **shear-thickening**, energy absorbing materials, for example D30) are used as materials to create foam-filled clothes that cushion, absorb and dissipate the energy resulting from a high impact blows. The shear-thickening property means that greater the force acting on it, the more solid the material becomes. This material is used in **ski clothing** and sports such as **motor racing clothing** to provide significant protection from injury against high impact incidents.

Compression clothing (page 46) works by supporting and protecting body tissues, increasing circulation, assisting in the removal of lactic acid and thereby reducing DOMS.

Footwear, braces and strapping

Sports footwear is the most important item of equipment for most sports. When choosing sports footwear, several factors must be taken into consideration including the **sport** involved and the **surface** used.

For example, in long-distance running the **weight** of the shoes can be of importance. They should not, however, be so light that their **stability** is impaired.

Elite athletes are often provided with **bespoke footwear**. The foot is scanned to capture its shape, then footfall is analysed (using forceplate technology). This indicates how the foot lands and moves and leads to the development of personalised footwear, whose aim is to make movement more efficient, improve performance and reduce the likelihood of injury (figure 2.11).

Proper fitting and sport-specific footwear reduce the risk of injury to the soft tissues, bones or joints of the lower limb.

The risk of a sprained ankle and other such injuries has been shown to significantly be reduced by wearing **braces** such as ankle supports (as worn by tennis star Andy Murray - figure 2.12).

There are a few items that can be used in training, but **not allowed** in competitive situations. For example, **strapping** a shot putter's fingers or hand helps prevent finger knuckle sprains, but is not allowed in competition.

There are many other examples of protective equipment, all of which contribute in the prevention of sports injuries.

The environment and safety hazards

A hazard is something that is potentially dangerous to an individual or activity or both. For example, if a sports hall roof leaks the floor may become wet and so it will need to be coned off and dried to prevent people slipping during a physical activity.

Temperature, **wet and windy** conditions can also be responsible for injury, and particularly cyclists should take care when cycling on wet, greasy roads.

The ability to perform vigorous exercise for long periods is limited by **hyperthermia** (over heating) and **loss of water and salt** in sweating. Athletes should know the hazards of vigorous exercise in hot, humid conditions particularly in ultra endurance events, and should be able to recognise the early warning symptoms that precede heat injury.

Managing risks

Managing risks refers to the practice of identifying potential risks in advance, analysing them and taking precautionary steps to reduce/curb the risk. This is known as a **risk assessment**.

Injury prevention and management is an important component of a coaching programme for participants in many sports and activities. An important function of a coach is to **identify**, **evaluate** and **refine** an injury risk coaching strategy programme for everyone in the coaching group, in addition to managing injury recovery strategies.

Coaches must also take account of guidelines and assessment opportunities from national governing bodies, experts and their own prior experience when designing and delivering injury prevention and management strategies.

figure 2.11 – Dan Hipkiss - with specially moulded shoes

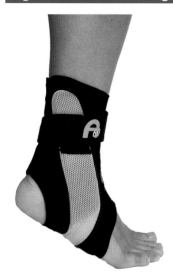

figure 2.12 – ankle bracing

Managing risks

Scientific experts at Loughborough University Sport and Technology Institute have developed a running kinematics assessment facility that uses motion analysis technology (figure 2.13).

This technology objectively assesses the running efficiency of the athlete and so can identify poor running technical elements that could potentially injure the athlete.

figure 2.13 – running kinematics, Loughborough University Sports Technology Institute

Another example of risk management, is that of physiotherapy **screening** services which are designed for sports persons of all ability. Standard tests are used to assess strengths and weaknesses in key areas, such as strength, flexibility (figure 2.14), core control and balance. This information can be used in exercise prescription for musculoskeletal conditioning, thereby decreasing the risk of getting injured.

figure 2.14 – sit and reach test

To be effective, injury prevention management has to be properly integrated into the participants' programme.

In summary there are several key progressive stages that will assist a coach and athlete to minimise the risk of injury as outlined in table 2.2

Table 2.2 - stages for prevention of injuries

	progressive stages for injury prevention
1	analyse the athletes' current risk of injury in relation to their level of development, previous history and the demands of the sport
2	select and plan activities, information and advice that will help the athletes minimise the risk of injury
3	where necessary, seek the support of other specialist staff
4	ensure that the strategy for injury prevention effectively supports and integrates with other training programme components
5	provide planned activities, information and advice to minimise the risk of injury
6	evaluate and review the success of the strategy for injury prevention
7	monitor and refine the strategy for injury prevention as part of the athletes' programme

Safety measures

Safety measures, which are intrinsic to sports coaching and teaching, include understanding the rules, having the kit and equipment appropriate to the sport and making use of technologies as illustrated in figure 2.13.

Coaches, athletes, teachers and officials must abide by set rules that are intended to minimise the chances of getting hurt or injured, by taking precautionary measures.

Safety measures

For example, in throwing activities, such as javelin, hammer and discus a **risk assessment** would include:
- Correct age-related, type, weight and dimensions of throwing equipment is selected by staff.
- Athletes wear appropriate **clothing** and **footwear**.
- The athlete should always check that the **predicted line of flight** and **adjacent** area are clear of individuals.
- Implements **should not be retrieved** until supervising staff directly instructs the thrower (or field official) to do so.

Although the chances of injury in sport can never be fully eradicated, preventative measures and procedures can minimise the risk of injury for sports' performers.

Rehabilitation from injuries

Rehabilitation programmes

Rehabilitation is the process of **restoring full physical function** after injury.

A rehabilitation programme should be designed with individual **short-term** and **long-term** goals in mind. The overall programme and individual exercises should progress safely and effectively (figure 2.15).

Traditional treatments of muscle/joint and ligaments injuries include rest, ice, elevation, compression (**RICE**), rehabilitation exercises, and anti-inflammatory medications. In recent years, advances in understanding of **muscle injury physiology** and **healing**, have led to the development of contemporary recovery methods.

figure 2.15 – injury rehabilitation

The **timescales** and **treatment options** involved in rehabilitation from injury depend upon the age of the person, severity of the injury, fitness levels and active daily lifestyles.

Immediately following an **acute injury**, the injured person should cease activity and the injured area must be immobilised to prevent further injury. The most important physical therapy used at this stage is **cryotherapy** (cold therapy) usually accompanied by protection, optimal loading, rest, ice, compression and elevation. This combination is known as **POLICE** (page 51).

An acute, inflammatory phase can last several days. The use of compression, elevation, alternating hot and cold therapies, and treatments such as **hyperbaric oxygen therapy** HBOT (page 47) and light massage can be used to stimulate the growth of new blood vessels and begin the stretching and strengthening of the damaged body part. **Therapeutic** exercise may be beneficial during this early stage to minimise de-conditioning. For example, isometric exercises assist in the increase in ROM and **minimise strength loss** in the injured part and related muscles.

The repair and healing process of the injured area takes place from anywhere between 3 weeks to a year after injury, but could be less depending on the extent of the injury.

Example 1: healing of a ligament in a sprained ankle
- The healing of a **ligament** in a sprained ankle joint can take between 2-8 weeks, depending on the severity of the impact and the extent of the injury.
- When the injured athlete can tolerate **pain** on moving the ankle joint, rehabilitation training can start.
- **Proprioceptive training** is very important, otherwise the ligament is likely to be stretched again, and **strengthening** of the peroneus longus and brevis muscles will reattain pre-injury strength levels.

Example 1: healing of a ligament in a sprained ankle

- During this recovery period the ankle joint should be **protected** from further overstretching with the help of adhesive strapping, an elastic bandage or tape or an ankle brace.
- Proprioceptive ability can be trained through specific exercises, such as the use of a **wobble board** (figure 2.16) most commonly used in the rehabilitation of ankle injuries, such as ankle sprains.
- In the case of the injured athlete, the improvement can compensate for the loss caused by injury.
- This has the effect of decreasing the chances of re-injury.
- It is recommended to start balancing on two legs, before progressing to one leg wobble board balances.
- Wobble board training can be introduced to the rehabilitation programme once swelling and bruising have disappeared and the injured athlete has regained bipedal balance.

figure 2.16 – wobble board exercise

Example 2, recovering from anterior cruciate ligament (ACL) surgery

The ACL is one of the **restraining** ligaments in the knee, as it prevents excessive forward movement of the tibia. It provides important information about **balance** to the joint and surrounding muscles, and gives the knee stability during rotational movements like twisting, turning and sidestepping.

A ruptured ACL is a common injury sustained in team sports such as soccer, rugby, netball, hockey and basketball. When it has been torn it is unable to heal and the **balance information** it carries is also lost.

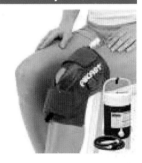

figure 2.17 – a knee cryocuff

- A **reconstructed** ligament involves replacing it with a **graft** taken from one of the hamstring tendons.
- Following the immediate surgical reconstruction of the ACL, rest, regular application of a **cryocuff** (figure 2.17) on the knee provides iced water compression to help reduce pain and swelling.
- **Within 24 to 48 hours** following the operation the patient is encouraged to walk with the aid of crutches (used to off-load weight bearing on the injured leg) and a fully supporting **leg brace** (figure 2.18) and is discharged as an outpatient for regular outpatient physiotherapy appointments.
- **Between 5-7 days** after discharge the patient should be able to flex the knee 60-90 degrees at the first physiotherapy appointment.
- For the **next 2 weeks** the aim is to regain **ROM** and start balance re-education by working through a series of exercises.
    - For example, in a lying position lift the leg 2-3 inches only keeping the knee straight.
    - Hold for 5 seconds and repeat 10 times, 4 times per day, after any sutures/clips have been removed.
- **After 2 weeks**, the wound should be healed, swelling reduced, walking with a limp and flexion improved to 110 degrees.
- **Between 2-6 weeks**, the aim is to continue the balance activities and commence light strength and endurance training.
- Goals include working on full range of movement, **balancing** on one leg, single leg squats and step ups, minimal activity related to swelling and clinical review.
- **Between 6-12 weeks**, the quadriceps/hamstring tone and definition will be poor. The graft fixation will be more secure within the femur and tibia enabling more vigorous strength training to commence. The goal during this phase of recovery is to improve strength in all leg muscles, so that equality between limbs is near.
- **Between 3 to 6 months**, **running** and **twisting** manoeuvres are introduced, building up to light sports. Gym work is encouraged until leg strength is equal (between limbs).
- The **6 month goal** aims to have rehabilitated the knee to near normal function, to be able to return to **non-contact sport**/training and have a final review at the clinic if all is good. Return to contact sport is recommended when the leg is at least 85% the strength of the other.

figure 2.18 – hinged knee bracing

Physiotherapy

The role of physiotherapy in sports medicine is one of participation in both **prevention** and **treatment** of injuries. The aim during injury rehab is to restore **original function** to the affected part.

Physiotherapy uses a range of physical recovery methods for musculoskeletal injuries that includes **heat treatment**, **massage** and **exercise** prescription. This is a big section to cover and so a restricted number of contemporary recovery methods are discussed.

Ultrasound therapy

Ultrasound is a **deep heating** process that uses acoustic sound waves to generate mechanical disruption of tissues. A gel is used on the surface of the skin to reduce friction and assist transmission of the ultrasonic waves. The treatment head is then moved over the surface of the skin, in the region of the injury, providing gentle massage as it transmits the **energy** into the tissue with no added strain to the injured area. Although ultrasound therapy was a popular treatment used by physiotherapists up to 10 years ago, it is used more sparingly within modern sports' recovery methods.

Ultrasound also acts as a **pro-inflammatory** process to stimulate the presence of **macrophages** (a type of white blood cell that engulfs and digests cellular debris). Macrophages also play an important anti-inflammatory role and can decrease immune reactions through the release of pro-inflammatory cytokines (small proteins, such as interferon, that are important in cell signalling). Their release has an effect on the behaviour of cells around them.

Ultrasound therapy increases the **extensibility** of structures such as ligaments, tendons and fibrous scar tissue inside and outside the joint capsule, resulting from the build up of mature collagen fibres which may form after the injury.
This **softens any scar tissue**, within muscle tendons and/or ligaments, without any strain.

figure 2.19 – medical support

Ultrasound therapy is beneficial immediately following the **acute stage of an injury** and should be discontinued when pro-inflammatory agents are no longer needed.
There is a possibility that the ill-advised use of ultrasound can damage nervous tissue.

Joint mobilisation and massage of soft tissue

Sports massage is defined as a collection of massage techniques performed on athletes or active individuals for the purpose of **aiding recovery** from exercise sessions or rehab from injury.

*   Massage techniques assist in **soft tissue mobilisation**, muscle function and **reduce local pain** (figure 2.19).
*   Muscle and joints can be **passively moved** to full range.
*   In addition sports massage **reduces DOMS** symptoms following intense anaerobic training.
*   Sports massage needs to be regular and can be **expensive**.
*   There are much cheaper ways of gaining the above benefits. For example, a **foam roller** massage has many of the same benefits as a sports massage done by a practitioner, including reduced inflammation, scar tissue and joint stress, as well as improved circulation and improved flexibility (figure 2.20).
*   Rolling preps muscles for stretching and so is a valuable part of a warm-up and cool-down for both rehab and regular schedules.
*   Sports massage can only be used for treatment during the **acute stage** in terms of **lymphatic drainage** in order to reduce swelling.

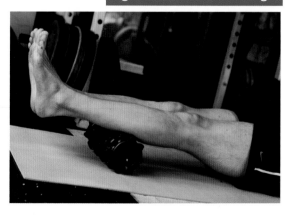
figure 2.20 – roller massage

*   However sport massage treatments are mainly carried out at the **repair stage**.
*   Care should be taken that excessive forces are not applied to traumatised tissue.

Electro stimulation

Electro stimulation (ES) also known as **neuromuscular electrical stimulation** (NMES), is a training technique used for injury prevention, injury treatment, toning, pain relief, muscular recovery and physical preparation.

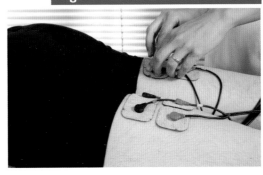

figure 2.21 – electro stimulation

Electrodes are placed on the muscle groups such as the abdominal muscles, hamstrings (figure 2.21), calf muscles, plantar arch muscles and lower back muscles. An electric current is produced which is sent to the nerve fibres causing a mechanical response in the muscle. The current settings can vary depending on the clinical pathology requirements.

ES is thought to affect the body with associated **therapeutic benefits** that:
- Stimulate muscles to **contract**, by stimulating muscle fibre recruitment.
- Stimulate nerves to **decrease pain** by stimulating larger nerve fibres that can override the smaller nerve fibres that produce pain.
- Increase **blood flow** to speed healing.
- Reduce **inflammation**.
- Stimulate cells to reproduce and speed **healing**.
- Assist the **removal of lactic acid** following a training session or competition and hence reduce **DOMS**.

- ES can be used early on in the recovery process when a wound has healed but the injured body part is not ready for loading.
- ES in combination with physical activity, serves is to stimulate weaker muscles to contract and improve strength more quickly.

Exercise programmes to strengthen weakened muscles/joints.
- In the case of a planned surgical procedure, the physiotherapist can be valuable both before and after.
- For example, prior to an ACL or meniscus operation, it is essential for the patient to exercise his or her thigh muscles as they are responsible for stabilising the knee, and if they are well-trained before the operation, subsequent rehabilitation is facilitated.
- Assessing an individual's functional state is part of the physiotherapist's work. By analysing the causes and consequences of a functional impairment, the physiotherapist can draw up a programme for the treatment of muscles, joints and ligaments.
- The treatment methods used are flexibility, strength and coordination in prescribed portions, together with encouragement, rest and pain relief.

Strength training

One of the major detraining effects that occur during long-term injuries is **muscular atrophy** of the unused limb. It is therefore essential that these particular muscles increase their size back to normal. Within the early stages of muscle rehabilitation, muscular size can be increased by effective electrical stimulation to the muscle.

figure 2.22 – the plank

Core stability exercises should not be neglected and can be combined with the start of performing some more traditional weight training exercises. The **plank** (figure 2.22 and figure 2.7, page 36) is one of the best body weight training exercises for improving core conditioning (which is often compromised following injury) but it also works gluteal and hamstring muscle groups, supports posture and improves balance.

As soon as the injured athlete can tolerate increased loading, he can progress through his rehab process back into more traditional strength and conditioning training programmes. For example, free squats can progress to single leg squats.

Strength training

Strengthening the quadriceps and hamstrings will directly result in increased stability of the knee joint and in turn further reduce the reoccurrence of hamstring injuries such as tears. During this period, the injured athlete will start to benefit from anatomical adaptations, such as **muscular hypertrophy** as he or she gradually progresses to pre-injury strength levels.

Elastic band training and tubing

figure 2.23 – Thera Band exercise

Elastic resistance is a unique type of resistance training that can be safely used in injury rehabilitation. The resistance provided by the latex **elastic band** or **tubing** is based on the amount that the band or tubing is stretched. Thera Band (a brand name for a type of elastic band of varying strength) elastic resistance training increases strength, mobility and muscle function, as well as reducing joint pain.

For example, following a shoulder injury, the main focus is to increase the **range of movement** and **muscle strength**, especially the rotator cuff which is a group of muscles that rotate the arm (figure 2.23).

Note that in this example the resistance is light, but sufficient to create the required adaptive physiological response.

Rest and active rest

The physiotherapist will include rest and active rest to give stressed body parts time to recover prior to the next part of the rehabilitation programme.
- Modern rehab includes **rest** as essential recovery time after trauma. **Active rest** means that low level exercises are undertaken in order to improve the blood flow through affected areas without physical stress, and therefore to promote healing via blood carried nutrients, particularly oxygen.
- Cell to cell activation is really important, since it stimulates the healing process.
- This also has the effect of preventing a muscle or other soft tissue from healing at a shorter length than it was before the injury. This is because post-trauma muscle length is unpredictable depending on joint flexibility and nutrition.
- Low level activity also has the effect of keeping muscle fit enough to exert force once an injury is healed.

Compression clothing

Compression clothing works by applying a constant pressure on the body part, which adds **external pressure** to the **veins**.
- By squeezing the muscle, **venous return** is enhanced, which may reduce the potential for **venous pooling**.
- And a reduction in post-exercise symptoms such as light headedness/dizziness.
- Increased venous return facilitates an increase in **cardiac output** (Starling's Law of the heart), resulting in increased **transportation of oxygenated blood** to recovering tissues.
- An increased blood supply will carry nutrients to the muscles and help **remove waste materials** more quickly.
- Recovery is improved and **DOMS** is reduced.

Compression clothing is also said to potentially enhance sporting performance by:
- Reducing **muscle oscillation** (vibration of leg muscles due to the repetitive impact loading).
- Increasing **proprioception**.
- Improving **body aerodynamics**.

Products include socks, short and long tights and short-sleeve and long-sleeve tops. Compression stockings are worn by runners, basketball players and other athletes hoping the socks will boost their performance and reduce the risk of muscle soreness, injuries and muscle cramps.

Compression clothing

Compression stockings are known to decrease post-exercise soreness, by increasing circulation and reducing the lactic acid build-up during the exercise period, thereby reducing **DOMS** and preventing medical conditions such as **deep vein thrombosis** (DVT).

figure 2.24 – compression tights

Compression tights (figure 2.24) may be useful for people with certain existing injuries, by providing support to minimise undesired movement of underlying tissues. Faster recovery means being able to train for longer periods sooner, and basically doing more of it. But to get the full benefits for recovery associated with compression tights, they must be worn during and after exercise for up to 24 hours.
When the compression clothing is too tight it can cause tissue damage by restricting blood flow and ROM. It is recommended to seek specialist guidance on fabric specifications.

The rationale for wearing compression sportswear is solid, but the evidence is weak.

Climate chambers

Environmental chambers replicate different climates at the press of a button with precise and harmonious control of altitude, temperature and humidity.

Hyperbaric chamber
A hyperbaric oxygen chamber is an example of a chamber that provides a controlled climate in which sporting injuries can be treated.

Research has found that healing is promoted by increasing the oxygen partial pressure surrounding affected areas. The various techniques employed to promote this are:

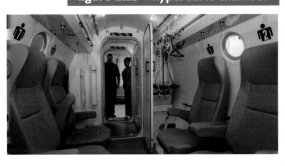

figure 2.25 – hyperbaric chamber

* Oxygen tents.
* Sleeping in a greater than normal proportion of oxygen in breathed air.
* Hyperbaric (meaning high pressure) chambers (figure 2.25), in which an injured athlete will spend periods of time in a zone in which the air pressure is above normal.
* Therefore forcing oxygen above normal pressure into the body. This is called **hyperbaric oxygen therapy** (**HBOT**).

HBOT is a treatment which enhances the body's natural healing process by inhalation of 100% oxygen in a **total body chamber**, where atmospheric pressure is increased and controlled. Initially HBOT served to provide a means of therapy to facilitate a speedier resumption to pre-injury activity levels as well as improve the short and long-term prognosis of the injury.

HBOT sessions can commence as soon as the injured athlete has recovered from the initial treatment phase.

HBOT is now commonly used as a regular therapy within professional sports such as rugby, soccer and cricket, with its known benefits listed below. Such benefits allow athletes of every level to recover faster, perform sharper, and train longer.

HBOT benefits
* Delivers up to 25 times normal levels of oxygen to body tissues.
* Stimulates the **growth of new blood vessels**, thus improving blood flow to areas with an arterial blockage that may have resulted from an impact injury.
* Reduces **fatigue** from inadequate oxygen supply to body tissues.
* Speeds up **recovery** from fatigue such as DOMS.
* Boosts **immune** system function by stimulating white blood cell activity, thereby controlling infection.
* Decreases swelling and **inflammation**.
* Promotes **regeneration** of injured tissues.
* Decreases ligament and tissue **healing time**.
* Aids the **repair** of stress fractures and breaks.

HBOT benefits

HBOT is an example of a secondary therapy used to treat sports injuries and its purpose is to assist the primary treatment received, for example, from a physiotherapist or doctor. HBOT assists in the recovery of acute traumatic injury to muscle contusions and sprains and strains thereby reducing recovery time.

figure 2.26 – a hypoxic tent

Hypobaric chambers

A hypobaric chamber or an **hypoxic tent** (low oxygen tent, figure 2.26), provide a hypoxic environment that contains a reduced amount of oxygen in the air compared with sea level atmospheric pressure (hypobaric means low pressure).

Hypoxic simulation occurs in cells and tissues that are in a hypoxic state and so is responsible for a number of adaptive responses that enable the body to make better use of the limited oxygen available. The main adaptive response is an increase in manufacture of red blood cells (**erythropoietin** production), alongside increases in **myoglobin**, **mitochondria** and **oxidative enzymes** levels.

These responses support an increased **oxygen** and **nutrient** delivery to body tissues undergoing repair, such as the healing of bone fractures. This is of great value to the process of rehabilitation from injury, particularly when the athlete is exercising within the hypobaric environment during the active phase of rehab.

In addition, this **hypoxic microenvironment** acts as a protective mechanism for recovery by stimulating the repair of a variety of proteins, fibroblasts, endothelial cells and osteoblasts used in the healing of fractures.

As with the HBOT recovery method, hypoxic sessions can commence as soon as the injured athlete has recovered from the initial sedentary treatment phase to the active recovery phase of rehab.

Sauna and steam heat room therapies

- **Heat therapies** should not be used immediately after an injury as this will increase body temperature and increase bleeding in the surrounding area and so will not be beneficial until after 48 hours after the injury and during rehabilitation.
- Within a climate chamber, such as a sauna or steam room, depending on the heat and humidity, core temperature starts to increase within 5-15 minutes.
- It is important to limit the time spent in heat chambers (hot or cold) otherwise body tissues become damaged.

- Heat creates a stress response in the body.
- As temperature rises, the body responds by rerouting blood flow to increase blood vessel dilation and secreting a number of hormones, including the **growth hormone** (GH, or **somatotropin**) which assists in increasing the rate of musculoskeletal tissue repair.

- Heat therapy reduces cellular oxidation rates (high rates of oxidation may compromise the recovery rate and cause damage to cell membranes).
- Heat therapy also stimulates **heat-shock proteins**, which play a role in organising other proteins that are thought to play a role in the growth/repair of muscle tissue.
- Heat therapy provides an ideal environment for regaining the ROM of joints and muscles.
- With heat therapy's ability to enhance muscle growth and limit oxidation, it should also enhance the injury recovery processes alongside other contemporary recovery methods.

Cryotheraphy

Cryotherapy is the treatment by means of applications of **cold temperatures**, and can be used as soon as the wound has healed (i.e. no broken skin). Cryotherapy treatment decreases skin, subcutaneous and muscle temperature, causing narrowing of the blood vessels (**vasoconstriction**). Its goal is to decrease cellular metabolism, decrease **inflammation**, pain and muscle spasm. A variety of cold applications can be used to treat sports injuries.

Whole body cryotherapy (WBC)

WBC involves exposing individuals to extremely cold dry air (below -100°C) for two to four minutes in a **cryogenic chamber**.
Reduction in skin and muscle tissue temperatures reduces blood flow to the arms and legs (**vasoconstriction**) and divert blood flow to the body's central core.

On leaving the chamber, blood flow returns to the arms and legs (**vasodilation**) reinstating normal oxygen levels, thus aiding the healing process.
WBC relieves muscle soreness and **inflammation** following high intensity training, as a result of reduced muscle metabolism, and is a popular recovery method used by professional sportspeople. WBC is a much quicker alternative to ice baths, but does require specialist expensive equipment.

Alternative cold therapy methods

Various alternative and cheaper cooling therapies are used in acute sports injuries as well as rehabilitation of the injured athlete, injury prevention and recovery from training and competitions.
For example, ice packs, ice towels, ice massage and frozen gel packs.

Ice baths

Ice baths (figure 2.27) use the fact that **chilling** the affected area can **reduce local inflammation**. The ice bath is thought to constrict blood vessels, flush waste products such as lactic acid and reduce swelling and tissue breakdown.

Total cold water immersion

Studies have shown that total cold water **upright immersion** (at an optimal temperature of 10 degrees and up to 10 minutes immersion) **decreases inflammation** following injury and aids recovery from training. The effect is best when the water pressure is greatest. In addition, it gives the athlete a feeling of perceived freshness.

Precautions should be taken because prolonged application of very low temperatures could have detrimental effects.

Contrast therapy

This is the alternating use of hot and cold application to an injured muscle or body part for therapeutic effect (for example, increasing blood flow to speed up the recovery process).

Hydrotherapy

Hydrotherapy is a therapeutic whole-body treatment that involves moving and exercising in a warm water pool. The temperature, pressure and movement of water are controlled and changed according to who's using the pool.

For example, **aquajogging** (figure 2.28) has proven to be a very good form of injury rehabilitation. This is because of its **low impact** on the muscles and the use of water resistance as an effective way of applying force to the lower limbs.

This combination avoids muscle soreness, stress fractures and aching joints and enables an injured athlete to **maintain fitness** during a rehabilitation programme. This method of hydrotherapy can be used as an alternative option to training on hard running surfaces, in addition to supporting recovery from hard impact training.

Nutrition

By choosing the right diet and supplements, recovery from injury can be enhanced. Eating a diet that achieves a the balance between allowing the immune system to function normally, whilst preventing the inflammatory response from becoming excessive, will speed up the process of rehabilitation from injury.

figure 2.27 – ice bath

figure 2.28 – aquajogging

Nutrition

Some foods contain **anti-inflammatory agents** as found in leafy green vegetables, avocados, fish (mackerel and salmon), mixed nuts, seeds and garlic. Tumeric is an anti-inflammatory spice that contains curcumin, an agent that suppresses the breakdown of protein and enhances the uptake of glucose into muscle, all good for injury rehabilitation.

A diet planned for injury recovery should avoid pro-inflammatory foods, such as processed foods high in saturated fats, and foods containing trans fats found in cakes, pies and cookies.

figure 2.29 – a balanced diet

Getting the optimal **energy intake** is important. When the body is healing it requires more calories (CHO) than when completely sedentary but not as much as it would require than when training at full fitness. The **basal metabolic rate** (BMR) can be a useful guide to work out a required calorie intake. Usually the main adjustment to be made is in reducing pre- and post-workout carbohydrates (in the case of injury this is a rehab workout).

Having plenty of good quality **protein** such as quality meat, whey and dairy products is important. Protein provides essential **amino acids** that provide the building blocks for recovery (figure 2.30).

figure 2.30 – sources of protein

Increase oily fish intake and consider taking a **fish oil supplement**, such as omega 3 fish oil capsules. Helpful foods include oily fish such as salmon tuna and mackerel, olive oil, nuts and seeds and avocado.

Eat foods that are rich in **vitamins** and **minerals** (figure 2.31). The immune system can be suppressed following injury and is important in supporting the body through the healing process.

Foods that contain essential **micronutrients**, like **vitamins** B and D, copper, calcium, and magnesium, as well as other compounds. **Bromelain** (in pineapple) and **curcumin** (in turmeric) are known to be effective in healing body tissues.

figure 2.31 – sources of vitamins and minerals

Supplementing the diet with **whey protein** and essential amino acids, such as **glutamine**, may be useful in providing some of the building blocks for tissue repair. While a good rehabilitation programme is a must when recovering from injury, having the correct **nutritional strategy** also plays its part.

POLICE and RICE

There are two recognised first aid methods that are used to assist the healing process:

RICE

RICE (Rest, Ice, Compression and Elevation) is a traditional procedure applied to soft tissue injury. Apply the frozen object to the area for 20 minutes three times a day for the first 48 hours.

*   **R**est: by **resting** the injured body part, further damage is prevented and the healing process is speeded up.
*   **I**ce: applied to injured body part, **reduces internal bleeding** and swelling. Ice can help to reduce acute pain.

RICE

- **C**ompression: reduces swelling by **supporting** soft tissues, minimising the danger of further damage and speeding up recovery. Compression is used in conjunction with ice to cool and compress the injury, for example the use of a cryo-cuff (figure 2.17, page 43).
- **E**levation: elevating the injured area above the heart aids the **drainage** of any liquid/leakage caused by the injury, reducing swelling and inflammation to the injured site.

POLICE

The **POLICE** method is another simple acronym to help ensure that the injured body part is protected, optimally loaded, and receives the benefits of ice, compression, and elevation. POLICE (**P**rotection, **O**ptimal **L**oading, **I**ce **C**ompression and **E**levation) is a more recent procedure for injuries, though not necessary soft tissue injuries.
The main difference between RICE and POLICE is the inclusion of Protection and Optimal Loading in POLICE.

- **Protection**: includes rest and protection for the injured area during the first few days following an injury.
- If it hurts to bear weight on the injury, use assistive devices, for example, crutches or a hinged brace (figure 2.18, page 43).
- If it hurts to move the area, **immobilise** it with a splint.
- These aids offer protection for the injured area.
- After a few days, gentle motion can be started whilst maintaining a level of protection.

- **Optimal loading**: whilst protecting the injured body part, gentle motion can, and should be started as soon as possible during the repair phase of a rehab programme.
- For example, after a shoulder injury the injured person would be able to progress from a few days of rest to passive ROM, active ROM, and finally, rotator cuff strengthening exercises (figure 2.23, page 46).
- This **progressive loading** of the injured body part can help promote optimal healing of the injury, and it can prevent delays in returning to normal due to joint and muscle tightness or muscle atrophy.
- Progressive optimal loading is highly supported by medical practitioners.
- POLICE is much better than RICE as rest is not always required.

Summary of advantages and disadvantages of rehabilitation strategies

Table 2.3 - **advantages and disadvantages of compression clothing**

advantages	disadvantages
compression clothing increases venous return and transportation of oxygenated blood to body tissues	compression clothing is expensive to buy
removes waste products such as lactic acid	if clothing is too tight, it can cause tissue damage and decrease ROM
recovery is improved and DOMS and cramping are reduced	need to seek specialist guidance on fabric specifications
compression stockings help prevent DVT following surgery	the rationale for wearing compression sportswear is solid, but the evidence is weak
reduces muscle oscillation	
muscle and joints can be passively moved to full range	
increases proprioception	
body shape is more aerodynamic	

Table 2.4 - **advantages and disadvantages of nutrition as a therapy**

advantages	disadvantages
in association with a controlled rehab programme, eating the right foods and supplements and required intake will aid the recovery process	

Table 2.5 - **advantages and disadvantages of physiotherapy**

advantages	disadvantages
physiotherapy offers a range of recovery methods that treat both acute and chronic musculoskeletal field injuries within a rehabilitation programme	physiotherapists rely on the experience of other team members that may not always be correct in their injury diagnosis
this ranges from joint, nerve and soft tissue mobilisations as well as other modalities which are underpinned by a scientific evidence base, such as ultrasound and electro stimulation (ES)	going privately for both physiotherapy and sports massage sessions is expensive
ultrasound reduces the healing time of certain soft tissue injuries, during the early rehab phase, by acting as a pro-inflammatory agent	ultrasound therapy has been associated with nervous damage and should only be applied during the early stages of rehab
ES serves is to stimulate weaker muscles to contract and improve strength more quickly	in acute injuries, taping may restrict circulation
sports massage assists in soft tissue mobilisation, muscle function and pain reduction during the repair stage	massage cannot be used on soft tissue injuries such as tendon ruptures and open wounds
muscle and joints can be passively moved to full range	
sports massage can be used as a gentle recovery method during the acute stage of an injury to assist in lymphatic drainage in order to reduce swelling	tape may cause may cause irritation by mechanical or chemical means or because of allergy and the effects may be exaggerated by sweating, itching and bacterial infection
taping and bracing are recovery methods used by physiotherapists to support a weakened part of the body, without limiting its function	taping may lull the athlete into a false sense of security, encouraging the athlete to resume his or her sporting activity too soon thereby making the injury worse
physiotherapists are part of a team which includes doctors, other therapists, sport psychologists and coaches who work together to maximise the athlete's recovery	

Table 2.6 - **advantages and disadvantages of climate chambers**

advantages	disadvantages
environmental chambers replicate different climates at the press of a button with precise and harmonious control of altitude, temperature and humidity	access to climate chambers may be difficult and therefore climate chamber treatment may be limited
to provide controlled environments where rehab of both acute and chronic injuries can take place from the initial injury phase to active full recovery	methods may be restricted to those who can afford it or elite athletes who are supported by a medical care scheme
HBOT facilitates a speedier resumption to pre-injury activity levels, following injury, due to increased delivery of increased amounts of oxygen to body tissues	not always 100% effective
hypobaric chambers stimulate erythropoietin production and hence oxygen uptake that can be used to stimulate the healing of bone fractures	

Table 2.7 - **advantages and disadvantages of cryotherapy**

advantages	disadvantages
less pain because nerve activity is slowed down	if an ice pack is too cold or applied for too long, it can actually damage skin and nerve tissues
less swelling because constriction of the blood vessels helps reduce blood flow to the area, reducing swelling	prolonged exposure in a cryochamber can give the athlete hypothermia, in addition to long-term tissue damage
faster healing because cellular activity slows down, which contributes to a faster healing process	the sudden drop in body temperature can be harmful, causing a sudden increase in heart rate and breathing rate
removes waste materials from the injured site	

Table 2.8 - **advantages and disadvantages of heat therapies**

advantages	disadvantages
a combination of hot and cold therapies dilates and constricts the blood vessels of the muscles thereby increasing the flow of oxygen and nutrients to musculoskeletal tissues, helping to heal the damaged tissue and removing waste products	heat treatment should not be too hot, as this may lead to the skin being burnt
heat stimulates voluntary muscles and the sensory receptors in the skin, decreasing the transmissions of pain signals to the brain and partially relieve the discomfort	heat treatments should not be used on damaged skin or on areas where circulation is poor
heat application facilitates stretching the soft tissues, including muscles, connective tissue, and adhesions that become stiff following injury	
hydrotherapy provides a safe, low impact form of heat therapy used in rehabilitation programmes	

Table 2.9 - **advantages and disadvantages of RICE and POLICE**

advantages	disadvantages
RICE is an established first aid procedure using during the initial injury phase	people can take the rest phase a little too far, and that can lead to decreased muscle strength and flexibility and so delay the restoration of normal functional mobility and activity
POLICE extends the remit of RICE to include protection and optimal loading and so deals with both the initial phase of an injury to the recovery phases of healing and rehabilitation	compressing an injury may reduce swelling, but when too tight it can cause numbness, tingling, or increased pain some experts believe that ice, applied initially after an injury, impedes the normal healing process

Summary of how coaches can assist athletes to manage and recover from injury

Table 2.11 - **summary**

coaches assist athletes by:
working with the athlete and specialist staff to evaluate the nature of the injury and its physical and psychological implications for performance and rehabilitation
working with the athlete and specialist staff to devise a strategy to assist the athlete to manage and recover from injury
ensuring the strategy is effectively integrated into the overall coaching programme
providing and supporting agreed activities that will assist the athlete to manage and recover from the injury
evaluating and reviewing the success of the strategy for injury management and recovery
monitoring and refining the strategy for injury management and recovery as part of the coaching programme

Practice questions

1) Sports injuries can be broadly classified as either acute or chronic.
   a) Explain what is meant by these two classifications, using examples where appropriate.   4 marks

   b) What are the common causes of chronic injuries?   3 marks

2) a) Describe the medical condition known as tendinopathy?   2 marks

   b) What are the similarities and differences between golfer's elbow and tennis elbow?   6 marks

Practice questions

3) Why are joint sprains a particular problem? — 2 marks

4) Screening is a key part of the professional sportspersons daily life.
   How can it be used in injury prevention? — 4 marks

5) Rapid recovery from injury is vital for elite performers and they now use a
   wide range of injury recovery techniques.
   For each of the following methods describe the treatment and its purpose.
   a) Cryotherapy. — 3 marks

   b) Proprioceptive retraining. — 3 marks

   c) Therapeutic massage. — 3 marks

6) Playing kit and equipment are major factors that an athlete needs to consider in injury prevention.
   Identify the key factors that affect the selection of their use. — 4 marks

7) Tiny tears and inflammation can develop near the site of an injury.
   a) Explain how cooling down and compression clothing can speed up the recovery process. — 6 marks

   b) Explain why it is important for an athlete to recover after exercise. — 4 marks

   c) Identify three other strategies used by athletes to speed up recovery. — 3 marks

8) Hyperbaric oxygen chambers and ice baths are aids to rehabilitation for elite performers.
   Briefly describe how each of these therapies assist in this process. — 6 marks

9) Describe a suitable method of treatment that is appropriate for an acute soft tissue injury. — 4 marks

10) Explain how periodisation could be used to minimise the risk of sports injuries. — 4 marks

11) Elite competitors often continue training with and through their injuries.
    Discuss the implications for coaches and sports medical teams in establishing an
    appropriate protocol for rehabilitation and return to sport from injury. — 15 marks

12) Discuss the advantages and disadvantages of contemporary rehabilitation strategies
    when dealing with sports injuries. — 8 marks

13) A basketball player twists his ankle in a game and has to leave the court.
    a) Describe the immediate treatment that they should use. — 4 marks

    b) The injury does not respond to the treatment. Identify two other treatments
       that could be used to help recovery. — 3 marks

14) Discuss the principles and guidelines for injury prevention. — 5 marks

15) Why should stretching be part of an injury preventative training programme? — 2 marks

16) Discuss the importance of nutrition as part of an injury rehabilitation programme. — 6 marks

17) Assess the use of POLICE rather than RICE as a rehabilitation strategy for
    sporting injuries sustained in a team game. — 8 marks

Answers link: http://www.jroscoe.co.uk/downloads/a2_revise_pe_edexcel/EdexcelA2_ch2_answers.pdf

CHAPTER 3: *Linear motion*

Linear motion

Linear means in a straight line. Chapter 3 attempts to put into perspective concepts involving movement in a single direction such as speed, velocity, acceleration and force (through Newton's Second Law of Motion).

> **STUDENT NOTE**
>
> Newton's first, second and third laws of motion are discussed in detail in AS/A1 Revise PE for Edexcel, ISBN 9781901424881, Topic 1 page 28 onwards.

Scalars and vectors

The ideas behind **scalars** and **vectors** are used extensively in maths and physics.

Scalar

A **scalar** is a quantity which has size or value only. Quantities like mass, speed, energy, power, and length have a value only. For example, a person could have a mass of 60 kg, or 1000 joules of energy are used up when performing an exercise.

No directional angle is required when talking about these quantities.

Energy is a scalar which has a value only, and the value of energy consumed daily by a Tour de France cyclist is 6,000 kilocalories - which has no direction.

Speed (measured in metres per second - ms^{-1}), distance and time are scalars which are linked by a simple equation.

  speed = distance travelled per second (ms^{-1})

  speed = distance travelled in metres (m) / time taken to travel in seconds (s)

Velocity is also defined as:

  velocity = distance travelled in metres (m) / time taken to travel in seconds (s)

  in a given direction, since velocity is a vector

Vector

A **vector** is a quantity which has **size** (called magnitude) and **direction**. By quantity we mean something like weight, displacement, velocity, acceleration, force, and momentum, all of which are vectors, and therefore have to have a direction connected to them as well as value or size. For example, a force could be 100 newtons downward (the downward specifies the direction), an acceleration could be 10 metres per second squared forwards (the forwards specifies the direction).

Usually in maths, the direction is specified by the angle θ (measured in an anticlockwise direction to the x-axis) in a graph of an arrow drawn on the graph, with the size (magnitude) represented by the length of the arrow (figure 3.1).

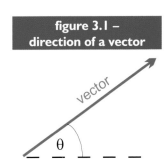

figure 3.1 – direction of a vector

Force as a vector

Force is a vector and therefore has a direction (shown as angle θ to the horizontal in figure 3.1, page 55) as well as a size or value. This point is very important to anyone thinking about what happens when forces are applied, because it enables a force in one direction to cancel out completely an equal force in the opposite direction so that, in spite of very large forces being involved in a given situation, forces cancel out to give a **zero** (or very small) net or **resultant force**.

A **resultant vector** is **two or more vectors added together**, taking into account their directions.

For example, consider the weight lifter in figure 3.2. As he pulls upwards on the bar, he exerts a force of 1000 newtons (N) upwards on the bar and gravity exerts a force of 980 newtons downwards on the bar.

The resultant or net force acting on the actual bar is therefore only about 20 N upwards, just enough to accelerate the bar off the floor.

The idea that net force causes acceleration is linked with **Newton's First** and **Second Laws** of Motion and is a fundamental property of force.

Also, it is possible for many forces acting in all sorts of different directions to cancel one another out. When this happens, from Newton's First Law we know that the object (or sportsperson) on which the forces act will either be stationary or moving at constant velocity (in a straight line). This situation is called **equilibrium**: where the object is stationary this is static equilibrium and where it is moving at constant velocity this is dynamic equilibrium.

Net Force

The point of this is that when more than one vector has to be taken into account, then they must be added together taking note of the direction of each vector.

In figure 3.3 for example, two forces of 500 newtons are acting, the green force acts upwards, and the red force acts downwards. Because they are acting in opposite directions, they add up to nil, in other words they exactly cancel out to give zero net force. Note that this gymnast is also in unstable equilibrium.

- In figure 3.4, the **vertical forces** acting on the sprinter are the weight (W = force due to gravity) acting downwards, and the ground reaction force (R) acting upwards. These two forces are identical in value but opposite in direction and therefore cancel out exactly to give zero net force vertically.

- The **horizontal forces** are the friction force (F) acting forwards, and the **air resistance** or **drag** (A) acting backwards. These two forces are equal in value but opposite in direction, and hence cancel out to give zero net force acting horizontally.

- Hence relatively large forces can act, but they can cancel out because of their direction. Note that zero net force does not mean that the sprinter is stationary, (from Newton's first law of motion).

- Equally, when the forces are added up and there is an unbalanced **resultant** (the forces **do not cancel out**), then there is a **net force** acting.

- The body on which this force is acting will then accelerate in the **direction** of this net force as specified by Newton's second law .

figure 3.2 – forces acting on a bar

Pull on bar
1000 N

Weight of bar
980 N

figure 3.3 – vectors cancel out

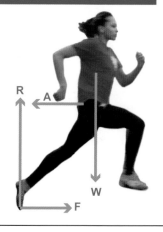
figure 3.4 – forces cancel out

R   A

W

F

Further notes on vectors

There are specific mathematical rules that enable you to add together vectors that are not in the same direction. You may notice from figures 3.5 and 3.6 that the resultant of two forces at an angle has been drawn by completing a **parallelogram** (in figure 3.5) or a **rectangle** (in figure 3.6, where the forces are at right angles). The resultant then lies along the diagonal of the parallelogram.

In figure 3.5, the resultant of the forces in the wires (T_1 and T_2) supporting the gymnast upwards **cancels out** exactly his/her weight (W) downwards (static equilibrium).

In figure 3.6, again, the **resultant** of the normal reaction force (R) and the combined friction forces (air resistance and friction with the ground) exactly cancels out the weight of the skier – note the geometric vector diagram (dynamic equilibrium).

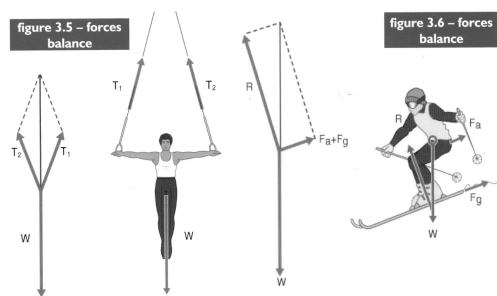

figure 3.5 – forces balance

figure 3.6 – forces balance

Figure 3.7 shows **resultants of forces** for the swimmer. His weight (W) is balanced by the upthrust of the water (U) and the forward thrust (T) cancels out the backward drag (D) of the water (again dynamic equilibrium).

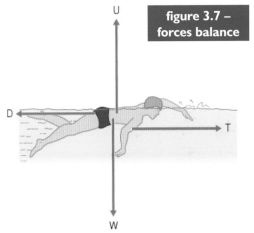

figure 3.7 – forces balance

Resultants

It is also possible to calculate the size and direction of resultant vectors using trigonometry. Looking at figure 3.8, in which **R** (the reaction force) and F (the total friction force) are at right angles, we note that angle α lies between F and the resultant **X** of the two vectors as drawn. Therefore using Pythagoras theorem on figure 3.8:

$$X^2 = R^2 + F^2 \text{ and}$$
$$X = \sqrt{(R^2 + F^2)}$$
$$= \text{the magnitude of the resultant } (\sqrt{} = \text{'square root of'}).$$

Also:
$$\tan \alpha = \frac{R}{F}$$

and α = the angle between **X** and **R**, which gives the direction of the resultant.

Hence, looking at figure 3.8, the normal reaction force on the sprinter's foot has the value 700 N and the forward friction force 200 N, so that the resultant total reaction force on his/her foot, **X**, has the magnitude:

$$X = \sqrt{(700^2 + 200^2)} = \sqrt{(530\,000)} = \textbf{728 N}$$

The angle α between X and the 700 N force will be:

$$\alpha = \tan^{-1} \frac{R}{F} = \text{the angle between X and R which gives the \textbf{direction} of R.}$$
$$= \tan^{-1} \left(\frac{700}{200}\right) = \tan^{-1} 3.5 = \textbf{74.06°}$$

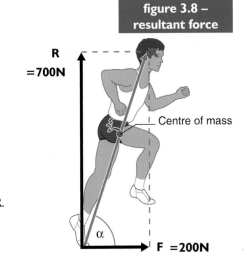

figure 3.8 – resultant force

R =700N

Centre of mass

α

F =200N

Resultants

Hence the resultant force has a **value** of 728 N acting at an **angle** of 74.06° to the 200 N force (horizontal). Note that this force X passes through the centre of mass of the runner and therefore would cause no toppling or rotation of his/her body during the running action. It is beyond the scope of this book to progress these ideas further (physics text books will provide many examples of the use and practice of the formulae).

Distance, position and displacement

Speed (a **scalar**) and **velocity** (a **vector**) are ideas that involve a body or object changing its position. For example, if an athlete starts a race – the stopwatch or electronic timer starts also – and he runs 10 m in 2 seconds, his position has changed by 10 m from the start line, the distance moved is 10 m and the average speed over this distance is 5 metres per second.

The same idea could be used in a game situation but now the position of the centre-forward might be 20 m out from the opposing goal, on a line 10 m to the left of the left-hand post (figure 3.9). At this point he might shoot for goal and the ball travels 25 m – the distance from the striker to the net at the back of the goal – in 0.5 seconds. In this case the speed of the ball would be 50 metres per second.

figure 3.9 – a striker 20 m from goal

So, you can see that distance is usually measured from one point to another point and the position of the points tells us where they are in space (or on a pitch or court). This distinction becomes important in races or games where starts and finishes are fixed.

The **displacement** of a sportsperson from the start of an event may also be important in some cases. For example, a triathlete may swim, cycle and run huge distances but he/she may only be displaced at most 2 km from the start position. So the displacement of the triathlete is the distance (as the crow flies) between the start position and the position of the triathlete – usually the direction is also taken into account.

Acceleration

Acceleration is the change of **velocity** per second or:

$$\text{acceleration} = \frac{\text{final velocity - starting velocity}}{\text{time taken to change}} \quad (ms^{-2})$$

Here, the velocity includes its direction, so we could have the velocity having the same value (magnitude), but just changing its direction. This happens for an object following a circular path (like the head of a hammer in the hammer throw). This means that the velocity is changing and therefore there is an acceleration towards the centre of the circular path. This also means that there will be a force (by Newton's Second Law) towards the centre of the circular path.

Weight and mass

These two ideas are often confused. **Mass** is a scalar and represents the total quantity of matter in an object. **Weight** is the force due to gravity on a mass (with a direction towards the centre of the Earth). Weight will vary slightly over the surface of the Earth depending on the gravitational field strength.

The gravitational field strength changes slightly depending on the thickness of the Earth's crust, the longitude, the proximity of large mountains, and the height above sea level.
Weight is approximately 10 newtons for each kilogramme of mass (the actual figure is 9.81 N kg^{-1} but it is usual to approximate this to 10 N kg^{-1} to simplify calculations), and will act on the **centre of mass** of a body (the point which represents the averaged position of all the mass of a body), as covered in the Edexcel AS/A1 book Topic 1 page 32 in this series.

Hence if the mass of a sprinter is 50 kg, then her weight would be 50 x 10 = 500 newtons **towards** the centre of the Earth.

Weight is also the predominant force acting on an object projected into flight.

Weight

Gravity is an example of a force field (others occurring in nature are electromagnetic and nuclear fields which are not relevant to this text).

A **force field** is a means by which a force can be exerted **without touching**. So, for example, a ball in flight is accelerated towards the earth's centre continuously and therefore has a net force acting on it without being in contact with the earth.

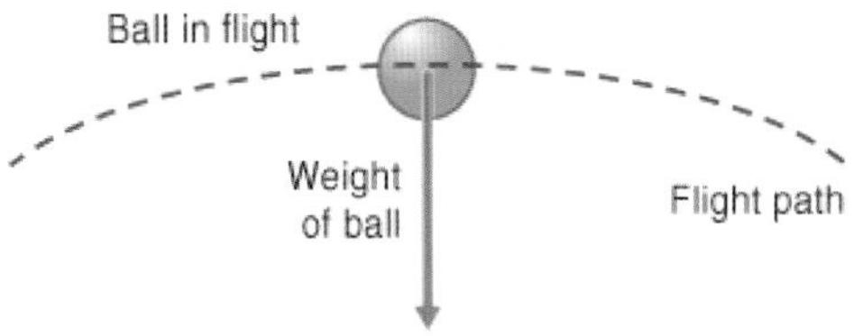

When thinking about this, you may be confused by the fact that the air surrounds the ball (figure 3.10, since the ball is in contact with the air, which in turn is in contact with the earth). However, experiments on falling objects have been done **in a vacuum**, which confirm the concept of the 'non-touching' force.

figure 3.10 – weight acting on a ball in flight

Ball in flight

Weight of ball

Flight path

Mass

Not only is mass related to the **total quantity of matter** in an object or body, and not related to the gravity field strength, but linked closely to the idea of inertia, as explained by Newton's first and second laws of motion.

Inertia is explained as **resistance to acceleration**. The more inertia an object has, the harder it is to accelerate when a given force is applied. This is why it is a good idea for any sportsperson who has to change speed or direction rapidly or accelerate from rest to have the least body mass possible consistent with the necessary strength. **Inertia** is derived from **Newton's First** and **Second Laws**, the quantity m in the formula $F = m \times a$ relates exactly to this, so inertia is therefore a property of mass and consequently a property of all objects. Inertia also applies to decelerating objects or people, so that, once moving, an object requires a force to slow it down or stop it. For example, at the end of an indoor 60 m sprint, runners have difficulty in stopping (figure 3.11), this is because of the inertia of their mass.

figure 3.11 – sprinters have inertia

Graphs and curves of motion

Graphs of distance against time

The following graphs of **distance against time** will show the progress of an object as it moves along. In graph 3.12A, the distance remains the same as time goes along - which means that the object remains in the same place, there is **no movement**, the object is stationary, with speed zero.

In graph 3.12B, the distance changes with time - meaning that the object is **moving forward**, and eventually it comes to a halt with zero speed, so it **slows down** as the speed reduces to zero.

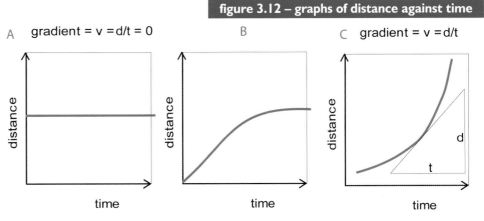

figure 3.12 – graphs of distance against time

A gradient = v =d/t = 0

B

C gradient = v =d/t

distance

distance

distance

time

time

time

d

t

Graphs of distance against time

What changes is the **gradient** of the graph, and this is explained in graph 3.12C, page 59. The gradient is defined as the rate of change of speed with time and this is the gradient as shown in the graph.

$$\text{speed} = \frac{d}{t}$$

So the steeper the gradient or **slope** of the graph, the faster the movement and the greater the speed or velocity.

Graphs of speed/velocity against time

Graphs of **velocity against time** show how velocity changes with time and here, the gradient is the acceleration of the moving object

$$\text{acceleration} = \frac{\text{change of velocity}}{\text{time taken to change}}$$

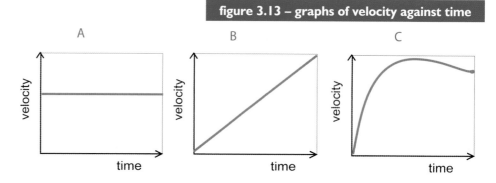

figure 3.13 – graphs of velocity against time

In graph 3.13A, the velocity **remains the same**, the gradient of the graph is **zero**, therefore the body's acceleration is zero. This body has **constant velocity** and is subject to Newton's first law.

In graph 3.13B, the velocity changes continuously with time, and the gradient of the graph is constant, and therefore the **acceleration is constant**.

In graph 3.13C, the moving object is a 100 m sprinter, whose **acceleration is largest** at the begining of the race, who reaches **maximum speed** at about half of the race, and who slows down slightly (**negative acceleration** or deceleration) before the end of the race.

This can be linked via **Newton's second law of motion** to the forces applied to the sprinter during the race.

Forces in sport

The sprinter

figure 3.14 – start, middle and end of a sprint

The sprinter

- At the **start of the race** (figure 3.14A, page 60), there is a steep upwards slope on her velocity time graph (figure 3.13C, page 60) which means a large acceleration. This corresponds with a large forward net force applied at the start when friction is a large forward force acting on the foot of the runner. From figure 3.14A, page 60, you will see that the vertical forces cancel out, and the friction force forward is much larger than the air resistance drag force backward. This produces a large net (resultant) force forward (marked in black on figure 3.14A, page 60). This force provides forward acceleration from Newton's second law.

- During the **middle of the run** (figure 3.14B, page 60), the velocity time graph is almost level, which means that acceleration is almost zero, therefore forces cancel out.

- At the **end of the run** (figure 3.14C, page 60), the velocity time graph has a small negative slope, showing that the sprinter decelerates, and that therefore there must be a net force backwards (shown in black) causing this deceleration.

Friction

Friction is a force which acts sideways between two surfaces which tend to slide past one another. This force enables sportspeople to accelerate, slow down, swerve, walk, and run.

The magnitude of friction depends on the **grip of footwear** on floor surface, and the **nature of the surface** itself (rough, smooth, slippy, greasy and so on), for example:

- **Studs and spikes** increase friction to enable better swerving and accelerating and decelerating in games or track situations. This applies to soft or wet surfaces.

- For **dry hard surfaces**, solid smooth rubber soles can give better friction as in discus or hammer shoes, rock climbing shoes, or tennis shoes for concrete surfaces.

- In **snow and ice**, long slender footwear (skates or skis) have low forward friction, but high sideways friction.

Note that friction acts forwards on the feet of the accelerating runner (figure 3.15).

Friction depends on the force pressing the surfaces together, but not on the area of contact.

For example:

- The inverted wings on racing cars increase the down force on wheels (figure 4.23, page 74). This increases cornering friction between the wheels and the ground.

figure 3.15 – friction

"ouch no friction"

friction acts forward on the foot of the accelerating sprinter

- Friction also enables swerving by players in rugby, soccer, hockey, and tennis. The friction force then acts sideways to the direction of motion, and changes the direction of motion.

- The direction taken after a bounce by a spinning ball depends on the direction of spin and the friction between the ball and the ground.

Rolling or sliding friction

- **Rolling friction** is the term which describes the force between surfaces which do not move relative to one another, like a wheel rolling over a surface, or a foot driving and pushing without slipping. The friction can be anything from zero up to a maximum just before slipping occurs. As soon as slipping occurs, the friction force falls, and would not be enough to keep a sportsperson upright (so he or she slips over).

- **Sliding friction** occurs when the two surfaces are moving relative to one another, and is always less than the maximum rolling friction. This is why ABS (**advanced braking systems**) will reduce braking force on wheels if sensors detect the beginning of sliding.

Fluid friction

Fluid friction (or **drag**) is a term applying to objects moving through fluids (gases or liquids). The force acts in the opposite direction to the direction of motion. This term applies to the **air resistance** experienced by objects moving through air.

Reaction forces within the body

Action and reaction forces within the body are caused when any muscle contracts. The two ends of the muscle pull equally on one another. In figure 3.16 the insertion of the muscle is pulled to the left and the origin to the right. The effect this has on the body shape or relative position of the different limbs and attachments depends on which of these are able to move.

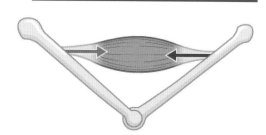

figure 3.16 – internal muscular forces

Muscle contraction within the body

Examples of muscle contraction causing changes in body shape, as origins and insertions are pulled towards one another, are shown in figure 3.17.

- Figure 3.17A - bending over the bar during the high jump.

- Figure 3.17B - stretching in the long jump.

- Figure 3.17C - tumbling by the gymnast.

- Figure 3.17D - arm action in the discus throw.

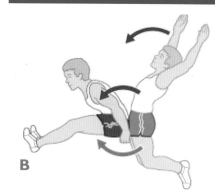

figure 3.17 – muscle contractions causing changes in body shape

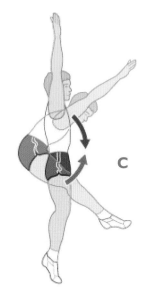

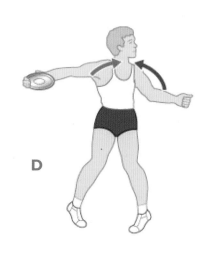

Reaction forces

STUDENT NOTE

Reaction forces are produced as a result of Newton's third law of motion, which is covered in detail in AS/A1 Revise PE for Edexcel, ISBN 9781901424881, Topic 1 page 29.

This is summarised here.

Newton's third law of motion describes what happens when **two bodies** (or objects) exert forces on one another. Action and reaction are equal and opposite and always occur in pairs.

Action acts on one of the bodies, and the **reaction** to this action acts on the other body. At a sprint start, the athlete **pushes back** on the blocks as hard as possible (this is the **'action'** - arrow in black in figure 3.18e), and the blocks **push forward** on the athlete (this push forward is the **'reaction force'**, arrow in red in figure 3.18e).

The reaction provides forward acceleration on the athlete. In figure 3.18c, a swimmer pushes backwards on the water with hands and feet (this is the force in **black**, the **action**).

At the same time, the water thrusts the swimmer forward (this is the force in red, the **reaction force**).

From figure 3.18:

- a, the jumper pushes down on the ground (black arrow), the ground pushes up on the jumper (red arrow - the reaction).

- b, the weight lifter pulls up on the weight (black arrow), weight pulls down on lifter (red arrow - the reaction).

- c, the swimmer pushes backwards on the water (black arrow), the water pushes forward on the swimmer (red arrow - the reaction).

- d, canoeist pushes backwards on the water (black arrow), reaction force thrusts the canoe forward (red arrow - the reaction).

- e, sprinter pushes back and down on the ground (black arrow), the ground pushes upwards and forwards on the sprinter (red arrow - the reaction).

- f, in cycling, the tyre on the rear wheel pushes backward on the ground (black arrow), the ground pushes forward on the rear wheel (red arrow - the reaction).

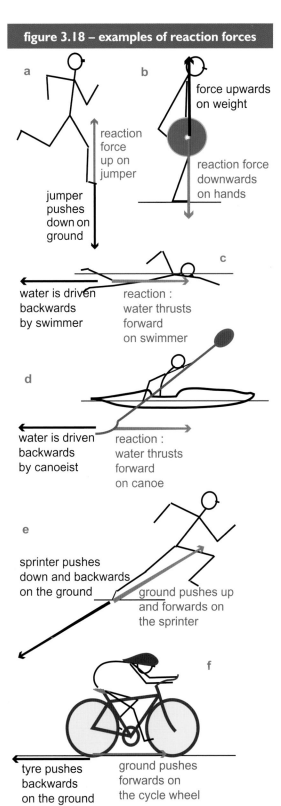

figure 3.18 – examples of reaction forces

a

b
force upwards on weight

reaction force up on jumper

reaction force downwards on hands

jumper pushes down on ground

c
water is driven backwards by swimmer

reaction : water thrusts forward on swimmer

d
water is driven backwards by canoeist

reaction : water thrusts forward on canoe

e
sprinter pushes down and backwards on the ground

ground pushes up and forwards on the sprinter

f

tyre pushes backwards on the ground

ground pushes forwards on the cycle wheel

Practice questions

1) Define what is meant by a scalar and a vector quantity.   2 marks

2) The table shows the speed of a 19 year-old male sprinter during a 200m race.

speed (ms⁻¹)	time (seconds)
0.0	0
6.0	1
7.5	2
8.2	3
8.4	4
8.5	5
8.5	7
8.4	8
8.3	10
8.2	13
8.1	18
8.0	22

a) Plot a graph of speed against time during this race.
When does he reach maximum speed and what happens to his speed between 8 and 22 seconds?   7 marks

b) Acceleration is the change of speed per second. Use the graph to establish his speed at 0.5 seconds and 1.5 seconds and calculate the average acceleration between 0.5 and 1.5 seconds.   3 marks

c) Successful games players are often able to change their velocity rapidly in the game situation. Explain the biomechanics behind this ability using examples from a game of your choice.   6 marks

3) A sprinter uses her calf muscles to push on the blocks at the start of a run.
Sketch a pin man diagram of the forces acting and use this to explain how this produces a forward force on her.   3 marks

4) Explain the nature of the reaction force which provides forwards impulsion for a cyclist.   4 marks

5) A weight lifter exerts an upward force of 2000 N on a barbell of 170 kg.
What is the vertical acceleration?   2 marks

6) a)   What characterises a vector quantity?   2 marks

b)   Figure 3.19 shows the forces acting on a runner at the start of a race. Use a vector diagram to show how you could work out the resultant force acting.   3 marks

c)   Sketch a pin man drawing of a person standing still showing all the forces acting on him.   2 marks

d)   Sketch a second diagram showing the vertical forces acting on a basketballer just before take-off while performing a jump shot. Represent the relative sizes of any forces you show by the length of the force arrows on your diagram.   2 marks

e)   Use this second diagram and your understanding of Newton's laws of motion to explain why the basketballer is able to take off. If the vertical upward ground reaction force on him is 2000 N, and his weight is 800 N, estimate the net upward force acting on him.   4 marks

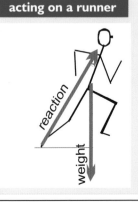

figure 3.19 – forces acting on a runner

Practice questions

7) Tennis players have to change direction quickly during a match to recover to the centre of the court.
Figure 3.20 shows a tennis player just after hitting a forehand and then starting to recover to the centre of the court in the direction shown.

a) Draw a pin diagram of the tennis player as he pushes off the court surface to recover to the centre of the court, showing all forces acting on the tennis player at this point. All forces must be clearly identified.   3 marks

b) Explain the factors that affect the horizontal force at this point. Apply Newton's second law of motion to explain the effect of this force on the player.   4 marks

figure 3.20 – a tennis player moves between strokes

8) Figure 3.21 shows the distance/time graph for a 100m sprint.

a) Describe the motion of the sprinter in sections A and B.   2 marks

b) Calculate the speed at points C and D and the average acceleration between the points.   3 marks

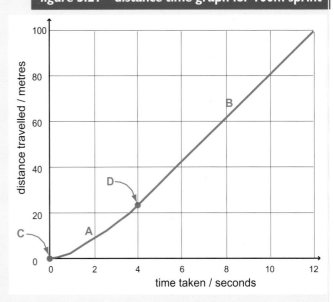

figure 3.21 – distance time graph for 100m sprint

Answers link: http://www.jroscoe.co.uk/downloads/a2_revise_pe_edexcel/EdexcelA2_ch3_answers.pdf

CHAPTER 4: *Angular motion, projectile motion and fluid mechanics*

Angular motion

Angular motion is defined as **the motion of a body which twists or turns about an axis** as explained in figures 4.1, 4.2 and 4.3. The twists, tumbles and turns involved in sports movements can all be described in this way.

Three imaginary axes of rotation

figure 4.1 – a hammer thrower turning around longitudinal axis

- **Longitudinal axis**
    - This axis runs vertically from the top of the head to a point between the feet.
    - Examples of sporting movements would be the spinning skater and the hammer throw (figure 4.1).

- **Transverse axis**
    - This axis runs horizontally from side to side across the body between opposite hips at right angles to the sagittal plane.
    - Sports movements about this axis include sit ups, and the high jump Fosbury Flop flight phase, and somersaults (figure 4.2).

figure 4.2 – a gymnast tumbling around the transverse axis

- **Frontal axis (also** called **the sagittal axis)**
    - This axis runs horizontally from front to back between belly button and lumbar spine.
    - Examples of sports movements about this axis are a cartwheel (figure 4.3), and the bowling action in cricket.

figure 4.3 – a cartwheel rotating about the frontal axis

Angle

Angle is a familiar concept to most people, so it is readily understood what is meant by 30°, 90°, 180° and 360°. In scientific terms, an angle is measured in radians. The radian as a unit of angle is defined as '**the angle subtended at the centre of a circle by an arc length of one radius**'. Suffice it to say at this point that one radian is approximately 60°.

Angular displacement

Angular displacement is defined similarly to displacement for linear systems and is the **relative angle** compared to some fixed position or line in space.

For example, if a golfer starts his/her drive from the presentation position (i.e. with club just touching the ball) and backswings to the fully extended position with the club behind his/her back, the club shaft would have an angular displacement equal to the angle between the starting position and the fully extended position of the backswing.

This would be a measure of the fluency and range of the swing and could be anywhere from 180° to 290° (or 3.142 to 5.06 radians).

Angular velocity

Angular velocity is the same thing as rate of spinning or twisting, and is defined as:

angular velocity (ω)　=　<u>angle turned (in radians)</u>
time taken to turn

This is a similar definition to that for linear velocity, except distance is replaced by angle in the formula.

Angular acceleration

Again in a similar way to linear systems, it is possible to define angular acceleration as:

angular acceleration　=　<u>change of angular velocity</u>
time taken to change

This concept applies to situations in which the rate of spin **changes with time**. Examples of this would be the hammer throw (in which the rate of spin increases throughout the movement up to the release of the hammer) and the tumbler, gymnast or diver (who speeds up the rate of rotation or slows it down by changing his/her body shape).

Torque

Torque is the twisting force which you could apply to a body to cause it to turn or spin. It is defined as the force applied to the body multiplied by the perpendicular distance to the axis of rotation (the moment of force about the turning axis).

This definition means that the bigger the force and the distance from the axis of turning, the bigger the turning effect.

Moment of inertia (MI)

This is the equivalent of mass (**inertia**) in the linear system, and is defined as:

moment of inertia　=　**sum of [(mass of body part)**
x (distance of body part from the axis of rotation) squared]
over all parts of the rotating body.

Mathematically:　　　$MI = \Sigma\, m\, r^2$

Objects rotating with large MI require large moments of force (torque) to change their angular velocity, and objects with small MI require small moments of force (torque) to change their angular velocity or ω.

Moment of inertia

The formula above means that moment of inertia depends on the spread of mass away from the axis of spin, so as the body shape changes, the moment of inertia of the shape changes. The more spread out the mass, the bigger the MI.

The unit of MI is kilogramme metre squared - kgm^2.

- Bodies with **arms held out wide** have large MI, the further the mass is away from the axis of rotation increases the MI dramatically.
- Sportspeople use this to control all spinning or turning movements.
- Pikes and tucks are good examples of use of MI, both reduce MI.

figure 4.4 – moments of inertia of different shapes

Values of moment of inertia

In figure 4.4 on page 67, I is the MI for the left most pin man and has a value of about 1.0 kgm^2 for an average male person. From this diagram you can see how control of the arms will make a big difference to the value of MI, and that a tuck or pike can also **change MI** dramatically.

Angular momentum

Angular momentum is a quantity used to describe what happens when bodies spin and turn, it is defined as:

angular momentum = **moment of inertia** x **angular velocity**
= **rotational inertia** x **rate of spin**

$$\mathbf{H} = \mathbf{I} \times \omega$$

Conservation of angular momentum

figure 4.5 – a spinning skater

The **law of conservation of angular momentum** is a law of the universe which says that angular momentum of a spinning body remains the same (provided no external forces act)

- This means that a body which is spinning, twisting or tumbling will keep its value of **H** once the movement has started.

- Therefore if moment of inertia (**I**) changes by changing body shape, then angular velocity (ω) must also change to keep angular momentum (**H**) the same.

- So, if MI (**I**) **increases** (body spread out more) then ω must **decrease** (rate of spin gets less).
- And conversely, if MI (**I**) **decreases** (body tucked in more) then ω must **increase** (rate of spin gets bigger).

- Strictly, this is only exactly true if the body has no contact with its surroundings, as for example a high diver doing piked or tucked somersaults in the air, but it is almost true for the spinning skater!

Sporting examples of conservation of angular momentum

- **The spinning skater**. If the arms are wide, the MI is large and the skater spins slowly. If the arms are brought in, MI is small and the skater will spin more quickly (figure 4.5).

- The third (lower) skater in figure 4.5 has contrived to have both arms and legs spread as far form the axis of rotation as possible, which will bring about the slowest possible rate of spin.

Sporting examples of conservation of angular momentum

- **The tumbling gymnast** (figure 4.6). With the body position open, the MI is large and the gymnast (or diver or trampolinist) will spin slowly. When he or she creates a tucked body position, the MI is small and he or she will spin more quickly.

- **The dancer doing a spin jump** (figure 4.7). The movement is initiated with arms held wide which would therefore have the highest possible MI. Immediately he or she has taken off, the angular momentum is conserved, and so by tucking the arms across the chest, this will create the lowest possible MI. This then means that he or she will acquire the highest possible rate of spin, so that more spins can be completed before landing.

- **The slalom skier**. The slalom skier crouches on approach to the gate and therefore will have a large turning MI. As he or she passes the gate, he or she stands straight up (reducing MI). This enables the person to turn rapidly past the gate, then he or she crouches again (figure 4.8) - increasing MI which will resume a slow turn between the gates.

- **The discus thrower** (figure 4.9). The discus thrower kicks his right leg wide at the start of the turn, thereby giving his lower body angular momentum with a large MI. As he moves to the centre of the circle he brings his right leg closer to the body (and therefore closer to the turning axis), reducing his MI. This increases the rate of spin of the lower body so that it moves ahead of the upper body in the movement.

Newton's laws of angular motion

The laws of angular motion are similar to Newton's laws of linear motion except that they apply to turning, spinning, or twisting system or bodies. They are:

- **Newton's first law of angular motion** states that a spinning or rotating body will continue with a constant angular momentum except when acted upon by an external force or torque.

- **Newton's second law of angular motion** states that the rate of change of angular momentum of the body will be proportional to the torque acting on it, and in the same direction (of spin) as the torque.

- **Newton's third law of angular motion** states that when a torque is applied to one body by another body, an equal but opposite in direction torque will be applied by the second body to the first body.

figure 4.6 – a tumbling gymnast

figure 4.7 – a spinning dancer

figure 4.8 – a slalom skier

figure 4.9 – a discus thrower

Projectile motion

Factors affecting horizontal displacement of projectiles

This section looks at the **motion of objects in flight**, such as human bodies (during the flight phase of a jump), throwing implements (shot, discus, javelin or hammer), and soccer, rugby, cricket, tennis and golf balls.

The flight is governed by the forces acting, the weight, air resistance, **Magnus effect** (page 74), aerodynamic lift, and the direction of motion. If weight were the only force acting, the flight path would be **parabolic** in shape, and some flight paths are similar to this (shot or hammer, the human body in jumps or tumbles or dives as in figures 4.10, 4.11, and 4.12, where weight is the predominant force acting).

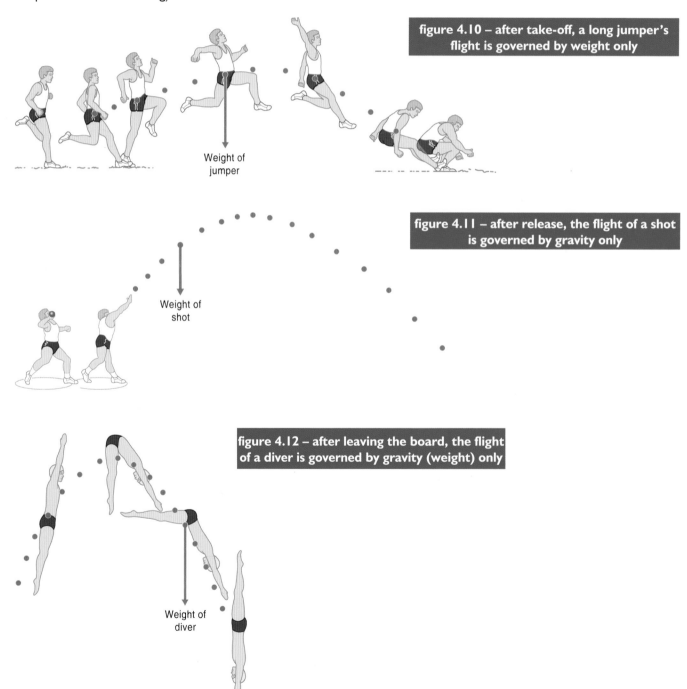

figure 4.10 – after take-off, a long jumper's flight is governed by weight only

Weight of jumper

figure 4.11 – after release, the flight of a shot is governed by gravity only

Weight of shot

figure 4.12 – after leaving the board, the flight of a diver is governed by gravity (weight) only

Weight of diver

Factors affecting horizontal displacement of projectiles

Figure 4.13 summarises the factors which influence the distance travelled, the **angle of release**, the **speed of release**, and the **height of release**.

The optimum distance moved before landing is acheived at 45° release angle.

If the height of release is about 2 metres off the ground, as in the shot put (figure 4.11, page 70), then the optimum angle of release (to achieve maximum distance) will be less than 45°, probably approximately 42°.

But if the landing of the object thrown is higher than the point of release (as in the case of a basketball shot), then the optimum angle of release will be greater than 45°.

figure 4.13 – factors affecting distance travelled

The relative size of forces during flight

The forces acting during flight are: the weight of the object, the air resistance or drag, (the faster the projectile travels the greater will be the air resistance), **aerodynamic lift** (page 72), and the **Magnus effect** or **Bernoulli effect** (page 74).

If the shapes of the flight path differ from a parabola then some combination of these forces must be relatively large compared with the weight (remembering that a flight of an object with only weight force acting would be a parabola).

For example, the badminton shuttle
For a badminton shuttle **struck hard** (figure 4.14a), the air resistance is very large compared with the weight, because the shuttle is moving quickly. The resultant force will therefore be very close to the air resistance. This would make the shuttle slow down rapidly over the **first part of the flight**.

Later in the flight of the badminton shuttle (figure 4.14b), when the shuttle is moving much more slowly, the air resistance is much less and comparable with the weight. This pattern of the resultant force changing markedly during the flight predicts a pronounced asymmetric path.

Figure 4.15 shows a badminton shuttle's flight path, which is markedly asymmetric, because of the change of predominant force during the flight.

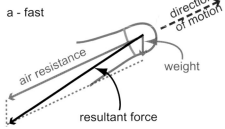

figure 4.14 – forces on a badminton shuttle

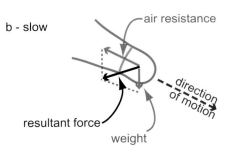

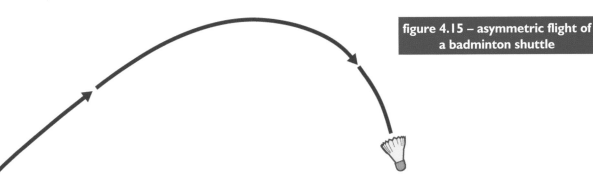

figure 4.15 – asymmetric flight of a badminton shuttle

Lift force

Dynamic **lift** (upward force) can be caused by the movement of the body. As the body moves forward, the angle presented by the lower surface of the body to the direction of motion (called the **angle of attack**) can cause the air molecules through which the object is moving to be deflected downward and hence would cause a downward force on the air through which the object passes (figure 4.16).

This **downward force on the air** would cause an **upward force on the moving object** in reaction to the downward force on the air (by Newton's third law).

This is the lift.

Such a force can explain the flight of a discus.

A discus is a symmetrical object, which would therefore not be subject to the Bernoulli force which explains the flight of a wing moving horizontally through air.

The **angle of attack** of the discus is such as to present its lower surface to the air flow which causes the lift as explained above.

There is a distinction between a force caused as a reaction to air (or water) thrown up or sideways to the direction of motion of for example a downhill skier or a cyclist.

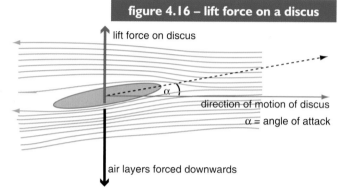

figure 4.16 – lift force on a discus

lift force on discus

α

direction of motion of discus

α = angle of attack

air layers forced downwards

Technique modification through the application of technology

In the case of putting the shot, the height of release and angle of release (figure 4.11, page 70) are critical to the displacement (total distance travelled) of the shot when it lands. The appropriate technique for shot putting will therefore need to optimise these factors.

Technology in the form of video analysis can be used to determine the values of the factors, and a coach would need to change the technique accordingly - taking into consideration the contribution of chest and leg muscle strength during the action.

A similar process should occur for the hammer throw, given that the optimum release angle here would be 45° (as opposed to 42° for the shot).

The technology would be similar to that shown in figure 4.17 which analyses the running motion of an endurance runner.

Angles and displacements can be produced quantitatively by these computer programmes.

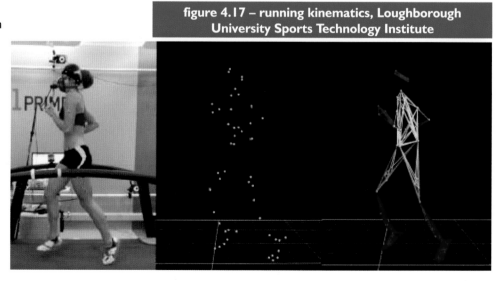

figure 4.17 – running kinematics, Loughborough University Sports Technology Institute

Fluid mechanics

Fluid friction force depends on the shape and size of the moving object, the speed of the moving object, and the streamlining effect (summarised in figure 4.18).

Drag and air resistance (fluid friction)

In order to minimise drag, the following developments affect sport:
- The body position and shape for a swimmer.
- The shape of helmets for cyclists.
- The use of lycra clothing.
- The shape of sports vehicles (cars or bikes).

Low values of fluid friction

This discussion concerns **low values of drag** compared with other forces. Examples are:
- Any sprinter or game player for whom air resistance is usually much less than friction effects and weight. Therefore streamlining is seen as less important.
- A shot or hammer in flight, in which air resistance would be much less than the weight, and therefore the angle of release should be around 45°.

High values of fluid friction

High values of drag will occur for any sportsperson or vehicle moving through water, and hence fluid friction is the critical factor governing swimming speed.

- Body shape or cross section, and clothing (surface material to assist laminar flow) are adjusted to minimise fluid friction.

A cyclist (figure 4.19) travels much faster than a runner and therefore has **high fluid friction**:

- He or she crouches low to reduce the forward cross sectional area.
- The helmet is designed to minimise turbulent flow.
- Clothing and wheel profiles are designed to assist streamlining.

Cross sectional area is the area of the moving object as viewed from the front. The smaller the better to reduce drag, hence cyclists crouch down, and keep their elbows in.

Laminar flow and drag

Fluid friction (or drag) depends on **laminar** flow, the smooth flowing of air or water past an object. Laminar means flowing in layers, and streamlining assists laminar flow. Figure 4.20 shows images of a streamlined helmet, and a non-streamlined helmet. The point of the streamlined shape is that the air moves past it in layers which minimises the drag or fluid friction.

Vortex flow

In the case of the non-streamlined helmet, vortices are formed where the fluid does not flow smoothly. When this happens bits of fluid are flung randomly sideways which causes drag.

The drag is caused by bits of fluid being dragged along with the moving object (the cycle helmet).

Some clothing (for example lycra running suits and shark suits in swimming) will minimise vortex creation (depending on the speed of movement) and maximise laminar flow of the air or water past the body.

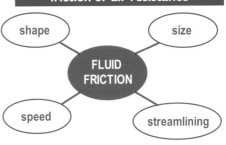

figure 4.18 – factors affecting fluid friction or air resistance

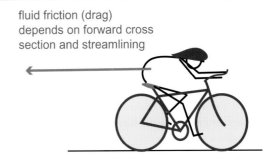

figure 4.19 – a cyclist needs good streamlining

fluid friction (drag) depends on forward cross section and streamlining

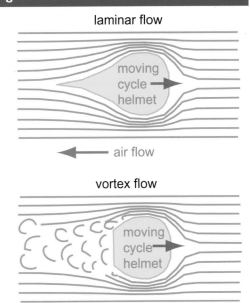

figure 4.20 – laminar flow and vortex flow

laminar flow

moving cycle helmet

air flow

vortex flow

moving cycle helmet

air flow

The Bernoulli effect

The force which gives lift to aircraft wings, and down-pressure on racing car bodies (figure 4.21, enabling greater friction between wheels and the road, and hence faster cornering speeds) is called the **Bernoulli effect**.

This effect depends on the fact that fluids which move quickly across the surface of an object cause a reduced pressure when compared with slower moving air across another surface.

Hence, in figure 4.21, the laminar flow of air across the **lower** surface of the wing (or car body shaped like an inverted wing) is **quicker**, because the air has to travel **further** in the same time as the air moving a shorter distance across the upper surface of the wing. Hence the shape of the wing is crucial to create the Bernoulli lift (in aeroplanes) or down force (in racing cars, figure 4.22).

The **Bernoulli effect** has been built into racing cars to increase the down force (which would therefore increase the friction force between wheels and the ground).

So, formula 1 racing car manufacturers build this **shape into the whole car** (figure 4.22), not just the artificial wings sometimes attached to the car upper surfaces.

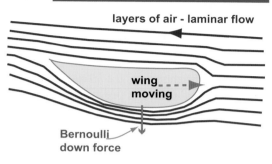

figure 4.21 – Bernoulli effect on an inverted wing

figure 4.22 – shape of a racing car body

The Magnus effect

The **Magnus effect** is the Bernoulli principle applied to spinning balls.

As a **spinning ball** moves through the air (from left to right on figure 4.23), the air layers which flow round the ball are forced into the path shown in the diagram. Here you can see that the air flow is **further** round the top of the ball, and hence the air flow is **faster** over the top of the ball than the bottom. This means that the **air pressure** will be **less** over the top of the ball than the lower half of the ball (following from the Bernoulli effect), hence the ball will experience a force upwards in the view of figure 4.23.

Hence **top-spin** as shown in figure 4.24, would cause a dipping effect on the ball in flight, the force is downward in this figure. Most tennis players use the top spin effct to cause a ball to dip into the opponent's court after a very firm hit of the ball. Rafael Nadal is a prime exponent of this technique.

Similarly, **side-spin** will cause a swerve in the flight whose direction is in the same sense as the spin of the ball. Golfers cause a ball to fade to the right or hook to the left by imparting side-spin to the ball during the strike.

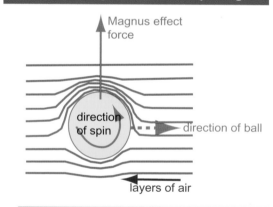

figure 4.23 – Magnus effect on a spinning ball

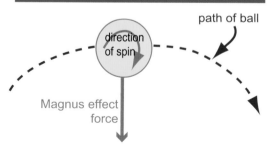

figure 4.24 – flight of a spinning ball

The Magnus effect

The diagrams in figure 4.25a show how side spin causes swerving sideways by the golfers.

The sense of swerve is in the same direction as the spin on the ball.

The sports in which back spin (figure 4.25b) and top spin (figure 4.25c) are used to the maximum are raquet sports such as tennis and table tennis.

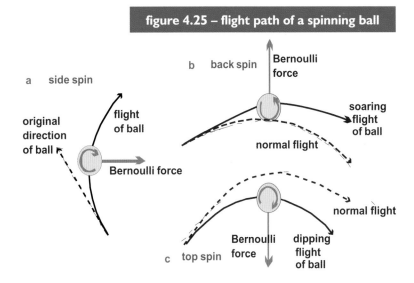

figure 4.25 – flight path of a spinning ball

figure 4.26 – golfers can control ball spin to place the ball on the green

Technological advancements in fluid mechanics and its influence on technique modification

In the section on fluid friction (page 73), we have briefly discussed how laminar flow and vortex flow influence the drag on the human body in sprinting and swimming, and how clothing or helmets (cycling) can influence this drag.

Wind tunnels

Factors investigated include:
- Wheel spokes and profiles.
- Width of handlebars.
- Riding posture, and hand position on the bars.
- Type of cloth and design of clothing.
- Forward cross-sectional area of frame and brackets.

Technology and drag

The computer programmes show how adjustments to shape can be made **before** construction, reducing expense and making more systematic the shape-making process. In addition to the cycling applications above, this is for:
*   Kayaking and rowing.
*   Bobsleigh, luge and skeleton.
*   Speed skating (helmets, costumes and body angles).

Further application of the same technology is used to **increase the drag effect** in order to improve propulsion in water based activities.

This applies to:
*   Improved patterns of pulling (hand and foot/leg positions and activity) in swimming.
*   Shape of blades in rowing and canoeing.

Sports boats

The drag on the hulls of yachts, sailing dingies, canoes and rowing shells depend on the surface area in contact with the water. If this can be reduced then the potential maximum speed which could be achieved can be markedly increased.

The main application of these ideas are in the military (cavitation, which creates a bubble of gas around the craft and is used in torpedoes, attack boats, underwater bullets and so on).

In a hovercraft, the body of the boat is suspended on a cushion of air, thereby reducing fluid friction almost to zero. The main reason why such craft are less popular now are the potential for lack of control during bad weather, a factor which also affects use of hydrofoil craft (which lifts the body of the boat off the surface of the water on special fins or wings).

Hydroplaning in sports boats (in which the hulls of speedboats are lifted off the surface to sit on a shaped bar at the rear of the boat) enable them to travel at speeds above 100 mph (figure 4.27).

figure 4.27 – sports boats at 100 mph

The latest speedboats have shaped hulls which reduce drag, the shaping being determined in a **flume** (a tank containing fast flowing water, and force measuring devices which can be attached to the boat shape body), in a similar manner to the shaping of a formula one racing car (as well as other more commercial vehicles) in a wind tunnel.

Practice questions

1) Define the term angular velocity.   2 marks

2) a) A diver can make a number of different shapes in the air. Table 4.1 shows three of these.
        Explain the meaning of moment of inertia (MI) in this context.   4 marks

Table 4.1 – **data for shapes of diver during flight**

phase of dive	shape of diver	time during flight	MI of shape kgm²
1	Z	0.0 - 0.5s	18
2	Y	0.5 - 0.7s	9
3	X	0.7 - 1.0s	3
4	Z	1.0 - 1.1s	18
entry	axis of rotation = ●	1.1s	

b) During a dive a diver goes through the shapes shown in table 6.1.
     Explain how the rate of spinning (angular velocity) would change through the dive.   5 marks

c) Sketch a graph of this rate of spinning against time. Your sketch need only be approximate. 4 marks

d) State the relationship between angular momentum, moment of inertia and angular velocity. 2 marks

e) Name the law of conservation which accounts for these variations in rate of spin.   1 mark

f) Explain and sketch the arc described by the diver as he or she falls.   3 marks

3) a) Describe in detail the body shape and movement within a chosen sporting situation where
        rates of spin are affected by body shape.   6 marks

b) How would you stop the spinning in this situation?   2 marks

c) Figure 4.28 shows a sportsperson's leg in two different positions.
     The values quoted are the moment of inertia of the leg as it rotates
     about the hip joint (shown as a red dot on each diagram).
     Explain the implications of these data for the efficiency of running style
     in a sprinter and long distance runner   7 marks

figure 4.28 – shape of leg

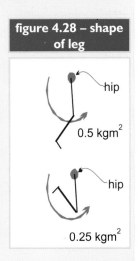

Practice questions

4) a) Figure 4.29 shows a gymnast undertaking a forward somersault following a run up.
Sketch three traces on a single graph to represent any changes in angular momentum,
moment of inertia and angular velocity for the period of activity between positions 2 and 9.   3 marks

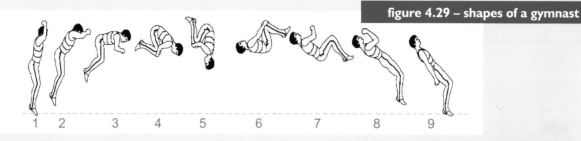

figure 4.29 – shapes of a gymnast

1   2   3   4   5   6   7   8   9

b) Explain the shapes of the traces on the sketch graph that you
have drawn.   6 marks

c) Table 4.2 sets out measurements of angular velocities
(rates of spin) of the gymnast at successive frames from
the start of the somersault.

Estimate from this table the ratio of angular velocities at
times X and Y.   1 mark

d) If the moment of inertia of the gymnast is 8 kgm² at time X,
estimate the moment of inertia at time Y, using data
from table 4.2.   2 marks

Table 4.2 – data for angular velocity of gymnast

	frame	angular velocity (degrees s⁻¹)
	1	650
X	2	750
	3	850
	4	1100
	5	1400
Y	6	1500
	7	1000
	8	850
	9	650

5) a) Figure 4.30 shows a spinning skater in various
positions. Under each diagram is an approximate value
for the moment of inertia of the skater spinning about
his or her central vertical axis.

The angular velocity of the skater in position **W** is
2.0 revolutions per second. What is the formula
for calculating the skater's angular velocity?

Calculate the angular velocity for the skater in
position **Z**.   2 marks

b) Sketch a figure showing a possible position which could
cause the skater to attain an angular velocity of 3.0
revolutions per second and calculate what the moment
of inertia of this shape must be.   2 marks

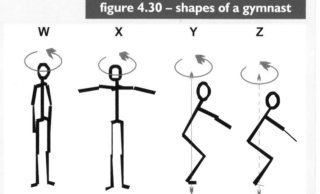

figure 4.30 – shapes of a gymnast

W   X   Y   Z

MI=1.0 kgm²   MI=2.0 kgm²   MI=4.5 kgm²   MI=6.0 kgm²

c) Principles of angular momentum can be used to improve performance in a variety of sports.
With the use of diagrams explain how a slalom skier turns through the gates at maximum speed.   4 marks

d) Explain with the use of diagrams how a dancer manages to complete a triple spin in the air
before touching the ground.   4 marks

Practice questions

6) a) Using examples, explain how the shape of an object can alter its flight path. 4 marks

   b) Explain the effect of air resistance on the flight of two badminton shuttles, one of which has been struck hard and the other gently. 10 marks

   c) Briefly explain why the flight path of a shot in athletics is so different from the flight of a badminton shuttle. 4 marks

7) a) Identify three physical factors (not skill factors) which govern a swimmer's speed and explain how one of these occurs. 3 marks

   b) Describe the factors which determine the amount of fluid friction acting on a swimmer. 4 marks

   c) Explain how you would minimise turbulent flow (high drag) of the water past the swimmer's body. 2 marks

   d) Give three examples, each from a different sporting context, to show how fluid friction affects the sportsperson. 3 marks

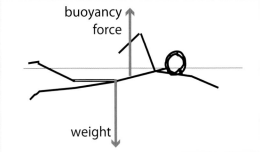

figure 4.31 – forces acting on a swimmer

   e) How would you attempt to reduce fluid friction? 3 marks

   f) Look at figure 4.31 showing the vertical forces acting on a swimmer during a stroke.
   Explain why it is difficult for a swimmer to keep a horizontal floating position. 4 marks

8) a) Fluid friction is a force which acts on a bobsleigh once it is moving. Identify the nature of the fluid friction in this case and explain how this might limit the maximum speed of the bob. 3 marks

   b) Explain the term 'turbulent flow', and how the bobsleigh is used to minimise this factor. 3 marks

9) a) Sketch a diagram to show the flight path of the shot from the moment it leaves the putter's hand to the moment it lands. 2 marks

   b) State and briefly explain three factors (excluding air effects) which should be used by the putter to optimise the distance thrown. 6 marks

   c) Explain why the turn in a discus throw produces greater horizontal range than the standing throw. 3 marks

10) a) The Magnus effect (the Bernoulli effect applied to spinning balls) states that a faster flowing liquid or gas exerts less pressure than a slower moving liquid or gas.
   Using figure 4.32, show how the Magnus effect explains the swerve of a spinning ball. 4 marks

   b) Use diagrams to show how your explanation relates to the flight of a table tennis ball with side, back and top spin. 3 marks

   c) Sketch a vector diagram of all forces acting on a table tennis ball in flight with back spin, and explain how the resultant force on the ball predicts the actual acceleration of the ball. 4 marks

figure 4.32 – Magnus effect on a spinning ball

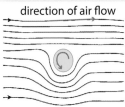

direction of air flow

   d) Identify one sport other than a ball game, in which the Bernoulli effect plays a part. 1 mark

Practice questions

11) What do you understand by the Magnus effect?
Explain how a knowledge of Magnus forces can assist a tennis player to
execute different types of spins.   15 marks

12) a) Give three examples from sport where fluid friction affects an object and a
sportsperson and state the effects of fluid friction in each case.   8 marks

b) Explain three factors that affect the amount of air resistance that acts on a body.   3 marks

c) State three ways in which cyclists reduce air resistance in order to maximise their speed.   3 marks

Answers link: http://www.jroscoe.co.uk/downloads/a2_revise_pe_edexcel/EdexcelA2_ch4_answers.pdf

CHAPTER 5
MEMORY MODELS

CHAPTER 5: *Memory models*

Information processing

The information-processing approach is a set of **theories** which seek to explain human action by showing how we take information from our surroundings and make decisions about what to do next on the basis of our **interpretation** of that information.

For example, the badminnton player in figure 5.1 has to take in the surroundings of the court, the positions and actions of his opponent in sending the shuttle over the net, and then decide what to do in returning the shot. He then has to activate his relevant muscles to perform this task, and perceive the outcome, where the shuttle has travelled to, and how the opponent has moved in reponse. This acts as feedback to inform the player what to do next as part of the subsequent phase of the game.

The **simplest model** of information processing is that shown in figure 5.2

Input

Input is the **information from the environment** received via the senses which the player uses to decide on a response to the situation.

Decision making

Decision making refers to the combination of recognition, perception and memory processes used to **select an appropriate response** to the demands of the situation.

Output

Output is the **response** which the player makes. In sport this is usually in the form of a movement of some kind. Output becomes a form of input or feedback.

Feedback

Feedback occurs because the player **perceives the outcome** of his or her response and this in turn becomes part of the input for the basis for further decision making.

Input

Almost any aspect of the immediate environment can act as input and is called a **display** from which the performer can select using his or her senses that which is relevant to his or her game or activity.

Senses

The senses used to collect information are collectively known as the **receptor systems**. When we are doing any physical activity we are aware of our surroundings. We use all our senses to locate ourselves in space and decide on the requirements of the task, whether it is to pass a ball or perform a gymnastic or dance movement. Taste and smell are not used to any great extent in physical activity but vision, hearing and proprioception are (figure 5.3, page 83).

Information is passed **to and from the brain** by the nervous system. This consists of two elements, namely the **brain and the spinal cord** which together form the **central nervous system** (CNS), and the **peripheral nervous system**, which comprises the nerves that connect the spinal cord with **all parts of the body**, radiating from (the **efferent** system) and returning to (the **afferent** system) the CNS.

figure 5.1 – decisions?

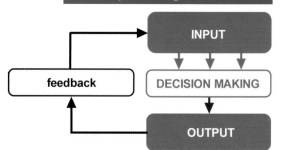
figure 5.2 – simplest information processing model

Senses

The **afferent** system transmits information to the CNS about events and processes that are happening both inside and outside the body. For example, if you are running a marathon on a warm day, you can both see the sunlight and feel yourself getting hot. The **efferent** system transmits information from the CNS to the muscles which are then activated to perform a skill or execute a movement.

Vision and hearing (audition)

Vision and hearing (**audition**) deal with information from the **external** environment. As light falls upon the retina at the back of the eye, it is converted into electrical impulses and so transmitted to the brain, which allows us to see the image through visual perception.

Hearing works in a similar way; in this case, sound waves cause the eardrum to vibrate and this is converted into electrical impulses and transmitted in a similar way to visual images, though dealt with in a different part of the brain.

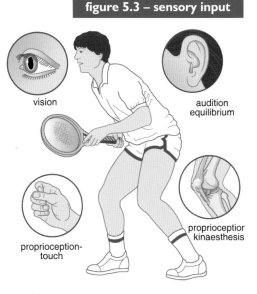

figure 5.3 – sensory input

vision

audition equilibrium

proprioception-touch

proprioception kinaesthesis

Proprioception

Proprioception is the means by which we know how our body is **oriented in space** and the extent to which muscles are contracted or joints extended; proprioception allows us to feel the racket or ball. The three components of proprioception are touch, equilibrium and kinaesthesis, and these are known as **internal** input.

Touch

Touch (or the tactile sense) enables us to feel **pain**, **pressure** and **temperature**. In sports and dance we are mostly concerned with the pressure sense to tell us how firmly we are gripping a racket, for example, or whether our climbing partner is on a tight rope or whether we struck the ball hard or 'stroked' it. If we are sensible we take heed of any pain warnings we receive.

Equilibrium or balance

Equilibrium is the sense that tells you when your body is balanced (figure 5.4) and when it is tipping, turning or inverting. It is important for divers, gymnasts and trampolinists, as well as dancers, to be able to orientate themselves in space. This is done by means of the sense organs in the vestibular apparatus of the **middle ear**.

Kinaesthesis

Kinaesthesis is the sense that **informs the brain of the movement or state of contraction of the muscles, tendons and joints**. A skilled performer knows whether a movement has been performed correctly or not not only from seeing its effect but also from sensing how the movement felt to perform.

This is known as **intrinsic feedback**. You may have experienced a foot or a limb 'going to sleep' and you will know how difficult it is not only to move the limb but also to know what is happening to it. The messages to and from the muscles have been interrupted and kinaesthetic sense impaired.

figure 5.4 – a sprint swim start, an example of balance

Decision making

Following the input, a performer must make decisions based on all the information available, but there usually will be so much of this that he or she must select that which is relevant.

This is done by a process called **selective attention**.

Perception and the detection, comparison and recognition (DCR) system

Perception (figure 5.5) is described as **stimulus identification**. As information is received from the environment, the performer needs to **make sense** of it, to **interpret** it and to **identify** the elements which are **relevant** and **important**.

Perception consists of three elements:

- **Detection** - the performer needs to be aware that something notable is going on around him or her. In a field game situation, this could be where the ball is, where the other players from both sides are in relation to the pitch dimensions, and what the goalkeeper is doing.

- **Comparison** - in which the performer will compare what is happening with his or her past experiences of similar situations, where are the players in comparison with set plays rehearsed in a training situation?

- **Recognition** - in which the performer realises that what is happening requires an activity in response. For example, what is the response to the rehearsed set play in the field game?

Attention

Attention (figure 5.5) relates to:

- **Amount of information** we can cope with, since the amount of information we can attend to **is limited**, and therefore we have limited **attentional capacity**.

- **Relevance of the information**. The performer must therefore attend to only **relevant information**, and **disregard irrelevant** information. This is called **selective attention**.

Selective attention

This is the process of sorting out **relevant** bits of information from the many which are received. Attention passes the information to the **short-term memory** which gives time for **conscious analysis**. A good performer can **focus totally** on an important aspect of his or her skill which **can exclude other elements** which may also be desirable. Sometimes a performer may desire to concentrate on several different things at once.

When some parts of a performance become **automatic**, the information relevant to those parts does not require attention, and this gives the performer **spare attentional capacity**.

This allows the performer to attend to new elements of a skill such as tactics or anticipating the moves of an opponent (figure 5.6). The coach will therefore need to help the performer to make best use of spare attentional capacity, and will also need to **direct the attention** of the performer to enable him or her to **concentrate** and reduce the chance of **attentional switching** to irrelevant information or distractions.

Developing selective attention

- Lots of **relevant** practice.
- Increase the **intensity** of the stimulus.
- Use **verbal** or **kinaesthetic** cues to focus on important information.
- For example, 'keep your eye on the ball' or a swimmer might selectively attend on the feel of the hand pulling through the water.
- Use **visualisation** or mental rehearsal techniques without movement.
- Watch performer's **video replays** to refine technique.
- **Observe and copy** the behaviour of a player who plays in the same position as the subject.

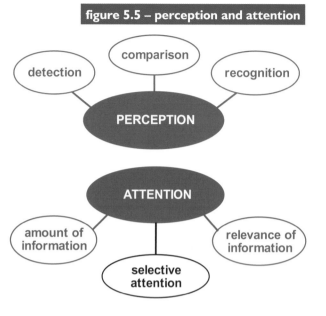

figure 5.5 – perception and attention

figure 5.6 – selective attention

Developing selective attention

- Coach needs to direct attention and give appropriate **feedback** to improve performer's motivation and alertness.
- Use **concentration** exercises, such as players scanning the field of play, followed by correct pass, alongside distracting background sounds or different instructions that may simulate the presence of noisy spectators that could distract players (figure 5.7).
- Develop **performance rituals** that automatically trigger focused attention that leads to good performance. Continue to **evaluate** and **reappraise** methods to ensure refinement and adjustments to selective attention techniques are an ongoing process.

figure 5.7 – distraction?

Benefits of selective attention

- Directs performer's attention on particular aspects of performance thereby **avoiding distractions**.
- Gives performer a better chance of making the correct **decision**.
- Improves performer's **reaction time** significantly.
- Hence helps performer to make **quicker** decisions.
- Helps **regulate** performer's **arousal** and **anxiety** levels.
- Reduces performer's potential **memory overload**.

Response selection and response programming

The term response selection refers to the next phase following selective attention. Now, the correct item has been picked out by the senses from the multiplicity of inputs available, then the correct response (what to do next) is decided. This is **response selection**.

Next the appropriate motor programme (which muscles to activate) is decided to acheive that response. This is **response programming**.

For the elite sportsperson, the selection is almost automatically linked to the programming and then the output.

Output

Output in this context refers to what the body actually does following information processing. The contraction of muscles, the movement of the body, the sequence of movements (figure 5.8), relevant to whatever sporting action is required.

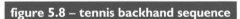

figure 5.8 – tennis backhand sequence

Welford's model of information processing

In Welford's model (figure 5.9):

- **Display** refers to the range of actions and things that are happening in the surrounding environment of the performer.

- **Perceptual mechanism** refers to the part of the brain which perceives the surroundings (via sight, sound and touch).

- **Decision mechanism** refers to the part of the brain which makes decisions.

- **The effector mechanism** is the part of the brain which carries out the decisions and sends messages to the limbs and parts of the body, which act out the relevant skill.

- **Intrinsic feedback** is the feedback as to what actually happens to the body via the proprioceptors, which inform the brain about balance, muscle tensions, limb positions and angles and so on.

- **Extrinsic feedback** is the feedback via the result (response) of the actions made, what happens in the game or performance or to a ball or the other players in a game, the results of which feed back as part of the display.

figure 5.9 – Welford's information processing model

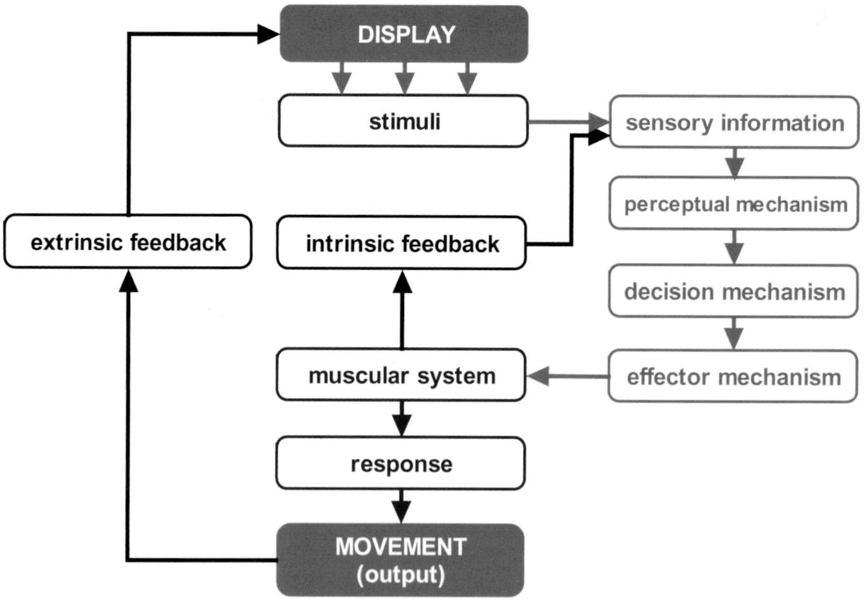

Whiting's model of information processing

This model (figure 5.10) describes in more detail how informartion is processed duning a physical activity.

- **Input data from display** involves information from the **environment** which enters the brain via the **sensory organs**. For example, before catching a ball, the catcher sees the ball and is aware of the thrower's movement.

- The **sensory organs** which receive information are referred to as **receptor systems** in the model.

- **Perceptual mechanism** is the part of the brain which perceives the surroundings and gives them meaning.

- The **translatory mechanism** consists of the part of the brain which makes decisions and sorts out and processes the few relevant bits of information from the many inputs from the surroundings.

- The **effector mechanism** is the part of the brain which carries out the decisions and sends messages to the limbs and parts of the body via the nervous system.

- **Output** involves the effector mechanism and the **muscular system**. The nerves send messages to the muscles which move in order for the ball to be caught.

- **Feedback data** is **information** which is used **during and after** an action or movement which enables a performer to adjust or change performance according to this new information.

figure 5.10 – Whiting's model of information processing

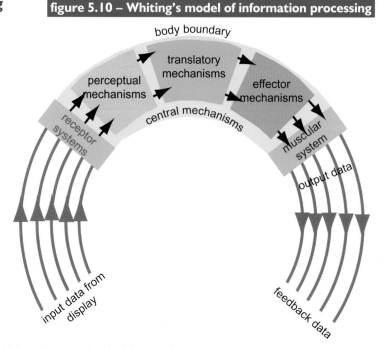

The memory system

All the senses feed a vast amount of information into the CNS. Think for a moment of all the aspects of your surroundings and your body on which you can focus your attention if you choose.

The games player can **switch attention** from the opponent to the ball to the grip on the bat very quickly (figure 5.11). He is able to do this because all the information that enters the sensory system is held for a **very short time** in a section of the memory known as the **short-term sensory store** (STSS) (figure 5.12).

Evidence suggests that there is a **separate store** for each sense. In these stores, the coded message for each stimulus is compared with all the information held in the long-term memory to allow it to be identified/recognised. This has to be done very quickly because the short-term stores have a **large capacity** but retain each stimulus for **less than a second.**

If the **perceptual mechanism** decides that the stimulus is not **relevant** or important, the sensory memory held in the short-term sensory store fades and is lost. All this happens before we are conscious of it.

The short-term sensory store has a very large capacity for information but a minimal storage time; its purpose is to **filter out irrelevant information** so the system is **not overloaded**.

Selective attention and processing capacity

If we are looking out for some particular stimulus **(intentional attention)** or if a particular happening catches our attention **(involuntary attention)**, then we focus on that by the process of selective attention. This focusing of attention passes the selected information into the short-term memory and allows more detailed processing.
The **short-term memory** holds the information for up to 30 seconds and allows it to be consciously analysed.

Memory model (figure 5.12)

- **Short-term sensory storage (STSS)** is the **area of the brain** which receives information and holds it for a **short time** (less than 1 second) **prior to processing**. Information deemed unimportant is lost and forgotten and replaced by new information.

- **Selective attention** is used to sort out **relevant bits of information** from the many which are received.

- **Short-term memory (STM)** is the **part of the brain** which keeps information for a short period (20 - 30 seconds) after it has been deemed **worthy of attention**. The STM can carry between 5 and 9 separate items of information which can be improved by **chunking** (page 92).

- The information can be used for problem solving (**decision making** in which it is decided what to do) or passed on to the long-term memory for permanent storage.

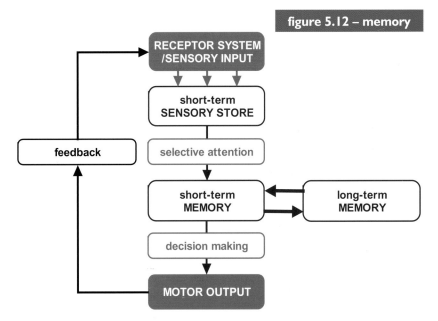

figure 5.12 – memory

RECEPTOR SYSTEM /SENSORY INPUT

short-term SENSORY STORE

feedback

selective attention

short-term MEMORY

long-term MEMORY

decision making

MOTOR OUTPUT

Memory model

- **Long-term memory** is the **part of the brain** which retains information for **long periods of time** - up to the lifetime of the performer. Very **well-learned information** is stored, and LTM is **limitless** and not forgotten but may require a code for the information to be recalled.

Definitions of reaction time, response time and movement time

Reaction time

Reaction time (RT) is the time between the **onset** of a stimulus and the **start** of the response. This is an **inherent ability** or trait. The stimulus could be kinaesthesia, hearing, touch, vision, pain, or smell. From this list, the fastest reaction times occur to stimuli at the front of the list, the slowest to those at the end of the list. This is also known as **simple reaction time**.

Response time

Response time is the time it takes to **process information** and then to **make a response**. **Response time = reaction time + movement time.**

Movement time

Movement time is the time it takes to **complete the onset** of a movement.

Choice reaction time

If **several stimuli** are given but only one must be selected for response, then a choice must be made of which stimulus to respond to. The **more choices** a person has, the **more information** needs processing, and the **longer it takes** to process the information, the **slower** the reaction time. This is **Hick's Law** (figure 5.13).

figure 5.13 – Hick's Law
showing increase in reaction time as number of stimuli increases

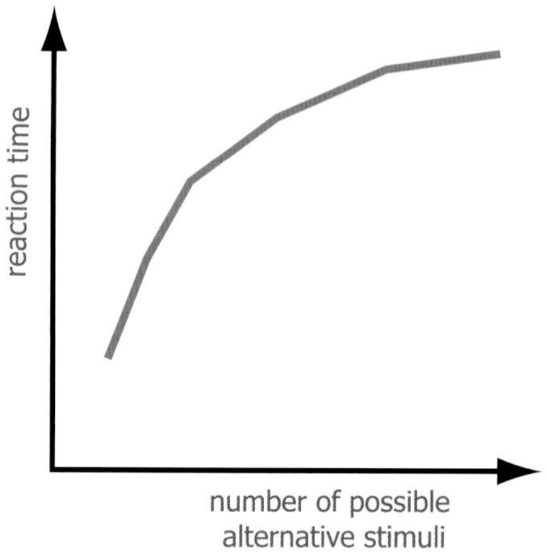

reaction time

number of possible alternative stimuli

Factors affecting reaction time (figure 5.14)

- **Age**: the older we get, the slower our reaction times.
- **Gender**: males have quicker reaction times than females, but reaction times reduce less with age for females.
- Increase in **stimulus intensity** will improve reaction time, a louder bang will initiate the go more quickly than a less loud bang.
- **Tall people** will have slower reactions than short people because of the greater distance the information has to travel from the performer's brain to the active muscles, short sprinters tend to win 60m races.
- **Arousal levels** affect reaction times. Arousal levels are best when the performer is alert but not over aroused.
- The performer must attend to the most **important cues** (which act as a stimulus).
- Factors like body language or position might give a cue which enables the performer to **anticipate** a stimulus by for example, identifying favourite strokes or positions, particularly if the play involves an attempted dummy or fake.

figure 5.14 – factors affecting reaction time

anticipation · age · gender · stimulus intensity · height · arousal levels · importance of cues → REACTION TIME

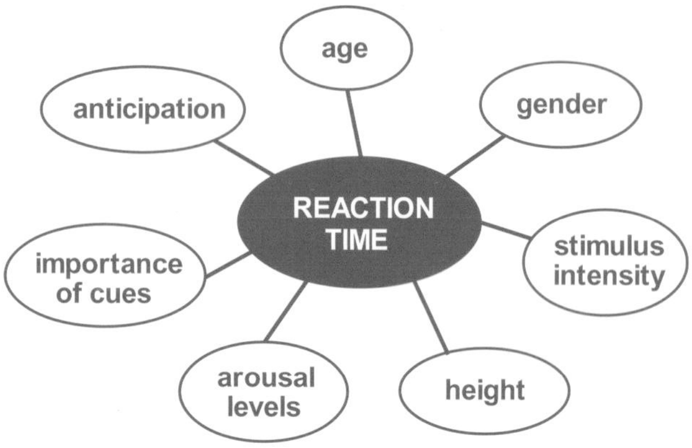

Implications to a coach of factors affecting reaction times

Performances can be affected by the factors listed in figure 5.14.

- Firstly in the selection of a suitable sport (for example, targetting a particular event in a group of events (shorter people in the 60 m sprint) for a sprinter).
- Use reaction speed drills that incorporate single and choice reaction times.

Implications to a coach of factors affecting reaction times

- Coach performers to **anticipate** and so reduce the time they take to respond to a stimulus.
- For example, the tennis player who anticipates the type of serve the opponent will use (spatial or event anticipation).
- In this case, the player has learnt to detect **certain cues** early in the serving sequence that predicts the potential type of serve.
- This means that players can start to position themselves for the return earlier in the sequence than usual and thus give them more time to play the shot when the ball arrives.
- For example, in a sprint start, get performer to focus on the starter's voice and the sound of the gun and separating this from background crowd noise and negative thoughts.

- **Decision making** working on set pieces and game situations. Provide opportunities to focus on different aspects of the game.
- For example, drills that switch quickly from concentration on the opponent to concentration on the field of play in invasion games.

- Ensure performers **warm-up** adequately to ensure the sense organs and the nervous system are ready to transmit information and the muscles to act upon it.

- Create a coaching environment that achieves optimum levels of **motivation** - 'psyching up'

Psychological refractory period (figure 5.15)

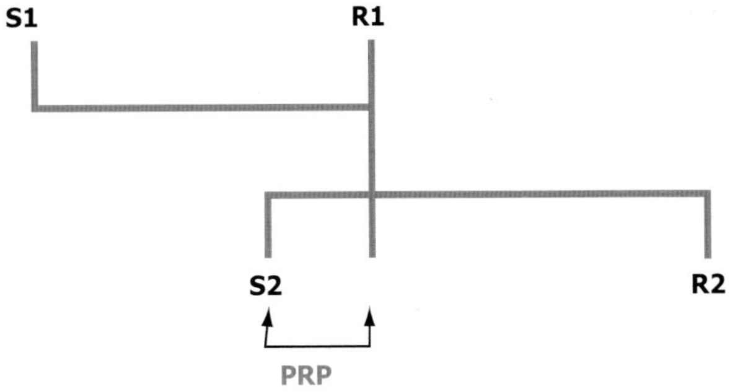

The **psychological refractory period (PRP)** is about what happens when following an initial stimulus (which may cause a reaction) there is a presentation of a **second stimulus**. The PRP is the time lag that occurs in responding to the second of two stimuli which occur close together, because a response to the first stimulus is still being processed.

Hence the **slowing down** of the processing of information between the relevant stimulus and an appropriate response. For example, defending a dummy in rugby (figure 5.16).

figure 5.15 – psychological refractory period

Psychological refractory period - example

Looking at figure 5.15, **S1** (1st stimulus) would be the dummy. **S2** (2nd stimulus) would be the definite move. If the dummy (**S1**) had been the only stimulus then the reaction would have been at time **R1**. In the meantime, **S2** has happened, but the performer cannot begin his or her response to this until the full reaction **R1** has been processed by the brain, so there is therefore a period of time (the **PRP**) after **S2** but before the time break to **R2** can begin.

A person who can do a multiple dummy (figure 5.16), can leave the opposition with no time to react and hence miss a tackle.

Single channel theory

This theory says that a performer can only attend to **one thing at a time**, so information is processed **sequentially**, that is one after another. Attentional switching would occur by **transferring attention** from one situation to another, so although attention would be **shared** between situations, only one situation would be attended to at a time (one then two then one then two .....). Therefore this can only be done if each situation requires **small** attentional capacity.

figure 5.16 – player sidesteps left then right

Anticipation

This is the ability to **predict** future events **from** early signals or **past events**.

Temporal anticipation is pre-judging **when** the future event will occur.
Spatial anticipation is pre-judging **where** and **what** the future event will be.

Reaction time can be **speeded up** if the performer learns to anticipate certain actions.
Good performers **start** running motor programmes **before the stimulus is fully recognised**,
they anticipate the strength, speed and direction of a stimulus, which would enable a
performer to partially eliminate the **PRP** (psychological refractory period).

However, **opponents** will also be trying to anticipate the performer's own actions, and a good
performer will attempt to **increase** opponents' reaction times by increasing the number of choices
of stimulus they have (this uses the choice reaction time theory, known as Hick's law - figure 5.13,
page 88). For example, increasing the number of fakes or dummies.

Strategies to improve response times

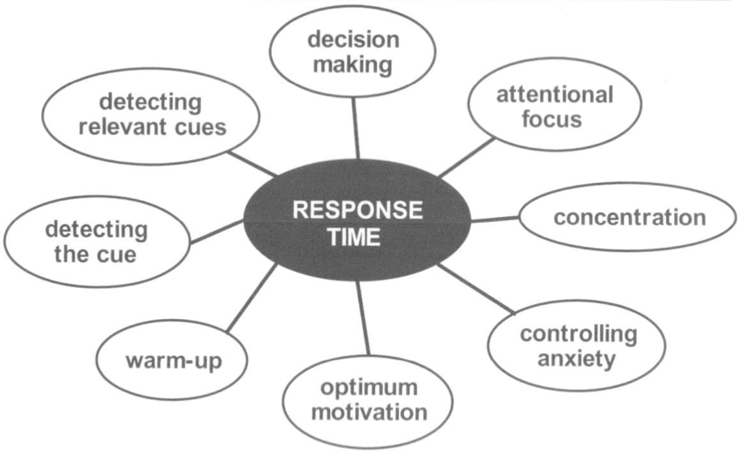

Response and reaction times can be improved using the
following tactics (figure 5.17):

- **Detecting the cue**: in which the **stimulus**
  (starter's gun) is sorted out from the **background**
  (spectator noise).

- **Detecting relevant cues**: in which the relevant
  stimulus is picked out from other possible ones,
  and **choice reaction time is reduced** by
  eliminating alternative choices.

- **Decision making**: in which performers work
  on **set pieces** in open skill situations so that an
  'automatic' complex response can be made to a
  simple open stimulus.

figure 5.17 – improving response times

- **Concentration**: in which there is a **change in attentional focus**, in which the
  performer practices **switches of concentration** quickly from one situation
  (for example, opponents in defence) to another (for example, field of play in attack).

- **Controlling anxiety**: Here, we know that anxiety would increase response times,
  so the performer would reduce anxiety by using **calming** strategies.

- **Creating optimum motivation**: in which the performer or team uses **psyching-up** strategies.

- **Warm-up**: which ensures that sense organs and nervous system are in their **optimum state**
  to transmit information and that the muscles are in an optimum state to act on it.

Schmidt's schema theory

Schema theory

Schema theory (figure 5.18) explains how sports performers can
undertake so many actions with very **little conscious control**.

The long-term memory **isn't big enough** to store all the motor
programmes required. **Schema** theory says that **generalised motor
programmes** exist which can be modified by taking in information while
a skill is being performed. Hence the LTM has to store **far fewer** motor
programmes, since any **new movement** can be performed by running a
schema which **closely matches** the needs of the new movement.
The **bigger** the schema the more **efficient** the movement, and large
amounts of **varied practice** are needed to improve a schema.

Feedback is very important to **correct** and **update** a schema.

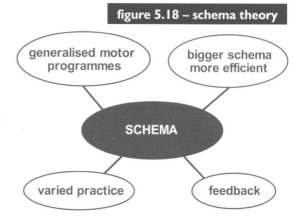

figure 5.18 – schema theory

STUDENT NOTE - SUMMARY OF SCHMIDT'S SCHEMA THEORY

1. **Knowledge of environment (initial conditions)**, for example, a basketballer who is aware of how far he or she is away from the basket.
2. **Response specifications**, for example, the basketballer recognising that he or she must carry out a jump shot because of an opponent.

3. **Sensory consequences**, for example, the basketballer is intrinsically aware of his or her body movements as the jump shot is being performed.
4. **Movement** or **response outcomes**, for example, the basketballer being aware of whether or not the shot has succeeded.

A schema is made up of two elements (figure 5.19).

Recall schema

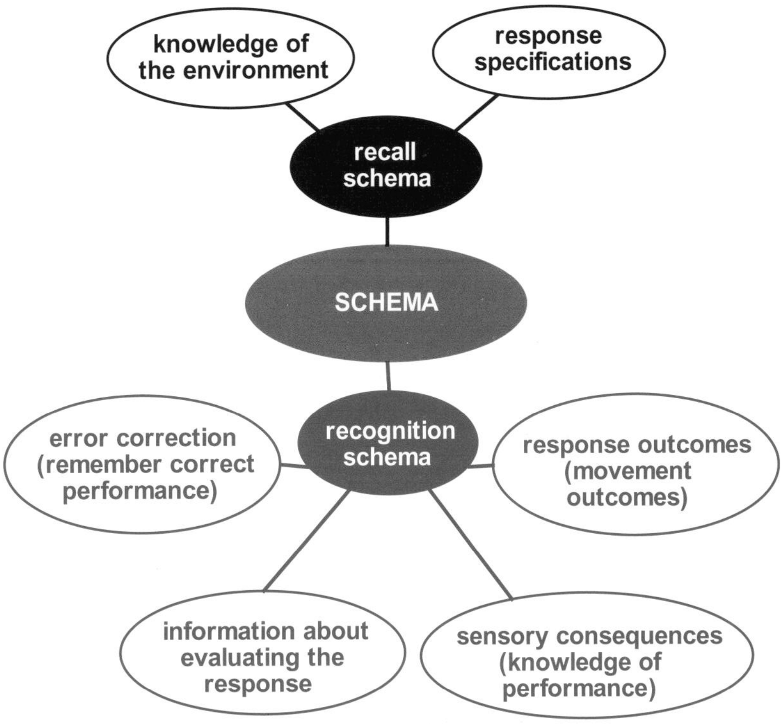

The first element of a schema is the **recall schema** which consists of all the information needed to **start** a relevant movement.

This includes the **knowledge of the environment** (initiial conditions):

- Playing conditions (pitch, playing surface, weather).
- Positions of team mates and opposition.
- Condition of equipment (kit, bike, car).

The recall schema also includes the **response specifications** (the correct technical model):

- Speed and force required.
- Size and shape of movement required.
- Techniques and styles used.

The recall schema is used for quick ballistic movements when there **isn't enough time** to process feedback.

Recognition schema

The second schema element is called a **recognition schema** which contains:

- Information needed to **correct errors** and remember **correct performance**.
- **Information** about evaluating the response.
- **Sensory consequences** (knowledge of performance) which would be the feeling and look of the performance.
- **Response outcomes** (movement outcomes) which would be the results of performance and the knowledge of results (how far, fast or many).

The recognition schema would be important when there is **enough time** to process feedback or for evaluating performance.

Sporting application of schema theory

In the case of a tennis first serve (Andy Murray, figure 5.20. page 92), a single schema could perform most of the movement required and the content in Andy's brain would click onto this single item rather than the thousands of tiny elements which make up the serve.

figure 5.19 – schema

Sporting application of schema theory

The **recall schema** includes knowledge of the court, the playing surface, and the position of the opponent. Further inputs would be the speed of the serve required, and the precise direction (wide or narrow down the T). This would be performed without feedback (during the actual movement which is so quick that there would not be time for feedback to reach Andy's brain),

The **recognition schema** would provide the elements of the sensory consequences (the knowledge of where the serve actually ended up - was it returned? Was it in the required direction (the response outcome or knowledge of results)? Did it enable Andy to recover and begin a response to the return if made?

At this point feedback would inform Andy of the next movement in the game.

There would be a **different schema** for the second serve, which although it looks similar to the first serve (and technically it would be similar - the movements, rhythms and timing would appear similar to the first serve), it would **feel completely different**.

This must be true, since if the schema for the second serve were **too similar** to that for the first serve, the performer might mistakenly use the wrong serve at the wrong time in the game.

Top players like Andy are able to switch between these schema, and use the first serve when normally the second serve would be played.

Also, this schema could be used for an overhead smash, given that this is in a more open skilled situation.

Strategies to improve information processing

Retention of information and facts in the memory (figure 5.21) can be improved by:

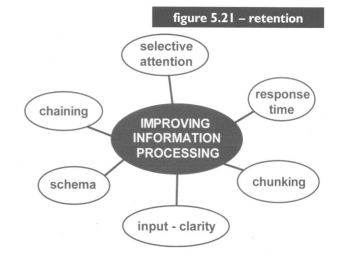

selective attention

response time

chaining

IMPROVING INFORMATION PROCESSING

chunking

schema

input - clarity

Input:

- **Educate** the performer about the details of a skill.
- **Explain** what to do and how to do it.
- Ensure that input is **clear** and **uncluttered**,
- Keep advice or instruction **simple** and **clear.**
- **KISS** - keep it simple stupid.
- Carefully **separate** similar skills to enable the performer to distinguish between them
- Organise the process of skill learning to ensure the information is **meaningful**.
- Be **brief** and do **not overload** the short-term memory which can only hold small amounts of data.

Chunking:

- More information can be held in STM if information is **lumped together**. This is called **chunking**.

Chaining or association:

- **Link new** information **with old** already learnt information.
- Multiple links can form a chain.

Strategies to improve information processing

figure 5.22 – practice makes perfect

Schema:

- **Practice makes perfect** (figure 5.22, many repetitions of this shot will improve its performance and percentage of success).
- The more **practice** that can be done to a **correct technical model**, the better the **schema** will be formed and the better the immediate performance.
- Perfect practice makes a skill perfect.
- **Repetition** of any information or skill will enable it to be remembered better.

Response time:

- See page 88 for details of how to improve response time in the context of sporting activities.

Practice questions

1) Identify the three main receptor systems used by a performer in sport.
   Where is the filtering mechanism found in an information processing model? Explain what happens with information as it passes through this mechanism.   8 marks

2) Identify and describe the three elements of perception.
                                                                    3 marks

3) Improvement in performance of a skill can be better understood by reference to the processes involved.
   Figure 5.23 shows Whiting's information processing model.

   a) Explain the meanings of the terms: perceptual mechanism, translatory mechanisms, and effector mechanisms, and relate these terms to stages in the Whiting model.   5 marks

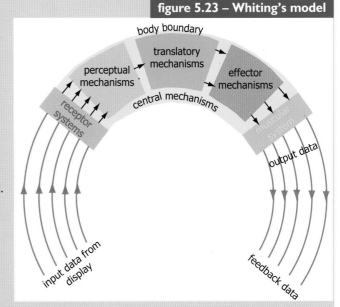

figure 5.23 – Whiting's model

   b) The diagram also shows five arrows entering the perceptual mechanism and only one leaving.
   What is the name given to this process and why is it necessary?   4 marks

   c) Identify three factors which might help a performer with his or her perceptual mechanisms.   3 marks

4) a) Using figure 5.24 representing the human motor control mechanism, explain what is meant by short-term memory and long-term memory.   2 marks

   b) How can information be retained in the long-term memory?   4 marks

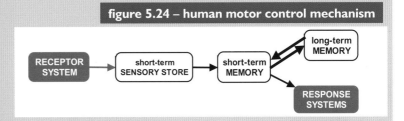

figure 5.24 – human motor control mechanism

5) What is meant by Hick's Law? Illustrate your answer by plotting a graph which represents this theory.
   How can performing a dummy move affect an opponent's response?   7 marks

Practice questions

6) a)   Using the example of a table tennis player receiving a serve, what information would be
held in the short-term sensory store and for how long?   4 marks

b)   Name and describe the purpose of the process by which information is transferred
from the short-term sensory store to the short-term memory.   4 marks

7) a)   Explain the difference between reaction time, movement time and response time?
What advice would you give to a sprinter to cut down on reaction time at the start of a race?   4 marks

b)   Sketch and label a graph to illustrate Hick's Law.
How does the number of choices available to a performer affect his or her performance?   4 marks

c)   When taking part in a badminton game, the shuttle occasionally hits the netcord during
a rally, and the receiver has to adjust his or her return shot. This causes a delay before
the final response can be made. What is this delay called and explain why it occurs?   4 marks

d)   What factors could affect response time in any game or sport?   4 marks

figure 5.25 – a javelin thrower

8) a)   Looking at figure 5.25, using examples from javelin throwing, identify four items of
information stored as schema.   4 marks

c)   Comparing the skills of throwing the javelin and taking a free throw at basketball,
explain how the skills are related using schema theory.   4 marks

d)   Briefly explain how the analysis of skills will influence a coach in organising training
for javelin throwing as compared with a basketball free throw.   4 marks

9) a)   Explain, using a sporting example, how the use of selective attention depends on
an athletes' level of ability.   3 marks

b)   How can a coach improve an athlete's selective attention.   3 marks

10) During sporting situations it may be necessary to process
information using memory systems.

What are the features and functions of the working memory?

Using figure 5.26 how can a single recall schema assist the
attacking player to decide on his next move?

What strategies could the player use to improve his memory
system?   15 marks

figure 5.26 – soccer player's attack

Answers link: http://www.jroscoe.co.uk/downloads/a2_revise_pe_edexcel/EdexcelA2_ch5_answers.pdf

SPORT PSYCHOLOGY

CHAPTER 6
ATTRIBUTION THEORY,
CONFIDENCE AND SELF-EFFICACY AND LEADERSHIP

CHAPTER 6: *Attribution theory,*
confidence and self-efficacy, and leadership

Attribution

Attribution is the process of giving **reasons** for behaviour and ascribing **causes** for events. For example, the player played badly today because the weather was poor.

Weiner's model

Weiner's model has four attributions, **ability**, **effort**, **task difficulty** and **luck** (see figure 6.1).

As in figure 6.1, these attributions are arranged in two dimensions, **locus of causality** and **stability** (with a possible third dimension, **controllability**).

figure 6.1 – Weiner's model of sports attribution		
	LOCUS OF CAUSALITY	
	INTERNAL	**EXTERNAL**
STABILITY — **STABLE**	ability 'we were more skilful '	task difficulty 'the opposition are world champions'
STABILITY — **UNSTABLE**	effort 'we tried hard'	luck 'the court was slippy'

Locus of causality dimension

Locus of causality is the performance outcome caused by:
*   **Internal factors** under the control of the performer such as ability and effort.
    *   **Ability** is the extent of the performer's capacity to cope with a sporting task.
    *   **Effort** refers to the amount of mental and physical effort the performer gives to the task.

*   **External factors** beyond the control of the performer such as task difficulty and luck.
    *   **Task difficulty** is the term describing the extent of the problems posed by the task including the strength of the opposition.
    *   **Luck** describes factors attributable to chance, such as the weather or the state of the pitch.

Locus of stability dimension

Stability refers to the performance outcome caused by stable or unstable factors:

*   **Stable** factors are fixed factors which don't change with time such as **ability** or **task difficulty**.
*   In a closed skill, such as pole vaulting (figure 6.2), the vaulter has learnt the specific movement patterns needed to create a stable technique. This is provided by a motor programme that contains all the information required to complete the skill.
*   Hence, although the pole vault is a difficult skill, the performance of it will be **habitual**, the **dominant habit** being stable.

*   **Unstable** factors are factors which can vary with time such as **effort** or **luck**.
*   If the pole vaulter **tries too hard**, the learned skill might break down (the inverted U hypothesis) and performance failure will occur. This is then unstable, and effort is a negative.

In attribution theory, **success** is explained by internal attributions, and **failure** is explained by external attributions. **Future expectations** are related to stability. If we attribute success to stable factors, or if we attribute failure to stable factors, then we expect the same next time.

figure 6.2 – a pole vaulter

Relationship to sports achievement

- **High achievers** (such as Andy Murray, figure 6.3) tend to attribute **success** to internal factors (such as Andy's incredible state of fitness), and attribute **failure** to external factors (such as the high temperature or strong wind during the match).
- **Low achievers** tend to attribute success to external factors (such as a favourable wind), and attribute failure to internal factors (such as lack of fitness or ability).

- The process of changing attributions is called **attribution retraining**. The point of this is to change a person's tendency to ascribe reasons for success or failure so that it is more like that of a successful performer rather than an unsuccessful performer.
- Attributions affect a sportsperson's **pride**, **satisfaction**, and **expectancy of success**. Some people exhibit **avoidance** tendencies when faced with a sporting situation (they try to avoid participating), and this is called **learned helplessness**.

Locus of controllability, the third dimension

The **locus of controllability** covers attributions under the control of the performer (and sometimes not under the control of the performer). The locus of control dimension relates to the intensity of a performer's feelings of **pride** and **satisfaction**, **shame** and **guilt**.

- **Pride** and **satisfaction** are maximised if success is attributed to internal controllable factors like ability and effort, therefore motivation would be enhanced.
- If **success** were attributed to **external** and **uncontrollable** factors such as luck or the fact that the task was very easy, then satisfaction would be less intense and there would be less motivation.
- If **failure** is attributed to internal controllable factors such as **lack of ability** and **lack of effort**, then the overpowering emotion would be dissatisfaction and motivation would be reduced.

The self-serving bias

- This idea crops up because **successful performers** tend to take credit for success. They do this by **attributing success** to their own overwhelmingly outstanding **qualities** (natural ability, **ability** to respond to the competitive situation), thereby enhancing their feelings of pride, self-worth, and self-esteem. They also tend to **blame external factors** for failure.

- Failure is automatically attributed to **avoid internal** controllable and stable factors (even if such factors may be true). This is the **self-serving bias**, people tend to give attributions to **protect their self-esteem** rather than look for true attributions which would reflect the reality of the situation.

- **Unsuccessful performers** do not always attribute failure to external factors and therefore do not protect their self-esteem. This tends to reduce motivation.

Figure 6.4 summarises the **attribution process**.

figure 6.3 – Andy Murray - high achiever

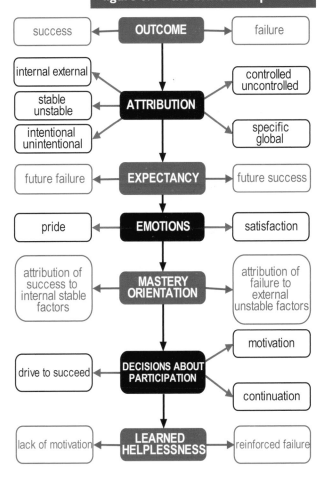

figure 6.4 – the attribution process

The link between motivation, attribution and task persistence

Table 6.1 – motivation, attribution and task choice and persistence

	high achiever	low achiever
motivation	high motive to achieve success low motive to avoid failure focuses on pride and on success	low motive to achieve success high motive to avoid failure focuses on shame and worry about failure
attributions	ascribes success to stable internal controllable factors ascribes failure to unstable external uncontrollable factors	ascribes success to unstable external uncontrollable factors ascribes failure to stable internal controllable factors
goals adopted	adopts task oriented goals	adopts outcome oriented goals
task choice and persistence	seeks challenging tasks and competitive situations and stays with them	avoids challenge, seeks very difficult or very easy tasks or competition and easily gives up
performance	performs well in front of evaluative audiences	performs badly in front of evaluative audiences

Learned helplessness (LH)

Repeated failure (or lack of success) can lead to a state known as **learned helplessness**.

This is explained as a **belief** acquired over time that one has no control over events and that failure is inevitable (for example, if a batsman repeatedly gets a duck, he may feel that he no longer has the skill to succeed at sport). It is characterised by a feeling of **hopelessness** in which a person with the physical potential to achieve highly at sport no longer feels that it is possible for him or her to do so (figure 6.5).

This is what is behind the common belief that if you fall off a bike, you must get back on straight away, otherwise you may never do so.

General and specific learned helplessness

*   **General (global) learned helplessness** occurs when a person attributes failure to internal and stable factors, and this feeling of failure is applied to all sports. For example, the comment 'I am useless at all sports'.

*   **Specific learned helplessness** occurs when a person attributes difficulties to internal and stable factors, and this feeling is applied to one specific sport. For example, the comment 'I am good at soccer but useless at racquet games'.

Attribution retraining strategies

Figure 6.6 summarises the process which must be undertaken if learned helplessness is to be avoided or recovered from. Following failure, low achievers need to learn to attribute success and failure to the same reasons as high achievers, namely:

*   Success should be attributed to stable internal factors.
*   Failure should be attributed to unstable external factors.

This would raise the **self-efficacy** (page 102) of the performer for his or her sport.

Hence attribution retraining will influence how the performer deals with a situation. During this process, the coach can provide encouraging feedback and set realistic achievable goals.

The positive and negative applications of attribution theory on performance and sustaining a balanced, active lifestyle is summarised in table 6.1.

figure 6.5 – get back on the bike straight away

figure 6.6 – attribution retraining

POOR PERFORMANCE

change from the
attribution:

of lack of ability

change to the
attribution:

of poor weather

change from the
negative emotion:

shame

change to the
positive emotion
or neutral emotion:

disappointment

change from the
behaviours:

helplessness,
avoidance of
competition

change to the
behaviours:

persistence,
seeking out
competition

figure 6.7 – failure needs retraining

figure 6.8 – a confident save

Confidence and self-efficacy

Confidence

Confidence is an element of mental preparation for sports performance, as outlined in figure 6.9.

Confidence arouses positive emotions which allow the athlete to:
- Remain **calm** under pressure.
- Be **assertive** when required.
- **Concentrate** easily.
- **Focus** on the important aspects of a task.
- Set challenging but realistic **goals**.
- Increase **effort**.
- Devise effective game **strategies**.
- Keep psychological **momentum**.

Confidence affects us by:
- Arousing **positive** emotions.
- Facilitating **concentration**.
- Enabling **focus** on the important aspects of a task.

Self-confidence is a feature of a sportsperson's attitude to his or her sporting activity which boosts personal self-worth and self-belief as outlined in figure 6.10. This belief centres around the notion that he or she can win or perform well.

Self-concept – a humanist approach

The term **self-concept** is a general term used to refer to how someone thinks about, evaluates or perceives themselves. To be aware of oneself is to have a concept of oneself.

Carl Rogers (1959) believes that the self-concept has three different components:
- The view you have of yourself (**self-image**).
- How much value you place on yourself (**self-esteem** or **self-worth**).
- What you wish you were really like (**ideal-self**).

figure 6.9 – confidence

calm — assertive — positive — concentration — CONFIDENCE — focus — playing to win — realistic goals — taking risks — never give up — effort

figure 6.10 – self-confidence and self-efficacy

belief that one can succeed — an attitude — SELF-CONFIDENCE — an aspect of self-esteem — perception of ability to perform a particular sporting task successfully — SELF-EFFICACY — a situation-specific form of self-confidence

Self-image

This does not necessarily have to reflect reality.
- For example, a person with anorexia (who is thin) may have a self image in which the person believes he or she is fat.
- A person's self image is affected by many factors, such as parental influences, friends, the media etc.

Self-esteem

Self-esteem is the **regard** you hold for yourself. Everyone has a concept of his or her person (**self-concept**). If you like your self-concept (who you think you are), then you have self-esteem. Self-confidence is different.

Self-esteem should be based on **who you are as a person** instead of how well you can perform in your sport or how high you go in a sporting career. Think about this: if you take away the part of you who is an athlete, how would you describe yourself? What are your **personal characteristics** that describe you? This is what self-esteem should be based on.

If you feel like you struggle with self-esteem, have hope, since this is a **learned capability** and it can change with practice, and the will to improve.

High self-esteem i.e. we have a **positive** view of ourselves. This tends to lead to:
- **Confidence** in our own **abilities**.
- **Self-acceptance**.
- Not worrying about what others think.
- **Optimism**.

Low self-esteem i.e. we have a **negative** view of ourselves. This tends to lead to:
- **Lack** of confidence.
- Want to be/look like **someone else**.
- Always worrying what **others might think**.
- **Pessimism**.

Ideal-self

This concept revolves around what you **would like to be** If there is a **mismatch** between how you see yourself (for example, your self -image) and what you'd like to be (for example, your ideal-self) then this is likely to affect how much you value yourself.

The coach, who should merely serve as a guide and not an authoritative figure, should demonstrate **empathy**, **understanding**, and **memories** of what it was like to be an athlete.

This relationship should be **athlete-centred** and **focus** on the athlete developing **self-awareness**, **growth**, and **development**.

Self-confidence is the **belief in your ability** to perform a task - it is not a judgment.

You can have self-confidence, but not self-esteem, and vice versa. Optimally, you want both high self-confidence in your abilities and self-esteem.

figure 6.11 – Jessica Ennis wins in London 2012, she had great self-confidence

Vealey's model of sport-confidence

A confident player plays to win even if it means **taking risks**, will take each point or play at a time, and **never gives up** even when defeat is imminent.

Vealey's **sport-confidence** is the level of belief a person has in his or her ability to be successful at sport.

- Success in sport could be related to winning (**outcome orientation**), or performing well (**performance orientation**).

- Different performers have different ways of enhancing sport confidence. Their **competitive orientations** can be varied according to the situation and whether a performer is motivated towards a performance goal or an outcome goal.

Table 6.2 – **sport-confidence**

factors influencing sport-confidence	definition and example
trait sport-confidence	the level of sport confidence a person usually has example, a discus thrower is generally confident about making a throw (figure 6.12)
competitive orientation	the perceived opportunity to achieve a performance or outcome goal example, the discus thrower is motivated by a challenging competition to throw well
state sport-confidence	the level of sport confidence a performer has in a specific sport situation example, the discus thrower feels confident because the wind is in the right direction
objective sporting situation	the performance takes into account the situation in which performance occurs example, the discus thrower competes well in the World Championships

Relationship of confidence to attribution

A performer's attribution of success or failure will relate to sport confidence. Attributing success to factors like ability and effort will increase a performer's sport confidence, by increasing his or her future expectancy of success.

Results of research

- **Males** (in the general population) have a higher sport-confidence than **females**.

- **Elite performers** have high sport-confidence.

- Elite sporting females have the **same level** of sport-confidence as elite sporting males.

- Therefore elite sporting females are **less affected** by **traditional female stereotyping** and roles.

- Elite performers are more **performance oriented**, which means that their feelings of confidence are based more on how well they perform than whether they win or lose.

figure 6.12 – discus throwers need to be confident

Self-efficacy

Self-efficacy is a situational form of self-confidence. It is specific to the sport or activity which a person is undertaking.

Bandura's self-efficacy

Bandura's self-efficacy model (figure 6.13) outlines **four** factors relevant to the self-efficacy of a sports performer.

Performance accomplishments
- **Performance accomplishments** consist of **past experiences**, for example, a previously performed skill at dribbling a soccer ball.
- If this is successful, then this leads to greater self-efficacy at this particular task in the future.

Vicarious experiences
- **Vicarious experiences** consist of what has **been observed in others** performing a similar skill (the sports performer experiences the same feelings of mastery and competence by watching another person perform a skill as if he or she has performed the skill himself or herself).
- For example, observing another player in your team dribbling a soccer ball. This is most effective if the model is of similar age or ability and is successful. This may lead to greater self-efficacy.

Verbal persuasion
- **Verbal encouragement** can lead to greater self-efficacy if the person giving encouragement is of **high status** compared with the performer.

Emotional arousal
- If **arousal** is too high, then **state anxiety** (anxiety produced by the specific situation of an activity - otherwise known as **A-state**) can be too high.
- This could lead to low self-efficacy. Mental rehearsal or physical relaxation techniques could lead to greater confidence and a calmer approach - this also contributes to greater self-efficacy.

figure 6.13 – self-efficacy (Bandura)

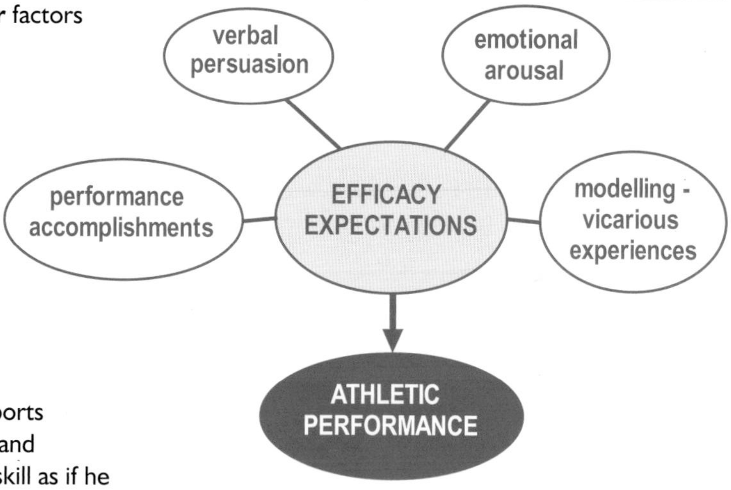

verbal persuasion

emotional arousal

performance accomplishments

EFFICACY EXPECTATIONS

modelling - vicarious experiences

ATHLETIC PERFORMANCE

Lack of confidence

Lack of confidence can cause **stress** under pressure. What tends to happen is that attention and concentration tend to focus on outside stressors such as mistakes (falling during an ice-skating or gymnastics programme), or spectators (shouted comments or applause on a neighbouring court).

- What also tends to happen is the setting of **goals** which are either **too easy** or **too hard**.

- Lack of confidence also causes the athlete to try to **avoid mistakes** (fear of failure or tendency to avoid failure).

- Non-confident athletes find it difficult to reverse negative psychological momentum, so that once things start to go wrong it is difficult to think positively.

Over-confidence or false confidence

Over-confidence is dangerous because it can lead to inadequate preparation (the athlete thinks he or she is better prepared than is actually the case, figure 6.14).

Low motivation and low arousal can occur, which are difficult to correct when competition is under way.

figure 6.14 – over-confidence can lead to injury

Strategies for the coach in building self-efficacy

Coaches can raise a performer's self-efficacy, resulting in a more positive and successful performance, as suggested in Bandura's self-efficacy theory (page 102):

- Build upon **successful experiences** by reminding performer of past successes. A previous performance is the strongest factor affecting self-efficacy and there is no reason why it cannot be repeated.

- Observe a **good demonstration** from a performer who shares the same characteristics, such as ability, gender and age, as the young performer. For example, a gymnast of similar age and standard, performs a forward roll on the beam. This performer will feel 'If she can do it, so can I'. Such a demonstration reduces worry and develops confidence.

- Use **role models** (figure 6.15) to inspire and motivate performer of potential long-term goals.

- Use **specific positive feedback**, such as words of encouragement and support, that may be related to a previous performance. The aim would be to convince the athlete of his or her ability to accomplish the task. Therefore, saying 'You can do it!' is not as effective as saying 'You successfully long jumped 4 metres, you can do 4.2 metres.' This positive talk or persuasion will elevate self-belief.

- **Break down complex skills** (whole-part-whole learning) into smaller specific components that challenge the performer but are within his or her current ability level, thus allowing the performer to have successful experiences which will over time increase the performer's self-efficacy.

- Use **mental rehearsal** or **imagery** techniques to reinforce skill learning.

- Control of **arousal levels** of the performer's internal feelings and physiological state, for example, increased heart rate and sweating. This may include **cognitive** and **somatic** strategies.

figure 6.15 – Johanna Konta

Leadership

Leaders play an important role influencing groups and individuals as well as setting goals. In terms of sport, leaders include team captains, coaches, managers and teachers. Successful teams have strong leaders.

A leader can influence the behaviour of others towards required and desired goals and will influence effective team cohesion. He or she will also help fulfil the expectations of a team, and will develop an environment in which a group is motivated, rewarded and helped towards its common goals. Recognised characteristics of successful leaders are summarised in figure 6.16.

Carron suggested that leaders emerge in two ways:

- **Emergent leaders** come from within a group because of their skill and abilities or through nomination or election.

- **Prescribed leaders** are appointed by a governing body or agency outside the group.

figure 6.16 – leadership chacteristics

CHARACTERISTICS OF EFFECTIVE LEADERS

knowledgeable · motivational · respectful · communicative · organised · patient · empathetic · firm · engaging · consistent · confident · fair · forgiving · fearless

The Chelladurai continuum

The **Chelladurai continuum** theory covers the notion that there are three types of leader, and that an actual leader may adopt all three of the types in different situations depending on the circumstances. These three types of leader are:

- The **autocratic authoritarian** leader who makes all the decisions.

- The **democratic** leader who shares the decisions (with members of a group or team), and seeks advice from the group itself. He or she will be prepared to change his or her mind based on this advice.

- The **laissez-faire** leader who lets others make decisions and is prepared to go along with whatever they decide.

Effective leadership

Table 6.3 - **effective leadership**

	autocratic style	democratic style	laissez-faire style
what is it?	the leader commands, and other team members have no input	team members discuss with leader what to do	leader has the same role as rest of the team, he or she is passive, but provides support where necessary
characteristics	leader makes all decisions leader tells them all what to do	team members give input social development encouraged	team members take responsibility for decisions lleader has very little input
when is it effective?	dangerous situations team performing badly team members not familiar with tactics or skills	small groups team members are highly skilled team members are all capable of being leaders	most people think this does not work but may function for very experienced team members

Theories of leadership

These theories centre around the **nature** or **nurture** debate.

The 'great man' or trait theory

This is the '**nature**' theory, that leaders are born not made, and have relevant innate personality qualities.

Social learning theory

This is the '**nurture**' theory, in which leaders learn their skills through watching and imitating other people (models). This theory says that leaders are formed throughout life by social or environmental influences.

According to this idea, learning to be a leader starts by observation of a model, then continues by imitation or copying of the behaviour of the model. The effectiveness of this process would depend on the model having high status.

figure 6.17 – Kate Richardson-Walsh

Kate Richardson-Walsh (figure 6.17) was the inspirational captain of the women's hockey team which won gold at the Rio Olympics 2016. She had 375 caps for her country and was captain for 13 years. She is an example of a highly successful leader.

Fiedler's contingency theory

Fiedler's theory states that there is a continuum between:

- **Task-centred leadership**, which would be best for the most favourable or least favourable situations.
- **Person-centred (or relationship-centred) leadership** which would be best for moderately favourable situations.

Fiedler's contingency theory

Whether or not the task-centred or person-centred approach should be used depends on whether relationships are warm, if the task has a clear structure, or if the leader is powerful and people will do exactly what he or she says.

There would also be the pressure of time which might affect the choice of leadership style.

Factors affecting leader effectiveness

Figure 6.18 summarises the three broad groups of factors affecting the effectiveness of a leader with any given group or team.

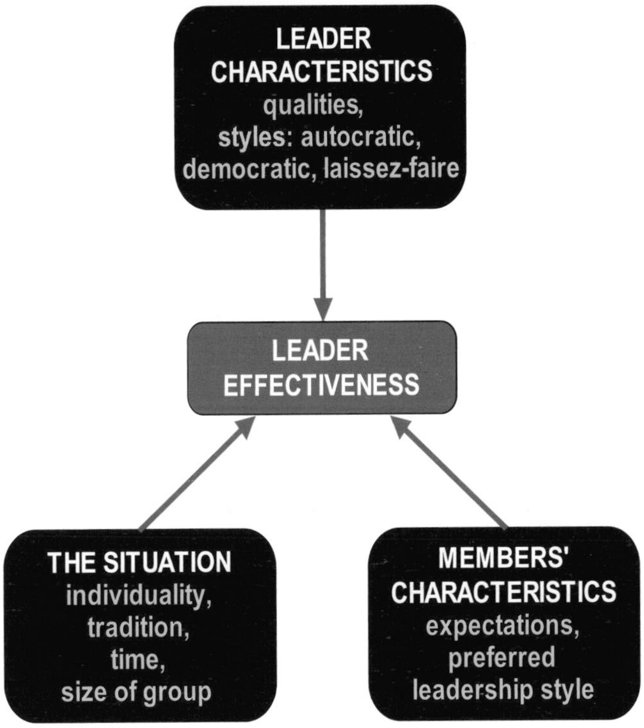

Leader characteristics

The following **leadership qualities** will determine a leader's effectiveness (this is expanded in figure 6.18):

- Ability to communicate.
- Respect for group members.
- Enthusiasm.
- High ability.
- Deep knowledge of the sport and techniques or tactics.
- Charisma.

figure 6.18 – factors affecting leader effectiveness

LEADER CHARACTERISTICS
qualities,
styles: autocratic, democratic, laissez-faire

LEADER EFFECTIVENESS

THE SITUATION
individuality,
tradition,
time,
size of group

MEMBERS' CHARACTERISTICS
expectations,
preferred
leadership style

Situational factors within leadership

- If things are going **well** for the team, or things are going **badly** (for example, there are poor facilities or no support), then a leader needs to be **task-oriented**.
- On the other hand, if things are going **moderately well**, then a leader needs to be **person-centred**.
- In **team sports**, a leader should be **directive** (task-oriented) and would organise and structure group tasks according to a plan (tactics or game strategy).
- In **individual sports**, however, we would look for a person-oriented leader, who would empathise with athlete problems and be sympathetic to individual difficulties.
- The **size of group** will affect leadership style, since the more members in a group, the less likely individual needs will be taken into account.
- If a **decision needs to be made quickly** (for example, in a dangerous rock climbing situation), then an **autocratic** style of leader would be essential to ensure that the correct action is taken immediately (people will need to be told what to do to avoid danger).
- **Tradition** can sometimes play a part in which style of leadership should be used, since within some groups, group members might tend to resent change. Sometimes change is essential, and it would be necessary to be **autocratic** and **task-centred** to implement change (the leader would not try and explain why change is needed, just that it needs to be done for the good of the team).

Members' characteristics within leadership

A good leader will adapt to the expectations, knowledge and experience of group members.

- If members of a group are **hostile**, then a leader would adopt an **autocratic** style.
- If members of a group are **friendly**, then the leader would adopt a more **democratic** and **person-centred** style.

Problems arise if the strategies for preparation used by a leader do not match group expectations (for example, if members of a team do not feel that the proposed strategy will achieve a win in the next match against a particular opposing team).

Chelladurai's multidimensional model

Chelladurai set out the model in figure 6.19, which sets out the links between **leader**, **situation** and **member** characteristics, and **required**, **actual** and **preferred** leader behaviour.

All these factors will affect the eventual performance of a team or group, and the satisfaction gained or perceived by both group members and the leader him or herself.

The point made by the model is that all the factors discussed above are linked in a real situation.

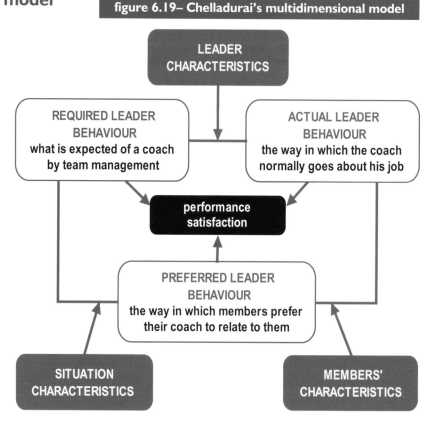

figure 6.19– Chelladurai's multidimensional model

Chelladurai's five types of leader behaviour

Training and instruction behaviour
This behaviour is aimed at improving performance. This type of leader behaviour is strong on **technical** and **tactical** aspects.

Democratic behaviour
This approach is one in which the leader allows decisions to be made **collectively**.

Autocratic behaviour
This approach is one in which a leader uses his or her **personal authority**.
This type would be least preferred if the leader or coach **does not show** that he or she is aware of sportspeople's needs and preferences.

Social support behaviour
This approach is one in which concern is shown for the **well-being of others**.
This might be preferred by youngsters.

Rewards behaviour
A leader uses **positive reinforcement** to gain the **authority** of leadership.

figure 6.20 – what type of leadership is shown here?

Practice questions

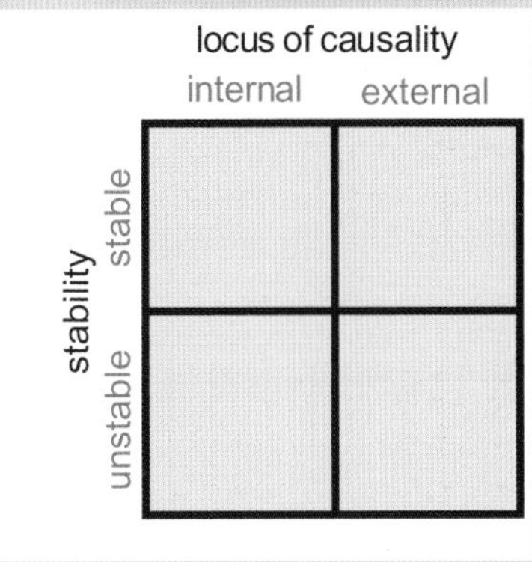

1) a) Figure 6.21 partly illustrates Weiner's model of attribution. Explain the term attribution using a sporting situation.   2 marks

b) Explain the terms locus of causality and stability when applied to attribution theory.   4 marks

c) Redraw the model and place on it relevant attributions for each of the four boxes.   4 marks

d) What attributions would you encourage if your team were playing well but often losing?   5 marks

figure 6.21 – Weiner's model of attribution

2) Using an example from sport, explain how attributions can affect a performer's future behaviour?   4 marks

3) a) Many young people claim to be hopeless at gymnastics. Suggest three reasons why these youngsters might have a negative attitude to gymnastics.   3 marks

b) What is meant by learned helplessness (LH) and how is it caused?   3 marks

c) How would you attempt to attract beginners to a gymnastics class, and then change any negative attitudes?   4 marks

4) Those who achieve little in sport often attribute their failure to factors outside their control and learned helplessness can result.
Using examples from sport, explain what is meant by learned helplessness and identify how self-motivational techniques may help to limit the effects of learned helplessness.   6 marks

5) a) What is meant by the term self-efficacy when applied to sports psychology?   1 mark

b) Bandura suggested that self-efficacy is influenced by four factors. Identify and apply these factors to a sport of your choice.   8 marks

c) As a coach of a sports team, how would you raise an individual's level of self-efficacy?   4 marks

6) How can self-concept affect performance in a sporting situation?   6 marks

7) Drawing on your knowledge and understanding of sports psychology, examine the theories and methods that you might use to raise the levels of confidence of a sports performer. Illustrate your answer with practical examples.   15 marks

8) a) How does self-efficacy explain performance?   4 marks

b) Describe each of the sections of self-efficacy theory?   8 marks

c) Provide a sport-based example of self-efficacy theory.   3 marks

Practice questions

9) a) What is meant by a leader and what sort of qualities would you expect to see in a leader within the context of sport?   4 marks

   b) Using psychological theories describe how an individual becomes a leader.   4 marks

10) a) Name three leadership styles.   3 marks

   b) What factors should be taken into consideration when deciding upon which leadership style to adopt?   6 marks

11) Fiedler's Contingency Model suggests that the effectiveness of a leader can change depending on the situation.
    Use sporting examples to explain this theory.   4 marks

12) Look at figure 6.22 of Chelladurai's multidimensional model of leadership.

   a) Explain each part of the model using examples from sport.   5 marks

   b) Behaviour of the group associated with leadership can be viewed from three perspectives. Briefly name and explain each of these perspectives.   5 marks

   c) Discuss the statement 'Good leaders are born not made', and explain whether you agree or disagree in the light of psychological theory.   5 marks

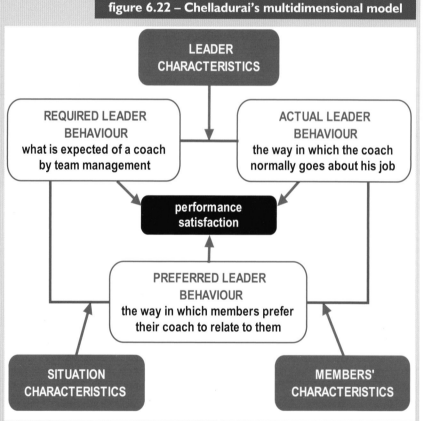

figure 6.22 – Chelladurai's multidimensional model

LEADER CHARACTERISTICS

REQUIRED LEADER BEHAVIOUR
what is expected of a coach by team management

ACTUAL LEADER BEHAVIOUR
the way in which the coach normally goes about his job

performance satisfaction

PREFERRED LEADER BEHAVIOUR
the way in which members prefer their coach to relate to them

SITUATION CHARACTERISTICS

MEMBERS' CHARACTERISTICS

Answers link: http://www.jroscoe.co.uk/downloads/a2_revise_pe_edexcel/EdexcelA2_ch6_answers.pdf

SPORT AND SOCIETY

CHAPTER 7: Commercialisation of sport

Commercialism and commodities

A definition of **commercialism** is **the treating of sport as a commodity, involving the buying and selling of assets with the market place as the driving force behind sport**.

Sport commercialism and British social history are intertwined as witnessed by the commercialisation of leisure pursuits during the **eighteenth century**, the growth in the spread of organised sport and physical recreation during the nineteenth century and the spread of television and the media coverage of sport in the latter part of the twentieth century and into the twenty first century.

The growth of commercial activity has increased participation and audience numbers, resulting in an improvement in sporting excellence (as witnessed by TeamGB's results since the 2004 Olympic Games) and improved sporting facilities (figure 7.1).

figure 7.1 – facilities as a heritage

The fact that **governing bodies** clung onto the concept of **amateurism** for so long, has in turn forced athletes into the arms of commercialism.

Nike - a case study

Nike represents a case study that illustrates the **growth** and **global** impact of a corporation.

Starting off as a small outfit selling Japan-produced shoes, it became a **global brand** employing labour and materials from the **developing world**, using the **media** to build recognition and forming **commercial alliances** with other organisations, including leagues and clubs.

It can be argued that, as a brand, Nike is more valuable that many of the sports clubs and characters it sponsors, and these include the likes of **Manchester United** and **FC Barcelona**, two of the most valuable sporting brands.

The **sporting media** can be seen as an expression of commercialism of sport in its **entertainment** style, its emphasis on **goals** and **spectacles** and its construction of performers as **celebrities**.

Sport as a commodity

Sport and its audience are sold as **commodities** to **advertisers**.

A **commodity** is something that is **useful**, has **value** and that can be turned to **commercial** or other **advantage**. The high price of the **advertising** slots during **major sport events** is based on the capacity of the sport to reach millions of potential **customers** for any number of products. The audience benefits from an increase in **televised** sport.

Sport is a **commodity** which simultaneously has evolved from **cultural** and **economic** activity.

Rules and codification

To become a commodity, sport not only has to be producible but also to be **reproducible** within a standard format, yet maintain **uniqueness** for each game, match or event. This requires that particular games within sport are played under identical and **stable rules** in both amateur and professional sports.

It requires the training of players to maintain the ethics of **sportsmanship** and the teaching of **fair play**, a basic underlying principle that underpins the **role** of sport in society.

STUDENT NOTE

For an introduction to this topic, refer to AS/A1 Edexcel ISBN 9781901424881, Topic 5, Chapter 16

The **codification** process was one of the first functions of early sports organisations and was important to **amateurs**.

Spectators

Spectators consume the sport commodity over a period of time, with different degrees of intensity of consumption and in a variety of ways:

*   Attendance.
*   Broadcast in TV or radio, but mostly TV.
*   Print, in tabloid newspapers.
*   Word of mouth.

Today, the **Olympic Games**, soccer's **World Cup** and **Formula 1** motor sport dominate all other sports competitions, attracting audiences in their millions.

Sports labour

Both professionalisation and rule changes push sports organisations into becoming involved in the **sport labour market** and the development of **elite sportspeople as commodities** within the global labour markets. Hence they have an economic value and players and coaches are under pressure from stakeholders to deliver.

Comparisons between advertising, sponsorship, endorsement and merchandising

Advertising

Advertising is a means of communication with the users of a product or service. Advertisements are messages paid for by those who send them and are intended to inform or influence people who receive them.

The selling or **merchandising** of products associated with sport is a major media objective. For example, electronic billboarding around an arena is aimed at the cameras. Advertising breaks on TV (although usually coincide with a break in play) attract large sums of money from the products they advertise.

These types of adverts not only get the general public interested in specific sports, but interest is also directed towards the advertised product.

Merchandising

Merchandising refers to the variety of products available for sale and the display of those products in such a way that it stimulates interest and entices customers to make a purchase. In the sports merchandising business, the property of value to a team is their name, logo and sports stars.

Merchandising

Through sponsorship and merchandising agreements the licensee is able to manufacture goods with logos, trademarks and trade names of the team, for example Manchester United merchandise (figure 7.2). The licensees believe that with the goodwill of the fans, they will associate with their clubs' identity and buy the merchandise.

A sponsor will expect to promote its products by using a performer's image in return for financial support. A contract will be commercial and dependent on the star status of the sportsperson.

figure 7.2 – MU merchandise

Advertising and merchandising

Advertising and merchandising are closely related concepts in the area of retail marketing and communications. Retailers use advertising to project a brand image and to drive traffic to retail **stores** or **websites**.

Merchandising is the strategic placement of products that attracts attention and contributes to sales once customers are in stores (figure 7.2 of the Man United shop).

Sponsorship

Sponsorship is when a person or organisation **pays the cost** of an activity or event.

Sponsorship advertising is a type of advertising where a corporation pays to be associated with a specific event, for example, Virgin Money London Marathon (figure 7.3).

figure 7.3 – Virgin Money London Marathon

Sports with the best sponsorship deals are sports with a **high fan base** such as football, tennis and snooker. During televised football games, the **half-time** TV adverts tend to have a heavy sports orientation.
Equally, many adverts are tennis based around the time of Wimbledon.

Sponsorship is varied and covers all aspects of the team sports and events/ competitions, stadium and grounds:

- **Team sponsorship** is one of the most prominent forms of sports advertising. Many businesses of all sizes choose to sponsor a sports team as a way to **promote** their company.

- The brand name will be featured on the kits of the player, for example, Chelsea' s £60m a season deal with **Nike**.
- Eclipsed by Manchester United's £75m a season deal with **Adidas**.
- Sponsoring a local team can generate lots of **revenue**, great publicity and create a huge amount of valuable goodwill for businesses of all sizes.

- Adidas has a long-standing relationship with Team GB (figure 7.4), which began 31 years ago at Los Angeles 1984 and extends to the 2024 Olympic Games.
- Adidas remains the British Olympic Association's (BOA) longest serving domestic sponsored partnership for team kit and footwear.

figure 7.4 – BOA Logo

TEAM GB

- Nowadays the **sponsorship of stadia** is a common occurrence and selling the stadium's naming rights can bring in massive revenue.
- For example, Stoke City FC announced (from the start of the 2016/17) the Britannia Stadium was to be known as the **bet365 Stadium** for the Premier League season.

- Stoke City Chief Executive Tony Scholes said: 'The Premier League is constantly evolving and to ensure that Stoke City remain as competitive as possible it's important we explore as many ways as possible of generating revenue'.

Sponsorship

- **Event/competition sponsorship** ranges from local to national to international level.
- For example, Aegon have been investing in **British tennis** since 2009 and crosses all levels of the game,
- From **nurturing young talent** through our Aegon FutureStars programme, encouraging amateur participation through tournaments such as the Aegon County Cup.
- Helping professional players reach **further potential** through the platform of the Aegon GB Pro-Series.
- And **supporting top players** through our national Davis and Fed Cup Teams.

Endorsement

An **endorsement** is a deal whereby a company will pay an individual for its brand to be associated with that individual.

Sporting role models (figure 7.5) often gain the attention of a corporation who wish to use the athlete's popularity and reputation to help **promote** a service or product. The sponsoring corporation will therefore pay that individual for him or her to endorse its product.

The individual will be seen to be endorsing the product by **wearing** the brand name, appearing in advertising campaigns both on television and in the print media for that particular product. Legally endorsements will be created through an **endorsement agreement** between the individual sporting star and the brand which they are endorsing.

figure 7.5 - Andy Murray, now endorsed by UnderArmour

Sponsorship and endorsements

Sponsorship is a **marketing** tool used by business where they pay for some or all the costs involved in a project in return for **recognition**. Sponsors aim to be **associated** with events and projects that are **directly linked** to their target audience as discussed.

Endorsement, on the other hand, has a much more personal twist.

When someone is endorsed by a brand they are publicly saying that they 'recommend' or 'suggest' you try a particular product because they think it's good.

For example, **Nike** was a main sponsor of the 2014 World Cup, but that doesn't mean that all the teams and players involved in the competition like or use their brand. Nor does it mean that FIFA recommend you use Nike.

Adidas, one of Nike's biggest competitors, also sponsored the World Cup and both only benefit from having their brand being exposed to potential consumers.

They sponsor the event, invest money in the competition and in return are able to **showcase** their **brand** to the world.

Nike also have endorsement deals with influential athletes that use their brand and believe it is the best product, for example, Roger Federer and Nike. Here the value comes from that athlete's influence in generating sales through a **recommendation**.

Sponsorship and endorsements

Now, the same athlete would not be able to be endorsed by Nike and Adidas **at the same time** for that results in a conflict of interest. Endorsement deals have to come across as authentic to consumers.

Advertising, sponsorship and endorsement deals and the sports star

Puma is Usain Bolt's largest sponsor (figure 7.6). In 2013, he signed an endorsement deal worth an estimated $10 million per year to remain with the company throughout his competitive sporting career. He is expected to earn $4 million annually to stay on as a brand ambassador after he retires.

Advertising, sponsorship and endorsements are packaged together when contracts are exchanged between corporations and celebrity sports stars.

Figure 7.7 lists how advertising affects the sports star.

However, the **motives** of the commercial media differ from sport motives, even though some products may be seen to help sport in other than financial ways.

The **sports performer** is helped by:
*   Provision of equipment.
*   Income.

The **sports governing body** or organiser is helped by:
*   Sport funding, which can be used to for example promote grass roots sport.
*   Positive associations between the product and the sport.
*   Greater exposure of the sport to the public via the media.

The **product** gains by:
*   Broadening the publicity given to the product.
*   Tax relief for the advertiser, since the exposure involves a cost which can be set against tax.

figure 7.6 – Usain Bolt and Puma

figure 7.7 – advertising

sport exposure · sport funding · positive associations · tax relief for advertiser · ADVERTISING and the SPORTS STAR · equipment for performer · product exposure · endorsement for performer · income for performer

In the face of the recent recession, several companies have withdrawn sponsorship because **profit** is their central motive.

Drug scandals have also have an impact on player's earning, for example, Nike and TAG Heuer cancelled their sponsorship deals with Maria Sharapova after she failed a drugs test.

Sports have **marketing managers** and promoters to generate income and athletes have agents and managers to look after their finances.

Sponsorship and merchandising

Through **sponsorship and merchandising** agreements the licensee is able to manufacture goods with logos, trademarks and trade names of the team, for example Manchester United merchandise (figure 7.2, page 112).

The **economic** factor is massive. In 1995, sport was the eleventh largest industry in the USA. Sport related activities account for 2% of **employment** in Britain. Sport has become increasingly **commercialised**, particularly over the last two decades, leading to growth in sports marketing, sponsorship, sports tourism and consultancy.

The historical and social context of commercialism

The **evolution** of commercialisation in sport has occurred through the past three centuries.

This began with tradesman **donating prizes** in kind at holy days to highly organised rural sports often sponsored by local publicans. Such **sponsorship** was supplemented in the eighteenth century with noble **patronage** or by a town or district that had **local government**.

This led to increased **gambling** and **spectatorism**, which in turn encouraged event organisers to seek further commercial development.

By 1900 the tradition had produced **folk heroes**, national **competition networks**, **international** championships and the popular interest of selling thousands of **newspapers** daily and bringing whole cities to a standstill.

Broken time payments

Opportunities for **working classes** to participate in sport were restricted by their long six-day working weeks and Sunday Sabbatarianism. In the UK, the Factory Act of 1844 gave working men half-a-day off, making the **opportunity** to take part in sport more widely available. Working class sportsmen found it hard to play top level sport due to their working hours.

On occasions, **cash prizes**, particularly in individual competitions, could make up the difference in los of earnings, with some competitors also wagering on the outcomes of their matches. As professional teams developed, some clubs were willing to make 'broken time payments' to players, i.e to pay top sportsmen to take time off work.

figure 7.8 – early rugby from 1850

As attendances increased, it became feasible to pay men to concentrate on their sport **full-time**.

A **spectator sport** is a sport that is characterised by the presence of spectators, or watchers, at its competitions (figure 7.8). In the late 1880's, the industrial North of England had many working class men, such as mill workers and miners, who started to play rugby. The **loss of earnings** that such a worker experienced whilst playing rugby on a Saturday was considerable and so became a major inhibitor. Some clubs began to make 'broken time payments' as compensation for the loss of income.

Many in the RFU (North and South) simply refused to accept the concept of broken time payments. A notable development was in 1893 when clubs in the industrial north of England put it to the Rugby Football Union that working players should be given 'broken time payments' to compensate them for pay lost while representing their club.

Many of the Northern administrators were ex-public school and strongly defended **amateurism**. The eventual outcome in 1895 was a split between twelve northern clubs who decided to break all links with the union and form the **Northern Rugby Football Union** (NRFU) on amateur lines, but with the acceptance of the principle of payment for broken time.

In the 1896/7 season the Northern Union introduced a challenge cup with all teams allowed to enter which caused great excitement. The final was held on May 1st 1897 between Batley and St. Helens at Headingley. Batley won 10-3 watched by between **13,000 to 14,000 fans** who paid £620 between them.

It was not until late August 1995, that **professionalism** in the Union game was agreed. The IRB did not really have a choice, with a lot of money beginning to flow into the game from advertising and TV. It was considered to be a complete injustice (by the players) that the players themselves were not able to share in this bounty.

Spectatorism

A spectator is a person who **watches** an event, and spectatorism is characterised by the presence of spectators at competitions.

Victorian Sport (1830-1901):
* **Mass spectator** sport began to take off.
* For the masses, **Saturday afternoon** free from work was the turning point, enabling them to play and spectate.
* For example, the **Heathens** (Newton Heath Football Club) - home ground at Belle-Vue Stadium Manchester (figure 7.9 shows large numbers of spectators surrounding the pitch).
* 'The Heathens' became a professional football team in 1885 and adopted its present name in 1902, **Manchester United** FC.

figure 7.9 – the Heathens in about 1880

Edwardian sport (1901-1918):
* Organised sporting involvement expanded rapidly across all classes.
* **Male working class** influence increased, notable for football in England and rugby in Wales.
* **Working class women** were largely excluded from sporting involvement.
* Sport was increasingly a matter of **national** concern.
* **Commercialisation of sport** continued with large numbers of spectators and increased number of **professionals** in major sports.

Between the wars (1918-1940):
* **Commercialisation** of sport expanded rapidly, especially the provision of spectator sport.
* Sport as part of a **national culture**, now extended to the majority of the population.
* Most sports were still **class oriented**.
* **Football** continued to increase in popularity and by the 1930s was the most popular spectator sport.
* Most spectators at professional soccer games were **men** who were able to **spend** some money at the turnstiles to support their local teams.

1940-today:
* An improved **standard of living** and working conditions has enabled **participation** and **spectatorism** for most social groups.
* **Amateur** administrators reluctantly allowed commercial forces to enter the world of sport.
* **Television** coverage increased in importance for sport, sponsors and spectators.

Developments in the media

Developments in the media are linked to **commercialisation** and sport - known as the golden triangle (figure 7.20 page 124).

The media include newspapers/magazines, radio and television broadcasting, with its main function to convey information to the general public.

Newspapers
The gradual emergence of the sports journalist can be traced back against a background of the expanding newspaper industry.

Clubs and NGBs were developed along with a sporting calendar for the spectator and player, and there was a dramatic increase in the range of sports available and in the number of people who played and watched them. This was followed by the introduction of the sports column and sports page. Bell's life (1822) and Sporting Life (1865) provided short, detailed sports reports.

Newspapers

By the 1920's newspaper sports reports could summarise sporting events and appeal to a mass and wide ranging audience.

Today there are two types of press that are also available online:
- **Popular tabloids**, such as the Daily Mail, the Express, the Sun and the Mirror, focus on popular male dominated sports. Hence football, rugby and cricket are given great exposure.
- More **high-brow broadsheets**, such as the Telegraph and the Guardian, and tabloids the Independent and the i, cover a variety of sports and analyse sport in more depth.

Magazines are a distinctive media form in their close connection to the social lives of consumers, and cover specific sports enthusiasms, for example, Athletics Weekly.

Radio

Radio broadcasting began in 1922 with the creation of the British Broadcasting Company (BBC), but sports commentary was not permitted until 27 May, 1925.

A rapid growth in radio audiences enjoyed the broadcasting of **popular sporting events** such as rugby and football matches, but many minority NGBs were fearful of radio's impact.

Television

The United Kingdom saw the first **live** television **broadcast** of a football match, with the BBC showing a specially arranged fixture between Arsenal and Arsenal Reserves on 16th September 1937.

World War II slowed down the development of TV to a mass audience.

Television developed from a very small number of networks addressing relatively undifferentiated mass audiences within national boundaries (1950s). This evolved into an era of expanded 'choice' with multi-channel systems gradually being added (1960s and 70s), to today's global broadcasting multi-channel systems (many of them originating from outside the UK) and their convergence with the internet.

During this development sports have had to change to make them more amenable to media coverage.

TV programmes can now be accessed via a range of interactive **computer devices** and watched on **multi-purpose screens** which vary from very small mobiles to large, flat, high definition screens.

The TV companies found sport fairly **cheap entertainment** compared with dramas or documentaries and so sport has been the beneficiary of media **growth**.

Roles of the media in terms of sport

The roles of the media, in terms of sport, are **fourfold** (figure 7.10).

- The basic function of the media has always been to give **information**. Radio and television give immediate **results, event descriptions** and **rankings**.
- **Education**. The media **inform**, **advise** and **critically analyse** issues through explanation, discussion and debate. Terrestrial and satellite TV have **documentaries** which give coaching advice, explain the risk of drug-taking, and give post-event discussions on games.
- **Entertainment**. A TV programme will give experience and pleasure to an armchair spectator almost equivalent to the live event. Attending live events is expensive, hence the popularity of screens in pubs, clubs or parks near to the venues, (Henman's Hill/Murray's Mound at Wimbledon for example).

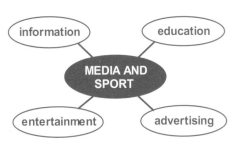
figure 7.10 – media and sport

information   education

MEDIA AND SPORT

entertainment   advertising

Roles of the media

- **Advertising**. The selling or merchandising of products associated with sport is a major media aim. An example of this is a tennis player wearing a certain make of headband, sports shoe or shirt. Each club in both rugby and soccer displays sponsors' names on its shirts. Electronic billboarding around an arena is aimed at the cameras. Advertising breaks on TV (although usually coincident with a break in play) attract large sums from the products being advertised.

The impact of the media on sport

The impact of the **media on sport** is extensive. They can **promote** balanced, active, healthy lifestyles and lifelong involvement in physical activity. This is via the people it presents, the way these people act and the messages they give. These messages could be given in children's programmes as well as in adult news and documentaries.

Hence the media's **selective** use of visual and written material can have a major influence. Most important is the **balance** of the message, not just the hero worship of sports stars, but help in recognising the **problems** as well as the pleasures of achievement. The media can give insight into the effort needed for success, and a belief in the ideal of fair play.

20th/21st century developments

During the twentieth century there has been a widespread erosion of **amateurism**. This has been caused through the influences of **internationalism** which offers the national governing bodies the prospect of **enhanced prestige** for their sports, and television **broadcasting rights** which provide huge **financial incentives** for them, their constituent clubs and their players.

The prospect of television revenue and consequent sponsorship, designed to further the excellence of performance in elite groups, persuaded amateur governing bodies such as those of athletics, rowing and rugby union to allow **deferred payments** to players, thus undermining their **amateur** credentials.

- This demand led to a business exploitation of commercial potential which is only reaching its fullest extent today in the age of global **commercialism** channelled through the media.

- The innovation of **satellite television** has brought the elements of international prestige and financial gain to bear upon sport simultaneously by offering staggering **fees** for participation in global events.

- The enduring popularity of **football** has made it the **biggest business** in sport.

- Much of the income football clubs receive is spent on wages for **highly paid professional players** who can supplement their income through product **endorsement** and other commercial ventures. Today the earning potential for 'sporting stars' is unprecedented.

- Television sport offers **business investment** in **advertising**, **endorsement** and **income** from ticket sales.

Influence of technology

Technological advances have revolutionised the ways in which humans **communicate**. The advancement of technology has brought together detailed coverage and faster action.

For example, **Spidercam** (a system which enables film and television cameras to move both vertically and horizontally over a predetermined area) is used to give additional viewing angles, thus enhancing the spectator experience.

HawkEye visually tracks the trajectory of the ball and provides action replays that can be used by umpires and players, as well as providing spectator entertainment.

Influence of technology

Mini cameras are fitted to racing cars, used in under-water events and on bikes and helmets to give the viewer at home a privileged viewing position.

Communications satellites enable **live** broadcasting on a global scale which has increased viewing audiences. Spectators can easily view at any point or dip into the action without losing the plot.

Technology lends itself well to **social media** as a means of communication and interaction including **email**, **social networking**, instant **messaging** and chat via tech gadgets such as **tablets** and **phablets** (phone + tablet,). Fans can **share** sporting moments **instantaneously** and these high tech gadgets provide another outlet for the **commercial** sector to exploit.

Media technological innovations are developing alongside and are fuelling the insatiable appetite of the sports spectator. Ultimately, production teams are the people who decide how best to use them.

Sports commentators

In sports broadcasting, a **sports commentator** (announcer) gives a running commentary of a game or event in real time, usually during a live broadcast. The sports commentator describes and analyses the action for the viewer at home. Their style of presentation usually reflects the **culture** of the sport.

figure 7.11 – Sue Barker

The role of the sports commentator has evolved over time. Much of today's sport is hyped-up in a **pre-game show** or just prior to the event commencing. The media presents its sports stars in conflict with each other as commentators discuss potential match outcomes. Some sports commentators are **celebrities** in their own right, for example, Sue Barker (figure 7.11, tennis) and Harry Carpenter (boxing).

Media and social values

Television often concentrates on the **conduct** of the participants and the spectators (aided by CCTV) and is generally **sympathetic** towards **officials** such as umpires and referees.

figure 7.12 – the Wimbledon queue

The media reinforces the contrast between the **high** and **low** **cultures** in sport. For example, Wimbledon's ticket policy aims to be both egalitarian as well as elitist as tennis fans line up for a British tradition, '**The Queue**' (figure 7.12). There is no place for deviant behaviour that is often present and publicised within more popular sports, such as football.

Gender inequalities in sport are often reflected by the media. A case in point would be to compare men's and women's football on British television. The women's game is yet to be given the same polished production quality that the BBC affords the men's game.

Despite technological innovations, conventions in the televising of sport appear resistant to change, indicating that these conventions carry high connotative value.

Media and social values

Today's media are able to promote equality of opportunity as sportspeople from ethnic minorities can become potent role models for example, Nicola Adams.

Nicola Adams has told of her joy at being a role model for female boxers (figure 7.13). The media has done much to enhance the profiles of sports stars.

The media coverage of a major sporting event generates a sense of **nationalism**. For example, London2012 was a highly emotive event that boosted national pride thanks to Team GB's success in the medals table.

Sports are expensive to run and so sponsorship deals and additional publicity, via the media, benefit both performers and spectators, a win-win situation.

figure 7.13 – Nicola Adams, Olympic champion

Impact of the Olympic Games on the Commercialisation of sport

The events of 1968, 1972 and 1976 and their impact on the 1984 Los Angles Olympic Games

The summer Olympics Games of 1968, 1972 and 1976 were turning points for both political and economic change that has impacted and secured the future of global sporting events.

The Olympics provide examples of the use made of sport by politicians and businesses who appreciate that sport has **political** and **economic** dimensions to be **exploited** when they can.

The '**shop window**' effect is the notion that the display of talent and excellence in both athletic **endeavour** and **organisation** of an event such as an Olympic Games, should be held up to demonstrate the high quality of **worthiness** of the national and political systems in which the games is held. This process was first promoted by Hitler for the 1936 Games in Berlin.

Mexico City 1968 'Black Power' demonstration

On the16th October 1968, US athlete Tommie Smith won the 200 metre race with a World record time of 19.83 seconds. Australia's Peter Norman finished second with a time of 20.06 seconds, and the US John Carlos won third place with a time of 20.10 seconds.

After the race was completed, the three athletes went to the podium for their medals. The two US athletes received their medals shoeless, but wearing black socks, to represent **black poverty**. Smith wore a black scarf around his neck to represent **black pride**. Both US athletes intended to bring black gloves to the event, but Carlos forgot his, leaving them in the Olympic Village. It was Peter Norman who suggested Carlos wear Smith's left-handed glove. For this reason, Carlos raised his left hand as opposed to his right, differing from the traditional Black Power salute when the Star-Spangled Banner played (figure 7.14).

Smith and Carlos delivered the salute with heads bowed, a gesture which became front page news around the World. As they left the podium they were booed by the crowd. Smith later said, 'If I win, I am American, not a black American. But if I did something bad, then they would say I am a Negro. We are black and we are proud of being black. Black America will understand what we did tonight'.

figure 7.14 – black power in Mexico 1968

In 2005, San Jose State University honoured former students Smith and Carlos with a 22-foot high statue of their protest which has become a globally recognised symbol of the Black Power movement that has helped to **reshaped American culture**.

The event is regarded as one of the most overtly political statements in the history of the modern Olympic Games.

Munich 1972 Palestinian terrorism

In **Munich 1972**, The Black September Palestinian terrorist
organisation (figure 7.15) organised and carried out the kidnap
and then murder of 11 israeli athletes and coaches from the
athlete village in Munich. One policeman was also killed.
The German antiterrorist police attempted to release the
hostages but failed at the airport as the group prepared to fly out.

The hostage-takers had demanded the release of 234 Palestinians
and non-Arabs jailed in Israel, along with two German insurgents
held by the German penitentiary system. Israel's official policy at
the time was to **refuse to negotiate** with terrorists under any
circumstances.
In the wake of the hostage-taking, competition was eventually
suspended for the first time in modern Olympic history,
after public criticism of the Olympic Committee's decision to
continue the games. On September 6th a memorial service
attended by 80,000 spectators and 3,000 athletes was held in the
Olympic Stadium.

The following day the Olympic programme resumed.

The incidents at these two games (1968 and 1972) illustrated to the media
world the power of the Olympic motif and structure.

Montreal's Summer Olympics in 1976

Montreal's Summer Olympics in 1976 was a turning point in Olympic history. It was the
Games' first highly visible security operation due to the terrorism act in 1972.

The **commercialisation** of the Olympics can be explained in terms of funding and
sponsorship. The funding of the Olympic Games up to 1980, was largely the **responsibility**
of the **host state or city**, which raised money out of local taxation.

This nearly caused the **bankruptcy** of the City of **Montreal** after the 1976 Games.
Following the terrorist tragedy at Munich four years earlier, the security bill ended
up running to $100m and the final tally of the cost for the Olympics was $1.6bn
which took the city 30 years to pay off.

By the 1980s many observers worried that the Olympics tottered on the verge of extinction.
Plagued by boycotts, terrorism and intractable national rivalries and beset by financial
shortfalls, cost overruns and the expenditure of vast sums for 'white elephant' facilities,
the list of potential suitors for hosting the games dwindled until only Los Angeles remained.
The world had seemingly abandoned the Olympics as too costly and too controversial. Some
forecasters predicted that Los Angeles would signal the death-knell of the modern games.

Peter Ueberroth and the 1984 Los Angeles Olympic Games

The USA federal government and the California State government refused to fund the
Olympic Games in Los Angeles in 1984.

Peter Ueberroth (figure 7.16) was a highly successful businessman and had witnessed
the financial problems associated with the Montreal Games (the Games in Moscow of
1980 were state-funded by the Soviet Union).

The Los Angeles Games were to be the first privately funded Olympics, and Ueberroth
made a point not to take charity. He realised that sales of anything in connection with
the Games could bring in a huge income, and that global commerce would willingly pay
large amounts in direct sponsorship of the Games.

The 1984 Los Angeles Olympic Games

- TV rights, clothing, logos, advertising at the venues and special edition postage stamps were all sold to bring in revenue for the Los Angeles Olympic Games.
- His aggressive recruiting of sponsors for the 1984 Olympics is credited as the genesis for the current Olympic sponsorship programme.
- Not only did he avoid the debilitating loss of Montreal, but he generated a surplus of approximately $250million.
- Fuelled by **television** broadcasting **funds** and the billions of **viewers**, **global television** transformed the modern Olympic Games into a spectacle, and transformed the modern Olympic movement.
- Ueberroth's legacy created the blueprint for the commercialisation of sport that has safeguarded the future of global events.
- The underlying features of his **blueprint** were that business people and entrepreneurs could be used to generate ideas, opportunities and solve problems as part of organising committees.
- The net result was that the sponsors brought in vast sums of money that covered the cost of the Games and more.

Since 1984 the IOC has used surplus income in several ways:

- **Safeguarding Olympics** and **Paralympics** mega-events.
- **Supporting** Olympic **Human Rights** initiatives and projects.
- For example, today host countries must sign a contract that requires protections for human rights, labor and the environment.
- If future host countries fail in their duty to uphold rights, the IOC is obliged to enforce the terms of the hosting agreement including the ultimate sanction of withdrawing the Olympics from the host nation.
- The development of the **youth sport** such as the Youth Olympic Games.
- The IOC invests in projects. For example, the 'Sport for Hope Programme' (figure 7.17) that targets developing countries and provides young people and local communities with positive sports development opportunities.
- Funding for the World Anti-Doping Agency (WADA) the IOC matches Government funding dollar for dollar.

figure 7.17 – Sport for Hope

Despite commercialisation, the IOC retains a complete ban on all on-site advertising in or close to Olympic venues.

Today, **Ueberroth's commercial blueprint** has political, economic, sporting and social impacts as first class sporting facilities, new housing, shopping malls and new transport links for people to live, work, play and visit form part of a debt-free legacy – a city's reward for staging a successful global sporting event, as was the case in London 2012 (figure 7.18).

figure 7.18 – the Olympic Park

Franchises in sport (USA and UK)

Sports franchise means **the contractual right granted to any person or persons to own or operate a sports team in a specified location**.

For example, Malcolm Glazer (estimated worth: £1.6bn) owns Manchester United and Tampa Bay Buccaneers (NFL).

In America, a club, or rather a franchise, exists to please the fans and provide entertainment. But above all, a franchise is a business to make money.

Franchises in sport

In the UK and Europe that order is reversed. As not a few Arsenal supporters might feel
right now, what is the point of being profitable if the team is indifferent?
'Football is not a matter of life and death, it's far more important than that'
Bill Shankly is famously reputed to have said, invoking irrational sporting passions
that mirror the win-at-all-costs ethic across the Atlantic.

The major US sports, gridiron football, basketball, hockey and baseball operate closed
leagues. The same teams (either 30 or 32 of them, depending on the league) play each other,
year in, year out. Only if their owners so decide, is their number increased in a process called
expansion, dictated not by the excellence of a new team, but the potential of a new market.

The same principle underlies relocation, whereby owners can move a franchise from one city
to another. Chelsea supporters are up in arms at the notion of moving a couple of miles from
Stamford Bridge, whereas in 1958 Walter O'Malley moved the baseball Dodgers 3,000 miles
from New York to Los Angeles.

Table 7.1 - **outlines of the pros and cons of franchises in sport:**

pros	cons
teams are on a more level financial playing field	the cartel structure of the leagues blocks new entrants
more teams have a realistic chance to win championships	regional monopolies allow owners to charge excessive prices
stadiums and spectator amenities are excellent, even when the resident teams are not	communities can lose their team as a franchise moves markets
franchises are bought and sold on the global commercial market enhancing their commercial status	professional sport is about generating wealth and like it or not it is commercial advertising which powers modern sport

The power shift from governing bodies to the media

UK governing bodies were originally based on the principle of **amateurism** and
even today many governing bodies remain decentralised, supported by voluntary
processes of organising and administering sport.

Today an NGB's role is to structure the sport and **oversee** and **organise** its
existing and future direction.

figure 7.19 – HawkEye in action

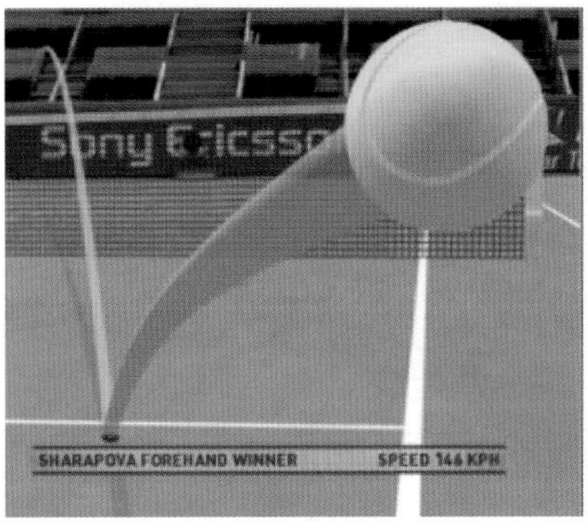

Over the years governing bodies have had to adapt to commercial pressures,
including the media, in order to maintain their status. Governing bodies have
commercially exploited their respective sports through the sale of media
rights or the conclusion of **sponsorship** agreements.

Governing bodies have **changed rules** as a result of media pressures.
Innovations such as the **golden goal** in football, the use of **HawkEye**
(figure 7.19)in tennis and cricket, and the review of incidents (foul play)
and the awarding of a try in rugby using the **fourth official** (the TMO,
who uses multiple TV views to make a decision), recreate more
excitement for spectators, which increases the sports' popularity and
hence the commercial revenue for both sponsors and the governing bodies.

Governing bodies have had to accept **TV commercial breaks** in play enabling sponsors to
advertise their products. Hence interruption of play is often controlled by such commercial
breaks. **Timetables** for events are often arranged to suit the armchair spectator, and at times
controlled by the TV network (USA).

Sport and its governing bodies have long considered themselves largely able to **self-govern**.
Governing bodies administer recognised **anti-doping programmes** and sanction those who
otherwise contravene the relevant rules of conduct and deviant behaviour that apply inside or
outside the field of play.

The power shift from governing bodies to the media

NGBs and IGBs may feel **less able** to **punish** players due to their **commercial** interests and **media pressures**.

The tabloid press have a habit of **creating stories** from the behaviour of sportspeople which may have no relevance to the standard of their sport. Such stories can completely overlay the sporting elements of a situation, particularly for female sportspeople. Press scandals sell newspapers.

Such scandals can detract from the purpose of a governing body in providing equitable conditions for the development of a sport.

Media exposure of corruption within NGBs

There has been alleged **corruption**, **bribery**, and **vote-rigging** relevant to the election of FIFA ex-president Sepp Blatter and the organization's decision to award the 2018 and 2022 World Cups to Russia and Qatar respectively. These allegations have led to legal prosecution in the USA and the increase in popular cynicism about the fairness and honesty of the whole international sport process. This was widely reported by the media, so that the integrity of the governing body (FIFA) was questioned.

Another example of media exposure, caused the manager of the England football team, **Sam Allardyce**, to resign in 2016 just two months into his job, apparently by mutual consent after being splashed all over the pages of the Daily Telegraph which linked him with allegations of impropriety.

The Allardyce 'sting' was the first part of what the Telegraph says is a series of stories yielded by a ten-month investigation into corruption in British football. The paper alleged that Allardyce, who was only appointed to coach England in July 2016, had used his position 'to negotiate a £400,000 deal and offered advice to businessmen on how to 'get around' FA rules on player transfers'.

The national governing body of cycling also came under the media spotlight in 2016 when the former GB track sprinter Jess Varnish made allegations about the former technical director Shane Sutton and claimed there was 'a culture of fear' in the organisation.

NGBs need to be aware of the need for new optimism in the sport sector, but a likely consequence is that less of the public purse will go to NGBs. Within this process there is a widespread acceptance that governing bodies must work with the media to maintain their future.

The Golden Triangle

The so-called '**golden triangle**' (figure 7.20) links and provides an overlap between the media, commercialism, and sport and its governing bodies. Without one, the other two cannot survive and increased media attention has led to sports becoming more exciting, which in turn leads to greater commercial sponsorship and greater participation in sport.

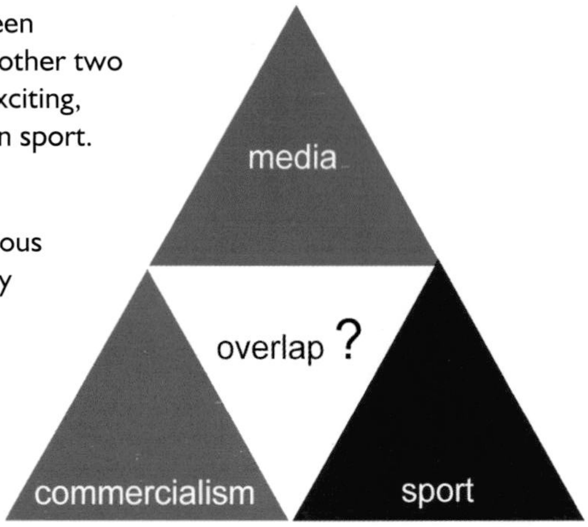

The media and sports communication

Sports communication provides a vital role and sports organisations utilise numerous media to reach individuals, groups or organisations that are affected by the activity of the business (called **stakeholders**).

Sports communication uses portals including television, radio, publications and internet providers. Social media have become popular in the sports industry and **platforms** such as Facebook, Twitter, Google, blogs and live chat rooms are reaching the stakeholders with **speed** and **efficiency**, carrying large amounts of **information** and **capacity for interaction** that connects with the public, building a brand, engaging fans and involving management, and management of reputations.

figure 7.20 – the golden triangle

The media and sports communication

Technology exists to keep everyone happy. Extra **choices** are available via the red button. **Web streaming** and **miniature cameras** positioned on helmets, bikes and inside motor racing cars, provide a different and more intimate perspective for the sport's fan.

Post 2017, the changing media and technology landscape will open up new opportunities, and so continue to further and strengthen the links between the media, commercialism and sport.

Sports stars as global stars

Sports stars became global stars with the growth of **satellite television** and the popularity of sport and sport **commercialism**.

Sports stars come and go, but some become legends and will remain in the public eye for decades. For example, **Muhammad Ali**, (figure 7.21) helped change cultural attitudes, as well as his own sport.

He was certainly sport's first and greatest trash-talker, the first to truly take advantage of television's mass-reach, and in terms of sheer impact, popularity and entertainment value worldwide remained untouched until Michael Jordan.

Some sports are only popular within their **cultural contexts**. For example, the four major **North American** sports, American football, baseball, ice hockey and basketball have relatively minor appeal in the rest of the world, consequently, there are few global stars within the Big Four sports, since the stars produced in these sports are specific within their cultural contexts. At home, these major sport stars have huge fan bases.

Global contemporary sports stars include **Usain Bolt**, **Mo Farah**, **Roger Federer**, **David Beckham**, **Serena Williams** and **Paula Radcliffe** who have sustained their global profiles as a result of the outstanding success and longevity of their sporting careers.

figure 7.21 – Muhammad Ali, the greatest

What is apparent is that sports stars have unprecedented earning power through sponsorship and endorsement (in the most popular sports). **Roger Federer** is the most marketable star in world sport, with Real Madrid superstar **Cristiano Ronaldo** only ranked eighth, according to the 2016 rankings.

The fierce competition between global clothing brands drives income for the richest ranked globally-known athletes. Despite being out of action for six months and just returning back to action for the start of the season in Australia in 2016, Federer amassed almost $50m in off court earnings in that year, with **Andy Murray** in 22nd and **Gareth Bale** in 29th position.

Male sportspeople still dominate the global sports scene, perhaps because they offer advantages to marketeers who want to tap into the traditionally hard to reach male consumer market.

Serena Williams and **Maria Sharapova** are 17th and 18th place respectively.

Global sports stars are athletes of influence and **role models** for others. The term role model is defined '**as a person whose behaviour, example, or success is or can be emulated by others, especially younger people**'. Role models may have considerable impact on a person's values.

Sports stars as global stars

It has become a truism that professional athletes, whether they like it or not, are **role models** for others. Talented sportspeople hardly win every time, and sometimes they do not exemplify fair play. But many sportspeople convey **attributes** about **performance**, **character** and **resilience** that draw admiration from fans.

Youthful **aspiring athletes** will emulate tries, wickets, goals, behavioural traits and sports fashion on the street or in their local parks. No surprise that sports stars are assumed to provide a '**role model effect**' for sport at community levels, whether by stimulating entry into organised activities or by catalysing ongoing participation.

The profile and outreach of sports stars has been enhanced globally by **social media**, such as **twitter**, **snapchat** and **facebook**. The **legacy** of London 2012 connected sport fandom and sport exercise. Team GB's high performance Olympic Champions help to inspire a generation of community-based sport participants.

High-profile global athletes are widely feted as **public figures outside of sport**, as happens with celebrities in other entertainment professions. In sport, though, such recognition is said to come with additional responsibilities, most notably in the assumption that athletes are, or must become, 'role models in the community'. In this respect they cannot expect to have the same level of privacy as someone without a public profile. So there is a trade-off, as happens with notable performers in other spheres of life, such as entertainers or politicians.

The off-field obligations of an international athlete involve significant surveillance and monitoring. For example, they must notify a National Anti-Doping Authority where they are every day of the year, and must be available for drug testing from 6 am to 11 pm. Clubs and leagues certainly have expectations that their global stars will conduct themselves 'appropriately' during their private lives.

The media typically thrives on scandal and sensationalism, so stories about public figures 'gone bad' are much more likely to appear in the press.

figure 7.22 – Tiger Woods and friend

- For example, the Tiger Woods negative press releases relating to his many love affairs during his sex scandal back in 2009 (figure 7.22).

- **Deviant behaviour** may result from the social controls of **competition**, **management** teams, **family** and **friends**.

- For example, the **doping** scandal of Lance Armstrong was widely publicised and presented him as a disgraced sports star.

- Celebrity, fame, criminal behaviour and deviant behaviour bring a loss of self and identity that is socially stigmatised in the media.

- Negative deviant behaviour may enhance the profile of the sports star in gossip columns and contemporary social media/web traffic.

Being a sport superstar doesn't automatically qualify a person to be a role model. Ultimately, when a small minority of athletes fail to live up to employer, governing bodies or community expectations, the wider sports profession is tarnished as disreputable.

The Americanisation of sport

Americanisation is the influence **American culture** and business has on other countries. Within the sporting context, it represents the **copying** of **American values** in sport (figure 7.23).

The persuasion of Americanisation of sports is so powerful that American culture is adopted in every respect of games, such as clothing, media technology, marketing and promotion strategies. Such issues are taken and implemented by other nations to draw attention to their local sports.

So why do other countries want to adopt American sports and their associated cultures?

figure 7.23 – Americanisation of sport

commercial sport
pathways to professional sport
Lombardian ethic
wealth performance management
AMERICANISATION OF SPORT
sports stars
role models
mass participation
the American dream
sports entertainment

Commercial sport

The development of **technologies** that underpin American sports are eminent features of the American **commercial sports world**. Other nations have adopted these techniques to enhance their sports industry.

USA sport has exerted a massive influence on **television** and the **media**. **Specialised channels**, such as the Entertainment and Sports Programming Network (ESPN), reap the benefit of sports programmes, selling advertising slots and greatly influencing television programming. A major example is the scheduling of an **Olympic timetable** to suit US prime viewing hours.

The adoption of commercial sports channels has spread globally. For example Sky Sports is a group of sports television channels operated by the **satellite** pay-TV company Sky plc. Sky Sports is the dominant subscription television sports brand in the United Kingdom and Ireland. It has played a major role in the increased commercialisation of British sport since 1991.

Professional sports like **baseball**, **basketball**, **football** (American football) and ice hockey have become massive industries and the economic centre of many US cities. Such sports have spread globally as a result of the player and coach migration/transfers, franchises and the influence of the media. For example, according to the **International Federation of American Football** (IFAF), there are 80 countries with organized federations governing the game, from China to Germany to South Africa. Overall, IFAF's best estimate is that there are thousands of leagues and hundreds of thousands of boys, girls, men and women playing at levels ranging from high school to soccer-like club leagues powered by player dues and local sponsors. Such is the impact of American sport.

USA sport is driven by business and was worth $60.5 billion in 2014. It is expected to reach $73.5 billion by 2019. Teams are bought and sold and in today's global market even the Americans have opened up to a worldwide pool of potential buyers, making sport that much more international.

USA commercial sport uses franchising to widen sport provision and spectatorship, and this is discussed on page 122. Pay-per-view (page 162) is another trend developed in the USA. Both ideas have been transmitted into the global market.

The **Golden Triangle** (page 124) is a concept developed in the USA, and you can see that its issues have evolved across the globe.

Lombardian ethic

The Lombardian ethic, **win-at-all costs**, supports the notion that **winning is everything** and is taken for granted by the American public. This is in contrast to the European and Olympic ideal that **taking part** is most significant and **fair play** an **essential** component.

American's **obsession with winning** leads athletes to do whatever is necessary to achieve victory. For some athletes this means training to the point of injury and irreparable damage. For others, the obsession leads to taking **performance-enhancing drugs** (PEDs), now a common world-wide phenomena. The damage athletes inflict upon themselves through **chronic drug abuse** is just one of many forms of violence that is evident in American sport.

American sport, such as football, ice hockey and boxing, are brutal and enormously popular.

Football's **unique violence** is not an unfortunate by product, it is what has made football into America's most **popular** and most **celebrated** sport.

Such is the pressure on winning, American professional coaches have highly paid but very insecure jobs, known as the '**hire and fire**' policy. This policy is now common with European soccer managers who are retained only as long as their teams are winning regularly.

The win-at-all costs ethic provides outright winners (**no draws**) and is against the participation ethic. The Super-Bowl league structure acts as a showpiece and a massive commercial venture, and has been used as a model by many global sports organisations, for example the European Heineken Cup for rugby union.

The **win-at-all-costs ethic** has been adopted by the UK's NGBs who allocate lottery funding to potential and existing sports men and women whom they consider to have the best chance at medalling at global sports events.

Pathways to professional sport

Sports are also a big **part of growing up** in the USA since these sports and others are prominent in youth leagues, high schools and colleges. The high prestige of **inter-scholastic sport** holds a major place in the American psyche. The win-at-all-costs ethic is paramount. This in itself attracts large groups of spectators and **sponsorship money**, which in turn pays for high quality **coaches**, sports **scholarships** and **facilities**.

The pathways to professional sport is via the '**pro-draft** system' which is the apex of the **American sporting pyramid** as set out in figure 7.24.

This is a system where **sports scholarships** are available for the most talented. Although the **pro-draft** system is highly unique to American sport, the notion that elite sports persons are able to be financially supported and to be able to extend their study time over a number of years and be offered a 'soft option' course, has to some degree been adopted in the UK.

For many years **American Universities** have attracted young talented overseas individuals to study, train and compete for them. Today this model has been accepted globally. For example, the 2017 Oxford Blues women's boat crew consisted of four British, three American, one Canadian and one New Zealander. The men's Oxford boat crew consisted of six British, two American, and one Dutch. Today, most prestigious universities offer **sports scholarships** that reflect the influence of American University culture.

figure 7.24 – the sporting pyramid in the USA

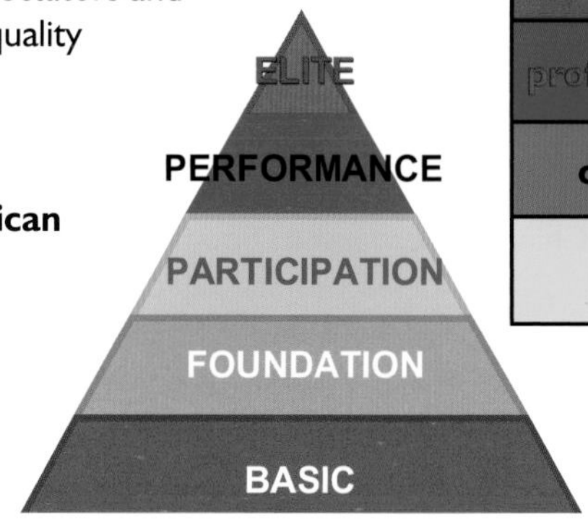

numbers of males participating in the **big four** sports 1994

	numbers	%
professional	3,155	0.164
college	90,629	4.7
high school	1,919,080	100

ELITE / PERFORMANCE / PARTICIPATION / FOUNDATION / BASIC

the big four sports are - football, basketball, baseball, ice hockey.

Sports stars, role models and wealth

Professional athletes have benefited enormously from lucrative **endorsement contracts** that transform them into international media icons. This trend started in the USA. Tiger Woods is an American professional golfer who has net worth of $740 million and an annual salary of $50-60 million. David Beckham's net worth is $350 million.

Roger Federer is the oldest player to have remained in the ATP World Tour top ten ranking over a period of two decades. Much of Federer's ongoing success as the world's highest-paid athlete endorser can be linked to several long-term deals he holds with premiere brands including Nike, Mercedes, and Rolex.

American sports have **high salaries** for coaches, administrators as well as the **performers**. This makes many performers multi-millionaires by the age of 30 (by which time their quality of performance, and hence salary, begin to decline).

Performance management

Performance management has been at the heart of USA sport which is underpinned by a sense of **vision** and **strategy**. It has taken time for other countries to catch up with this process. Performance management has had a significant impact in countries such as Britain who have gained an international **competitive advantage** in sports such as **cycling** and **rowing**. For example, under the stewardship of Performance Director Dave Brailsford, British Cycling (the national governing body) has been transformed into a world beater.

America sports entertainment

USA sport is **entertaining**, **sensational** and **intense** which arguably raises its status in popularity. This Includes entertainment off the pitch, for example, **cheerleaders** and **mascots** (figure 7.25), which are perceived as family entertainment, juxtaposed against skill and creativity as being more important than intensity.

figure 7.25 – cheerleaders and mascots as entertainment

The global presentation of cheerleading was led by the 1997 broadcast of ESPN's International cheerleading competition, and the worldwide release of the 2000 film 'Bring It On'. Due in part to this exposure, there are now an estimated 100,000 cheerleader participants scattered around the globe in Australia, Canada, China, Colombia, Finland, France, Germany, Japan, the Netherlands, New Zealand, and the United Kingdom. Can you explain why **females** accept this **role in sport**?

A **mascot** represents a **symbol** that brings luck. In the world of sports, costumed mascots were first used in the USA in leagues such as the NFL. Today mascots are seen at all major global sporting events as **family entertainment figure**s that add **excitement** for their spectators. Mascots are also used for **merchandising**. What makes a mascot great is as much about the audience as it is about the **franchise** it symbolises.

The American Dream

The American Dream is an ideal by which equality of **opportunity** is available to any American, allowing the **highest aspirations** and **goals** to be achieved.

Individualism is a core aspect of the American Dream and it has become a central tenet of the global sports culture shaped and promoted by the **golden triangle**. Contemporary sports stars typically embody values we associate with the achievement of the American Dream – that is, **effort**, **ambition**, **toughness**, **strength** and of course **winning**. This is not surprising, since the values of the American Dream are closely associated with the emphasis on individual **self-interest** and **materialism** that surfaced during the growth of entrepreneurial, industrial and **consumer capitalism** in the USA.

Mass participation

The **radical ethic** (an alternative life-route to the Lombardian ethic in American sport) makes the **excellence of the outcome** important, but more dominant in this ethic is the **way** it is achieved. This ethic is associated with **lifetime sport**, **health**, **fitness**, and **mass participation**.

The first city marathon was staged in Boston in 1897 following the inaugural Olympic marathon. John Graham, the manager for the USA's first Olympic marathon squad, was inspired to establish the Boston Marathon, with assistance from businessman Herbert Holton.

In 1975, Boston became the first major marathon to include a wheelchair division and female participants. In 1986, prize money was awarded to Boston Marathon winners for the first time.

The **Boston Marathon** provided a **template** for other cities to use, and today it is considered to be one of the world's most **prestigious** road races.

The idea of sports mass participation and its associated health benefits and fund raising capacity, is now a global commercial business that attracts professional and amateur runners from around the world to marathon events on all five continents. Certainly the last sixty years have shown the culture in American sport all its forms to be an extremely exportable commodity.

figure 7.26 – mass participation in practice

The concept of competitive sports fixtures and events played in other continents

Major American leagues have been working to establish themselves world wide to build global competitive sports fixtures and events.

When using terms such as globalisation and international strategy, there are many different factors which play a role in this process, such as location, television access, websites, social media, merchandise sales and player appearances.

NFL

It does appear that the NFL (figure 7.27) is strategically positioned to be the first league which includes a team located on a different continent. If this happens it could make the NFL a leader in the globalisation of professional sport.

The NFL has wrestled with introducing their league structure on both sides of the Atlantic since the 1980s. This started by the NFL staging the preseason American Bowls in a dozen cities around the world.

Since 2007, the NFL's **international** plans have centred on London, but recently the league has also been reaching its tentacles into Germany, Mexico and Brazil, with the idea of playing regular season games or the Pro Bowl at international sites outside the UK, too.

figure 7.27 – NFL logo

NFL

The NFL sees a **business opportunity** that raises the ceiling for the league's growth beyond what can happen in the USA. If **brands** of American football (figure 7.28) are developing in other parts of the world, the NFL wants its brand to be the main one.

For example, the NFL has worked aggressively to establish itself in London to help them grow their game internationally and develop a **fan base** to support a London-based **franchise** of the future. The NFL's latest business strategy has been a profitable one and has involved working with **Tottenham Hotspur** (10-year partnership deal) to play at least two NFL games per year at the English Premier League club's new stadium in North London, due to open in 2018.

The project involves building a retractable grass pitch over an alternative artificial playing surface. This venture represents the first of its kind in producing a stadium to cater for both British and American football. Germany could be next, but the league still has major hurdles to clear in its quest to become a truly a global brand.

Can it be done?
* The major concern is that the league is largely disconnected from the grass-roots efforts that might grow the game from the bottom up.
* **Specialised equipment**, such as protective pads and helmets represents a **financial challenge** at grass roots level, in addition to the associated risk of brain trauma associated with this violent game.
* There is an **international organizing body** for the sport (IFAF) but the infrastructure is not strong.
* In Europe, politics between different countries' own football organisations have interfered with unified growth.

* The **branding** of a super league needs **merchandising** and **TV deals** and the right **media availability** in place.
* NFL TV coverage in Germany, outside of the last few Super Bowls, has traditionally been restricted to a pay channel. This **media** coverage needs to be **expanded**.

* That's why the NFL is trying to build toward a permanent outpost overseas, thinking bigger than just a series of games to provide successful marketing opportunities.
* The NFL's immense wealth and current foothold in London certainly indicate increased international growth.

figure 7.28 – modern rules

NBA

The American-based NBA (figure 7.29) is another professional sports league that is keenly aware of its opportunities that accompany growing their brand internationally.

It has a rich history of playing games overseas with the regular occurrence of **exhibition games** against European teams since 1984. NBA regular season games outside of North America began in 1990 in Japan and have spread to China and Europe.

Like the NFL, London has played a significant role in the NBA's **globalisation** campaign, hosting the first international exhibition game between two NBA teams in 1993 and the first regular season contests in 2011. In 2016 it grouped all its overseas initiatives under the banner NBA Global Games.

Basketball is already a **global sport** and is very successful in Lithuania, Spain, Argentina and China in addition to being recognised as an Olympic sport.

In 2016, there were more than 100 foreign leagues from 37 different countries playing in the NBA, providing a strong foothold for **franchising expansion**.

figure 7.29 – NBA logo

Tour de France

The Tour de France (figure 7.30) is the global showpiece of the **Union Cycliste Internationale** (UCI - the governing body of world cycling).

The UCI categorises teams into three divisions.

The top 18 teams are the **UCI World Teams** and compete in the **UCI World Tour**.
The second and third divisions respectively are the Professional Continental teams and the Continental teams. These scheduled events take place throughout the world.

figure 7.30 – le Tour de France logo

A UCI World Tour event (an ongoing annual competition that includes thirty-eight road cycling events) awards points to create the UCI World Ranking, which means that the teams that compete in the Tour de France are mostly UCI World Teams, with the exception of the teams that the organizers invite.

The Tour de France is third largest sporting event in the world, and can boast of its longevity by being over 100 years old. Despite its huge commercial and global successes, it has only assumed the status of a global event in recent years.

Traditionally, the race is held primarily in the **month of July**. This an annual 3 week **multiple stage** bicycle race that is primarily held in France while also occasionally making passes through nearby countries. For example, in 2017 the race start was in Dusseldorf.

While the route changes each year, the format of the race stays the same with the appearance of time trials, the passage through the mountain chains of the Pyrenees and the Alps, and the finish on the **Champs-Élysées in Paris**.

The Tour is important for fans in Europe. Millions line the route, and crowds flank the course creating a festival atmosphere.

Doping
- Allegations of doping have plagued the Tour since around1903.
- Early riders consumed alcohol and used ether to dull the pain.
- On 13th July 1967, British cyclist Tom Simpson died climbing Mont Ventoux after taking amphetamine.
- In 2005, doping controversy surrounded Lance Armstrong, a month after Armstrong's seventh consecutive victory.
- Today the **World Anti-Doping Agency** (WADA) is responsible for the regular testing of riders for PEDs, such as blood doping transfusions and EPO use.

Race organisation
Parisian race organisers, the media, corporate sponsors, provincial host-towns and the race's professional stars have shaped the Tour de France as an **entertainment spectacle** from its inception.

figure 7.31 – Chris Froome four times winner

Over decades the race has evolved into a globally televised spectacle that has generated publicity throughout the world. Unlike the NFL and NBA, the Tour has stayed localised with the emphasis on Tour-related commerce, sponsorships and global sports stars. Tour organisers sold TV coverage to American television networks and used **sponsorship** funds from **American companies** like Coca-Cola and Nike to expand the race's budget.

Chris Froome (figure 7.31) achieved his fourth win in 2017, through the phenomenal strength of his team, but crowned with individual moments of drama and determination, demonstrating a **will-to-win** that runs as deep as Team Sky's resources. These strategies have kept the Tour de France grounded to a very successful **French cultural** phenomenon.

The future of commercial sport

- Sports are **expensive** to run and so **sponsorship** deals and additional publicity, via the media, benefit both performers and spectators, a win-win situation.
- **Entertainment** and consumption will be the major **organising principles** for the future.
- Financial **profits** and economic **expansion** will be the goals of most sports and corporations.
- The emphasis on entertainment will fuel the success of **professional sports** in forms of 'sportainment'.
- **Corporate conglomerates** will buy teams and link them to their media, entertainment, and Internet divisions.
- **Sport equipment manufacturers** will continue to sell the idea that involvement in sports requires highly specialised and **expensive** equipment and clothing.
- **Wealthy people** will use sports as contexts for announcing their status and identities through **appearance**, sport **ownership** and **visual display**.

But despite all such predictions it is to be believed that leisure pleasure sport will be an integral part of the **lifestyle** of masses of people to improve human **wellbeing** and **quality of life** as a form of everyday **healthy** activity compensating the demanding goals and objectives of our lives.

Commercialism, media and sport in today's world

Commercialisation creates employment opportunities in media, coaching, sport and event management, as well as stimulating businesses related to sport and benefitting the economy overall.

The following tables (table 7.1 and 7.2) set out the positive and negative impact on different aspects of sport (the performer, the coach, an official and the audience), of commercialisation, sponsorship and the media.

Table 7.1 - **positive and negative impact of commercialism, sponsorship and the media on sport**

positive impact on sport	negative impact on sport
the elite performer	
increased income from sponsorship in return for using or wearing the sponsor's goods	sponsorship and the media can be over-demanding of a performer requiring interviews at inconvenient times
the media can increase the awareness of the public of the skill, excellence and peronality of the performer (a role model)	increased pressure on a performer to obtain or change lucrative contracts for playing
improved facilities for training, coaching, TID and competition available through increased funding for a sport	the media tend to sensationalise lifestyle and non-sporting life choices by a performer instead of sporting excellence
increased participation level due to exposure of major event, people want to have a go at a new sport (eg rugby after England's World Cup victory in 2003)	there are inequalities of coverage (minority sports don't get much exposure), thereby performer cannot attract sponsorship
media led developments lead to more variations to sport (eg twenty20 cricket - summer season for Rugby League) leading to greater opportunities for income to the performer and financial gain to the sport	exposure of deviance (fighting, diving to cheat, arguing with officials) lowering role model status caused by 'win at all costs' attitude in media
increase of profile of performer and the sport	elite performers are often treated as commodities
unprecedented earning power for male athletes in most popular sports and for females in a more limited number of sports	psychological pressure on high profile athletes through excessive media attention
performers can concentrate on training without financial worries	performers are under pressure to perform when injured
positive role models encourage mass participation	

positive impact on sport	negative impact on sport
the coach	
can award contracts to performers which in professional sport gives him or her control over everything to do with playing strategy	sponsorship and the media pressure can be over-demanding of a coach
sponsorship can include coaches and enable travel to support performers at coaching camps and major events	an imbalance of salaries paid to coaches/managers of top professional clubs, such as soccer, and professional coaches/managers employed in amateur sports
an official	
media led developments lead to more variations to sport (eg twenty20 cricket - summer season for Rugby League)	NGBs lose control of a game, rule structure, timing of games and breaks are adapted to suit TV or sponsors
major help with decisions, the fourth official can review incidents (including scoring) on repeat TV	media can control location of events and kick-off times, technology (HawkEye, 4th official) not always available at lower level of competition
increased profile for full time professional officials, eg the tennis gold badge umpires	may have to call time out for advertising, for example NBA basketball
technology takes the pressure off officials when decisions are close	officials may become too dependent on technology
the audience	
increased investment improves quality of facilities, acquiring top players and entertainment eg cheer leaders to attract bigger audiences	excessive advertising could interrupt the viewing experience
certain sports (soccer, rugby, cricket, golf and tennis) are ring fenced into terrestial or free to view TV for primary events, therefore maintaining large audience for high status events (test matches, Wimbledon, cup finals etc.	pay to view TV can make some sports events expensive to watch
sports channels available (at a cost) for specific events	low attendance at events which are fully covered on TV
media led developments lead to more variations to sport (eg twenty20 cricket - summer season for Rugby League) leading to greater opportunities for fans and more exciting games	there are inequalities of coverage (minority sports don't get much exposure), thereby sports fans for that sport cannot see their favourite sport
technology, such as video screens and HawkEye for replays and match statistics, increase excitement, awareness and knowledge of the sport	more breaks in play can disrupt audience experience
commercial products are readily available for the spectator	player kit merchandise is regularly changed and disfavoured by some supporters due to expense
if the performers are able to work better with sponsorship, entertainment levels should rise	event schedules are planned to maximise USA viewing figures and so may not be timely for the UK arm chair spectator or athletes
	tickets to major sporting events are expensive

Table 7.2 – **positive and negative aspects of media coverage of sport**

positive aspects of media coverage	negative aspects of media coverage
players or teams gain revenue from sponsors	sponsorship companies usually only focus on high profile players or teams
sponsorship can provide teams with improved facilities and/ or equipment	sponsors can control event timings to suit peak-viewing times
teams or players gain publicity and promotion	players or teams can be restricted as to what products they can use
sponsorship can elevate new sports into the limelight via media publicity	sports can be overrun with sponsors – thus losing the nature of the game
more money for grass-roots teams	NGBs forced to alter rules to make games more exciting - in order to generate sponsorship interest
	more exciting events given priority over other sport
raises profile of the sport	leads to a squeeze on amateur sport
	media will not support minority sports, or low profile sports such as badminton with less identifiable role models

Practice questions

1) Identify three factors that have influenced the commercialisation of sport within the UK. 3 marks

2) Discuss the advantages and disadvantages of commercialisation in sport. 8 marks

3) a) Give a definition of sponsorship. Support your answer with an example. 2 marks

   b) Identify three factors that would influence a sponsor's decision to invest in a sport. 3 marks

4) a) What conditions are required for commercial sport to develop? 4 marks

   b) Suggest two reasons why commercial sports have become global commodities. 2 marks

5) Explain the differences between sponsorship and endorsement. 4 marks

6) How are advertising and merchandising linked together within sport's marketing? 3 marks

7) Write an argument for and against the suggestion that the commercialisation of sport has been beneficial for the performer and for the sport. 4 marks

8) a) With reference to association and rugby football explain the term 'broken time payments'. 2 marks

   b) What was the effect of broken time payments on the emergence of professional sportsmen? 2 marks

Practice questions

9) Explain how the modern Olympics between 1972 and 1984 revolutionised the
    commercialisation of sport.   8 marks

10) a) What do you understand by the term franchise?   1 mark

    b) Discuss the similarities and differences in sport franchising between the USA and the UK.   4 marks

11) a) Describe four different ways in which sponsorship operates in sport.   4 marks

    b) State three different ways a sports club can obtain funding.   3 marks

12) a) Describe four negative effects of media coverage on sport.   4 marks

    b) Describe four positive effects of media coverage on sport.   4 marks

13) Discuss the changes UK governing bodies have had to make in order to become
    financially viable.   4 marks

14) Describe three ways that sport benefits TV.   3 marks

15) Discuss the relationship between sport, sponsorship and the media.   15 marks

16) Many elite sports are now commercialised and seen as forms of entertainment.
    Discuss the suggestion that an increase in the commercialisation of sport has been
    beneficial for performers and the sport.   8 marks

17) Outline how global sport has changed over the past 20 years due to 'Americanisation'.   8 marks

18) Major leagues have been working to establish themselves globally.
    Using an example from sport, discuss how this development is affecting
    the growth of professional sport.   6 marks

Answers link: http://www.jroscoe.co.uk/downloads/a2_revise_pe_edexcel/EdexcelA2_ch7_answers.pdf

CHAPTER 8: *Ethics and deviance in sport*

Ethics in sport

Ethics are rules, often unwritten, that dictate an individual's **conduct**.

Amateurism

The term amateur comes from a French derivation of the Latin word '**amator**', defined as 'lover of'. In practice, it means a person engages in an activity for **pleasure** and feelings of **worthiness** rather than for financial benefit or professional reasons.

In 19th century Britain, rational sport was initially an exclusive development by the male upper and middle class and is normally described as the Gentleman Amateur period. Gentlemen members of the middle and upper classes were usually products of the English public school system that promoted an active policy of **athleticism** (goodness, manliness, restraint and discipline) perceived as character building qualities needed by the sporting gentleman amateur.

STUDENT NOTE

There is a section on Amateurism in 19th century Britain in AS/A1 Revise PE for Edexcel ISBN 9781901424881, page 176

Amateur sports are sports in which participants engage largely or entirely without **remuneration**. The whole subject of remuneration was controversial in 19th century Britain, when sports such as cricket paid leading amateurs **more in expenses**, than any lower class paid professionals (figure 8.1).

figure 8.1 – cricket by 1851

The elite amateur **Oxbridge sportsmen** initially took their games to members of their own social group, forming games clubs and sports associations and eventually National and International Governing Bodies. These clubs and sports associations were amateur and excluded the lower classes who only had popular festivals and professional opportunities to participate in sport.

Amateur games and sport became **codified** and **regulated**, **regular**, **respectable** and **rational**, and were refined to meet the supposed high moral standards that were accepted as the amateur code of conduct. For example, the FA was formed by these gentlemen and the early soccer sides (such as Sheffield Wednesday) were all gentlemen.

The FA Cup was won by old student clubs or urban gentlemen's clubs. Similarly, the early Athletic Clubs admitted middle class gentlemen who established and developed amateur athletics and gymnastics associations.

From the end of the 19th century and up to the 1990s in some sports (for example tennis, rugby union and athletics), amateur and professional sports developed **separately**. The **middle classes** were **administrators**, **agents** and **promoters**, the **working classes** were **participants**, and the **upper classes** were **sponsors** or **patrons**.

Examples of the **attitude of administrators** to performers included:
- The definition of amateurism in athletics, which excluded the possibility of earning any money through sport until the 1980s.
- The exclusion of rugby league (and therefore potentially professional) players from any part in rugby union until the 1990s.

Sporting amateurism was a zealously guarded ideal in the 19th century, especially among the upper classes, but faced steady erosion throughout the 20th century with the continuing growth of professional sport, the role of the media, monetary gain and commercialism. It is now strictly held as an ideal by fewer and fewer national governing bodies, even though some of them maintain the word amateur in their titles.

Amateurism

By the early 21st century the Olympic Games and all the major team sports had accepted **professional** competitors even though the Olympic Games still retains the ideals of amateurism in its Olympic **creed**, **charter** and **oath**.

However, there are still some sports which maintain a distinction between amateur and professional status with separate competitive leagues. The most prominent of these are golf and boxing. In particular, only amateur boxers (figure 8.2, Nicola Adams, double Olympic Champion, now turned professional) could compete at the Olympics up to 2016.

figure 8.2 - Nicola Adams, Olympic champion

The Olympic Oath

Written by Baron **Pierre de Coubertin**, founder of the modern Olympic Games, the oath is a solemn promise made by one athlete from the host nation at the Opening Ceremony of each Olympic Games.

'**In the name of all the competitors, I promise that we shall take part in these Olympic Games, respecting and abiding by the rules which govern them, committing ourselves to a sport without doping and without drugs, in the true spirit of sportsmanship, for the glory of sport and the honour of our teams.**'

figure 8.3 – Usain Bolt, millionaire superstar

The Olympic Oath is an oath of **sportsmanship** and **fair play**. By swearing the oath, competitors vow to respect all the rules that govern the Olympic Games and abide by them in the true spirit of sportsmanship.

The Olympic Games remain unique as a sporting festival representing the pinnacle of sporting achievement alongside its associated spirit of fair play and sportsmanship. It pitches the true amateur against millionaire superstars, such as Andy Murray and Usain Bolt (figure 8.3).

When athletes try everything from head-butts to kicking, and taking drugs to edge out an opponent, the spirit of the Games is questioned and the darker spirit of the Olympics is revealed. In some instances physical intimidation and violence, as well as time wasting, have become all-too routine features of increasingly intense sports contests.

At Beijing 2008, Chilean tennis player **Fernando Gonzalez** caused outrage when he refused to own up to a shot clipping his racket at a crucial stage in his semi-final with James Blake. Gonzalez claimed the point and went on to win a silver medal.

At the Seoul Olympic Games of 1988, **Ben Johnson** was disqualified and labelled a drug cheat 3 days after winning the 100 metres. Johnson's blood and urine samples contained the steroid stanozolol.

In 2016 over 100 Russian athletes were banned from the Rio Olympics after proof of a **state-run doping** programme. Athletes who use the performance enhancing drugs (PEDs), but are never tested and caught, are cheating the system.

Many sports writers and ethics professors have proposed lifting the ban on steroid abuse in the face of constant rule breaking. If there is no way to level the playing field and stop PED abuse, they reason, why not allow it and regulate it for safety?

Such **win-at-all-costs** sentiments are against the Olympic oath and stretch the rules to their absolute limit.

Sportsmanship

The idea of **sportsmanship** (figure 8.4) is not just what you play, but how you play in a sport. If the sporting activity involves competition, then it should always be performed with a spirit of sportsmanship. Sportsmanship involves conforming to the **rules** and the **spirit** and **etiquette** of a sport, and is known as the **contract to compete** concept (based on the Victorian ideas within the spirit of '**fair play**').

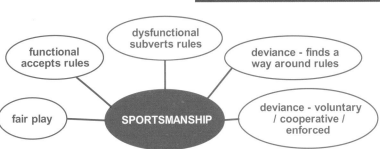

figure 8.4 – sportsmanship

- functional accepts rules
- dysfunctional subverts rules
- deviance - finds a way around rules
- deviance - voluntary / cooperative / enforced
- fair play
- SPORTSMANSHIP

Respect for an opponent is an unwritten code within sports where participants agree to '**do their best**', '**to strive to win**', '**to play within the rules**', and to do this with a degree of sportsmanship. Playing to win is said to be a good thing as long as it is within the '**spirit of the game**'. This implies that a person should allow his or her opponent to do the same, and not be unduly upset if that opponent wins. Respect is to be given to the rules, to opponents, and to officials attempting to administer a contest.

In sport, we have problems of **violence** on the field and the use of **PEDs**. This tells us that the ethic of fair play is under attack. Without fair play, sport as a noble pastime is doomed. It is possible to look at games on the television or during school sport and test the behaviour of performers.
The behaviour will vary from the high point of players making moral decisions to the other extreme of deliberate violence against others. Fair play will exist as long as you at least accept the referee, but it's better if you accept the rules of play.

- Perhaps there can be no true sport without the idea of fair play, where the spirit in which the activity is played is more important than a '**win-at-all-costs**' attitude?
- Sportsmanship is functional if the rules of a game or sport are accepted, or the decisions of a referee or umpire are accepted, and dysfunctional if a performer has no regard for others or deliberately subverts the rules of a game in order to gain advantage.
- Sportsmanship behaviour is still evident today, even within professional sports. For example, admitting fouls and shaking hands at the start of and end of a sporting contest (figure 8.5).

figure 8.5 – sportsmanship reigns

Encouraging sportsmanship behaviour
- Rigorous **drug testing**.
- Use of **technology**.
- **Punish** foul play using fines and sin bins.
- NGBs addressing required **rule changes**.
- **Awards** such as the Fair Play Awards are awarded to individual in recognition of remarkable acts of fair play or outstanding careers conducted in the spirit of fair play.

Gamesmanship

Gamesmanship (figure 8.6) is the term which describes behaviour **outside the rules of a sport** or game which aims to gain advantage over an opponent, and has been defined as: '**the intention to compete to the limit of the rules and beyond if you can get away with it**'.

Some professional performers and coaches maintain that '**you get away with what you can**', an admission that potential rewards, millions in sponsorship and wages, can outweigh moral considerations. Gamesmanship is driven by a '**win-at-all-costs**' attitude and shows no regard for the well-being of the opponent.

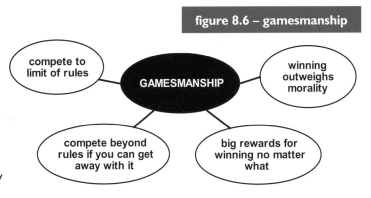

figure 8.6 – gamesmanship

- compete to limit of rules
- winning outweighs morality
- GAMESMANSHIP
- compete beyond rules if you can get away with it
- big rewards for winning no matter what

Gamesmanship

Examples of gamesmanship are:
- A boxer or fighter thumbing the eye of an opponent.
- A soccer player deliberately fouling an opponent with the aim of getting him or her off the pitch.
- A rugby player stamping on an opposing player.
- A cricket team 'sledging' their opponents when batting – extreme verbal banter – destroying confidence and concentration.

Win ethic – win-at-all-costs

- The win ethic is also known as the '**Lombardian**' ethic that is heightened by the needs of **professionalism** and a society that only acknowledges the winners.
- The Lombardian ethic is based on a statement '**winning isn't the most important thing-it's the only thing**', made by **Vince Lombardi** (figure 8.7), a famous American football coach.
- This suggests that **outcomes** over-ride the process of participating.
- The win ethic sits at the heart of sport in the USA .

- Elitism is at the heart of most sporting activity, and is, in effect, a programme of excellence as exemplified by Sport England's World Class Podium programme where medals success at major global sporting events, count towards NGB funding.
- The win ethic rejects the Olympic ideal that taking part is most significant and fair play as an essential component.
- The win ethic almost totally controls the professional sport scene, and remains a central philosophy in most athletic departments in schools.
- The win ethic is reinforced by the media, the hiring and firing of coaches and managers, a no drawn games philosophy and a high level of deviancy.
- Perhaps this win-at-all-cost culture is the reason why more children than ever before are choosing not to participate in youth sports.

figure 8.7 – Vince Lombardi, head coach of the Green Bay Packers 1959

Positive and negative forms of deviance and the performer

Deviance

The term deviance describes behaviour in which people find a way around the rules, however they are framed and can be institutional, group specific, or individual.

Deviant behaviour could be one of three possibilities:
- **Voluntary**, the performer decides to take drugs.
- **Cooperative**, the performer decides to take drugs, because all his friends are.
- **Enforced**, an East German swimmer took drugs provided by her coach.

Deviance in sport concerns the **intention to cheat** as part of deviant behaviour, and includes **aggression** and **violence** among competitors and spectators, as well as the issue of **doping**.

In **sociological terms**, deviance means the variation of behaviour from the norm (what is normal). This can be upwards (positive) or downwards (negative) deviance. Positive deviance is when someone will over-conform to norms with no intention to harm or break the rules.

Negative deviance

Negative deviance involves behaviour that fails to meet accepted norms and has a detrimental effect on individuals and on society in general.

Examples of negative deviance include using PEDs, cheating within a contest, using bribes to influence the outcome of a match, fan violence or hooliganism, illegal betting on the outcome of a contest, financial irregularities in the transferring of players and player violence (figure 8.8).

figure 8.8 – player violence

Positive deviance

Examples of positive deviance include training through injury, adopting a 'no pain, no gain' attitude which implies an 'over' commitment to sport. For example, it used to be a common occurrence within rugby union, to continue 'playing through' an injury in the interests of the team as a whole. This behaviour has largely disappeared with the advent of substitutions, but used to be the major reason for the ending of a promising career in the sport.

Causes of deviant behaviour

- NGBs may **feel less able** to punish players due to their commercial interests.
- Fear of the offending player taking them to **court**.
- Deviant behaviour may have become more **socially acceptable**.
- Individuals lack **moral restraint** to maintain an acceptable code of conduct.
- The **fact of winning** may have more value than the loss of respect or punishment that may occur.
- **Rewards** are great and so individuals may be prepared to take **risks**, particularly true of positive deviance.

Violence within sport

Player violence

This issue arises when **acceptable aggression** (assertion) in sport becomes **violence**.

Violence is normally where aggression goes beyond the agreed codification in that game or activity. There is an additional dimension, in that **acceptable aggression** in the activity may not match up with the **laws of the land** and so players can misunderstand their legal position.

Figure 8.9 summarises the issues affecting player violence.

Physical aggression and an unacceptable level of verbal abuse may be identified as part of player violence:

figure 8.9 – aggression and violence in sport

- The presence of **spectators** can **increase player arousal**.
- Many games require players to be **hyped-up to p**erform at their best, making aggression and outbreaks of violence more likely.
- More recently, the use of **drugs** may have increased this tendency.

- On the other hand, some sports require **calmness** and **focus**.
- For example, darts, snooker, dance and gymnastics, and players in these sports are less likely to be violent.
- **Gamesmanship**, aimed at putting an opponent off, can be equally unacceptable.

Aggression by sports performers is a part of their sporting life. The need to be **competitive** and the **frustration** felt at failure can lead sportspeople to be violent as an extreme expression of this aggression. The level at which aggression becomes violence varies according to the activity.

For example, **boxing** involves punching an opponent, which would be violence in any other sport. In this case, it is argued that the essence of boxing is 'the art of self-defence' and that boxing has its own code of acceptable behaviour with a referee to see that this is observed, as well as the safety precaution of gloves. There is also a difference here between amateur and professional boxing, and between junior and senior competitors.

This rules difference also is relevant to a variety of other activities and games, such as tag rugby with young children.

Causes of player violence in sport

The **causes of violence** among players are summarised in figure 8.10.

- The **crowd** response to player activity (chanting, booing, name calling) can affect player tendency to violence.
- The **confrontational nature** of most top professional games (the gladiatorial influence) can increase the tendency to violence.
- The popular nature of some sports can lead to **player expectation of violence** as part of the game **culture**.
- The presence of a **large number of spectators** and the significance of victory can increase the emotion of a sporting occasion, and again make violence more likely.
- The **failure** of sports administrators to adequately **punish** players who are persistently violent can cause players to cynically commit further violent offences on the field.

figure 8.10 – causes of player violence in sport

(CAUSES of VIOLENCE in SPORT: crowd, administration, players, facilities, popular, emotionally charged, gladiatorial)

Strategies for preventing violence between players

The solutions lie in the **code of behaviour** being part of the **tradition** of the activity from school onwards and the quality of **control by officials** during a game, and the efficiency of the administration of sanctions by NGBs on offending players.

Officials

- Officials should include an **explanation** of their action (figure 8.11).
- The use of the **television match official** (TMO - fourth official) during the match, advising the on-field referee, on close calls and post match video evidence, such as the Rugby League '**on report system**' that can be used by referees to review controversial play.
- The use of deterrents, such as **sin bins**.

Managers and captains

- Establish a clear **code of conduct** and expectation.
- Understand individual player's level of arousal and train players to **manage their own arousal** levels.
- Where possible ensure that **players**, who have a low flash point, are kept away from **high stress** situations.
- **Avoid** an attitude of **winning-at-all-costs**.
- Discuss **stress appropriate behaviour** during team talks.

figure 8.11 – is it worth arguing with the referee?

NGBs

- **Punishments** by controlling bodies should be seen to be **fair** and **consistent**, and should therefore fit the offence.
- Recognise players with a good disciplinary record as **role models**.
- The use of **educational campaigns** and awards, such as the Fair Play Awards that reward clubs with good disciplinary records.
- Train officials in **player management**, such as how to defuse situations between players.
- NGBs like to deal with violence themselves, but increasingly are getting more involved with the **legal system** (page 154).

But the most essential element is the **attitude** of each player.

Spectator violence

Spectators get very **emotionally involved**, desperately wanting their side to win.

A crucial feature of football followers is their **identity** with the team they follow. They refer to members of their team as 'us' and 'we', and members of the opposition as 'them and 'they'. This leads to the **emotional attachment** which can often be directed at opposition players on the pitch, and also at opposition supporters.

This can lead to **violence in the stadia** and on the streets, but can also involve **extreme verbal abuse**. In such instances the law is probably being broken, but access by the stewards and the police is not possible because of the crowd effect. The facilities of a stadium, in respect of the **mixing of the fans** of opposing teams, can be a cause of spectator violence particularly in **professional soccer**.

Hooliganism

The dominance of a youth culture, where gangs identify with a professional football club and are prepared to fight an opposition group in a chosen place, is a frightening extension of soccer hooliganism. Hooliganism is **anti-social** or **aggressive**, **violent** and **destructive** behaviour by troublemakers, typically in a gang.

Acts of hooliganism (figure 8.12) often overspill and impact local surroundings such as shops and bars, as witnessed between Russian and English football supporters in the 2016 European Championships in France. Although there is a strong working class peer group culture associated with soccer, this has, occasionally, involved middle class male groups. The media can encourage confrontational situations by highlighting players' comments about opponents and giving these hooligan gangs publicity.

But spectators certainly need to recognise that no matter how much they get worked up, their violence is measured in legal terms.

Causes of spectator violence in sport

There are numerous causes in what is naturally an antagonistic and often frustrating situation. For example, the tendency towards violence by a supporter group is linked to whether or not their team is winning. Supporters of a winning team are more likely to be benevolent and good natured, whereas supporters of a losing team can be violent, particularly in 'derby games'.

Spectator violence has been explained as a form of **social deviance** and it is caused by:
* Being in a crowd, where there is **confinement** and poor crowd control.
* **High emotion, diminished responsibility** and the likelihood of **shared aggression**.
* Consumption of **alcohol** exacerbates these problems.
* There is also an element of **depersonalisation** that a crowd gives an individual, where it is 'easy to be lost in a crowd'.
* **Poor officiating**.

In the case of hooliganism, the question arises as to whether these are **hooligans at football** or **football hooligans**.

In the case of the former, the solution lies in the **conditions and control** needed to prevent this anti-social behaviour. If, however, football makes them behave as hooligans, then one must look at the **behaviour of the players** and the causes of frustration.

Strategies for preventing spectator violence

Measures (figure 8.13) which have been taken to reduce the chances of spectator violence are:

- **Segregation** of home and away supporters.
- The introduction of **all-seater stadia** (outcome of the Taylor Report (page 157)
- Increase the '**family**' concept.
- Increase the number of **stewards** and police.
- Ensure that **alcohol** cannot be bought or brought into grounds.
- More responsible **media** reporting.
- Detect trouble by using **CCTV**.
- In addition, campaigns like '**kick racism out of football**', sponsored by major soccer clubs, player and Governing Bodies, can defuse unacceptable racial aggression.
- **Legal intervention** that punishes offenders.

figure 8.13 – preventing spectator violence

The impact of commercialism on the sportsmanship ethic and the growth of gamesmanship in the UK

The commercialism of sport is subject to the **market forces** of commerce. The rise of **professionalism** in sport has led to a rise in **commercialisation**.

- Increased availability of **professional** contracts, sponsorship, player endorsements and prize money has allowed UK athletes to train and compete as full-time professional athletes.
- **Lucrative commercial deals** put great **pressure** on athletes to do well.
- Without the **moral values** as guides, some athletes may decide the financial benefits from **winning** significantly overshadow the likelihood of being **caught** and so winning becomes an obligation and gamesmanship becomes part of the winning strategy.
- The commercial **rewards** for winning become so **significant** that a '**win-at-all-costs**' mentality has **eroded** away the concept of **sportsmanship** and increased the growth of **gamesmanship** within UK sport.
- Today, the **win ethic** almost totally controls the professional sport scene within the UK.
- Here, there is clear link to the impact of **Americanisation** of sport (page 127).
- Within **gamesmanship**, the need to win is associated with financial rewards.
- Increased level of **commercial finance** in sport will increase the need to win.
- Winning can secure a **position in the team** and its status.
- For example, a team winning a world cup creates global **superstars** and associated **wealth, fame, national pride, sponsorship** and player **endorsements**.
- An outcome of the need to win is that athletes will find different ways to help them to win and gamesmanship is seen as a **more palatable way** of **bending the rules**, without infringement of the rules.
- Some commercial sponsors may prefer to be associated with the more traditional clean image of sport. For example Andy Murray provides an impeccable image of sportsmanship for his sponsor Under Armour.

Performance enhancing drugs (PEDs)

A performance-enhancing drug (PED) is any substance taken by athletes to **improve performance**.
Doping refers to **the use of banned athletic PEDs by athletic competitors**.

Sportsmen have used PEDs, such as anabolic steroids, since the 1950s and up until the 1980s there were comparatively balanced discussions in the media about the value certain drugs might have for athletes.

Performance enhancing drugs (PEDs)

The **German Democratic Republic** (GDR known as East Germany) conducted a decades-long programme of coercive administration and distribution of PEDs, such as testosterone and other anabolic steroids to its elite athletes for the purpose of bolstering the communist state's image and prestige by winning medals in international championships (such as was the case in the 1972 Munich Games). This national programme was known as the **State Plan 14.25**.

It was not until the 1980s that **physicians** admitted that PEDs could improve performance. Most of the major scandals did not come until the 1980s. In 1988 Ben Johnson won the 100 metres at the Seoul Olympic Games, and was stripped of his medal for taking steroids. This high profile case tarnished the image of track and field athletics forever.

In the past 20 years, drug taking has become a very common part of top class sport.

A recent high profile case has involved more than 1,000 Russian athletes (competing in summer and winter Olympic, and Paralympic Sports and other global events across over 30 sports) who were involved in the manipulation of concealed positive doping tests and benefitted from a state-sponsored doping regime dating back to 2011.

The Russian Olympic team corrupted the London Olympic Games on an unprecedented scale and was involved in the ongoing use of prohibited substances, wash out testing and false reporting, supervised by the Russian Anti-Doping Agency (RUSADA).

The reasons people take drugs

The reason sportspeople take drugs (**performance enhancing drugs** or PEDs) or other nutritional ergogenic aids, is to attempt to gain an advantage over other competitors or players.

Some drugs are **against the law** and others against sporting regulations, but young people can be attracted to these unethical and dangerous substances because their heroes and role models are presumed to have taken them.

- Thus taking drugs ceases to be only a personal decision.
- This is part of the win ethic, the willingness to win at all costs, or simply a desire to excel in something as an unbridled ambition.
- The International Olympic Committee and International Sports Authorities view drug taking as **cheating**, and it is deemed totally unacceptable for the unscrupulous to be allowed to take unfair advantage. Let's not forget the Olympic oath sworn on behalf of all participant States.

Sociological, psychological and physiological, informed analyses of drugs abuse in sport requires an understanding the reasons why deviant drug abuse is prevalent on a global scale.

Elite athletes are full-time professionals and every part of their training and competitive life is geared up to enhancing his or her performance so that he or she can win. Yet some of these enhancements are banned.

Figure 8.14, page 146, provides an overview of the reasons why sportspeople should not take these substances, along with the reasons that people take these drugs.

Social reasons to aid performance

A major social reason for drug taking is the belief that **everyone else is doing it**. This belief makes drug taking acceptable and reinforces the **win-at-all-costs** attitude that success cannot be achieved without drugs and that the benefits of winning are greater that the risk of being found out.

Whilst the need for the athlete to win and their potential use of drugs is a personal affair, it has become a public issue because the use of PEDs has been banned. The importance of national pride, (as was the case with the GDR national programme State Plan 14.25) and the overriding need to win, impact on the decision of the individual athlete in relation to the use of PEDs.

figure 8.14 – performance enhancing drugs

The commercialisation of sport means that **profit** becomes the overriding **motivation**, **eclipsing** ideals of **fair play** and **sportsmanship**. Victory has become the ultimate goal of sporting clubs, coaches, and athletes and the **rewards** of winning are considerable.

Athletes must try and win and so are highly motivated, otherwise they will not get **government** support, sponsorships and endorsement contracts. **Tangible rewards** override moral values. If PEDs can offer that competitive edge (as observed in table 8.2, page 152) it is not surprising that contemporary athletes will use them at the expense of their known health risks.

Contemporary opinion **undermines** the ideals of **fair play** and **health** when it comes to sporting endeavours as today's sport is neither fair nor healthy.

Modern sociologists believe that commercialisation and commodification of sport has fundamentally changed sport. The pressures on young potential athletes with such a short playing career can only encourage the use of anything that might give them an advantage and lengthen their career. With the UK Pathway programmes, such as **Long-Term Athlete Development programmes** (LTAD, page 176) it is hoped that such schemes can overcome these social pressures.

Athletes are vulnerable and socially influenced by:
* **Media coverage**: in their attempt to sell newspapers the media tend to give extensive coverage to **doping scandals** within sport.
* This may give the athlete a misleading impression of the extent to which PEDs are used in sport.

* **Peer pressure**: athletes may directly observe or hear of the practices of fellow athletes who use PEDs and may be offered drugs by their fellow competitors or team members.
* There is a perceived suspicion that rivals are using something (PEDs?) that assists them in meeting the physical demands of intense training and competition.

* **Support team pressure**: family members and coaches may instil additional pressure on athletes to improve performance by any means available.
* It has been suggested that governing bodies 'turn a blind eye' to some drug takers in order to benefit from the commercial benefits that result from success.

* **Deterrence**: there are few deterrents that discourage an athlete from taking illegal drugs as drugs are readily available in gyms, over the counter and on the internet.

Athletes are vulnerable and socially influenced by:

- **Fame, salaries and sponsorship deals** which also tempt athletes to **cheat**. But when found out, professional sports careers can be shattered as was the case for Maria Sharapova (figure 8.15) after failing a drug's test in 2016 followed by a two year ban. In 2017, Maria was able to resume her professional career.
- Nike and Tag Heuer cut ties with Maria Sharapova. Up until that point Maria was the world's highest paid female athlete.

Psychological reasons why people take drugs to aid performance

- **Beta blockers** help to decrease anxiety and steady the nerves.
- **Anabolic steroids** increase arousal and aggressive tendencies, traits that are needed in sports such as weightlifting and contact team sports, such as rugby.
- **Stimulants**, such as amphetamines, increase mental alertness, concentration, motivation and confidence.
- **Perception of pain** is dulled, thus enabling an athlete to work harder and longer.
- There is the fear of '**not making it**'.
- **Motivation**: athletes are driven to succeed as a result of **internal** and **external** motivation.

- **External rewards** are central to competitive sports and are immense, where athletes receive publicity, awards, money and sponsorships for their sporting achievements.
- **Taking illegal drugs** is one way to achieve this success.

figure 8.15 – Maria Sharapova, ups and downs

Positive and negative implications of drug taking to the sport and the performer

Athletes don't take drugs to level the playing field, they do it to get an **advantage**. A vicious cycle of upping dosages to get a **bigger advantage** happens.

- The pay-off is now **fame, image and money** and the long term health consequences are minimised (figure 8.16).

- PEDs can cause **impotence, worsening acne, balding, 'steroid rage'**.

- **Females** acquire masculine traits such as a **deep voice, facial hair** and **breast reduction**. PEDs can also **stunt growth** in adolescents.

- More serious side effects include heart and **liver damage**, and an increased risk of blood clots.

- The risk of being caught is reducing. As undetectable drugs become more available, more athletes will choose to cheat.

figure 8.16 – regular injections to short-term success

Over the years there have been allegations of **doping in the Tour de France**. Lance Armstrong won seven Tour de France titles, because **blood doping** is the difference between being really, really good and being world class. When Armstrong finally admitted to blood doping, he actually said that he had to cheat just to be competitive at the top of the sport.

Other high profile drug cheats include the infamous sprinters Ben Johnson, Marion Jones and Dwayne Chambers.

Positive and negative implications

Athletes are allowed to use powerful drugs that deal with **health conditions**, such as asthma, providing they have a **therapeutic use exemption** (TUE) certificate. Recently Sir Bradley Wiggins (figure 8.17) has come under sustained fire from the media for using a prescribed drug called **corticosteroid** to deal with his chronic asthma and allergies. He says that he does not obtain an unfair advantage over his rivals. However, this drug can rapidly reduce an athlete's weight whilst maintaining power.

figure 8.17 – Sir Bradley Wiggins

The dilemma here is that, on the one hand inclusive sports participation shold be encouraged, but on the other hand this can facilitate drug abuse via the backdoor which is an unintended and undesirable consequence. As a result, WADA is considering a blanket ban on corticosteroids

Drug cheats can often tarnish a **sports image** and call into question the **validity of results** in competition. **Public respect** for all sports professionals suffers if there are frequent drug scandals. It becomes **harder to believe** that all athletes aren't cheats. That may cause all victories to be viewed with suspicion. This is hardly fair on the honest athletes, and it's no fun for the spectators either.

Uncovered drug cheats risk losing their **reputation**, professional **earnings**, long-term **career prospects**, as well as negatively impacting on their **social and psychological well-being**.

The essence of sport exemplifies values such as fair play, honesty, health and excellence in sport. The challenge is for role models, parents and coaches to influence these positive values.

Illegal ergogenic aids

Figure 8.18 summarises the categories of illegal ergogenic aids used by sportspeople,

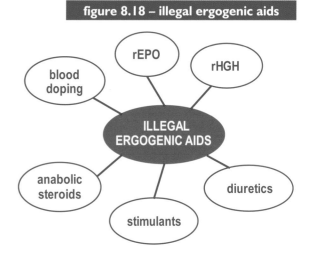

figure 8.18 – illegal ergogenic aids

Whilst the need for the athlete to **win** and their potential use of drugs is a personal affair, it has become a public issue because the use of PEDs has been **banned**.

The importance of **national pride**, (as was the case with the GDR national programme State Plan 14.25) and the overriding need to win, impact on the decision of the individual athlete in relation to the use of PEDs.

Doping control agencies, such as **WADA** (page 150) claim that the health of the athlete is a key reason why the use of drugs in sport is banned, with the health being a significant criterium used to determine if a substance or method should be banned.

As genetic therapy techniques develop, the opportunity to cheat begins to look limitless.

Future developments in PEDs may include:
* **New 'undetectable'** drugs.
* New ways to **administer** existing drugs without being detected.
* **Skin patches**, for example, can deliver a steady dosage of the drug, which is harder to detect.
* **Genetic therapy**, injecting genes directly into muscles, lungs or other target areas.

The nature of genetic therapy treatments means they will probably be almost impossible to detect. This is one of the points used in arguments for the legalisation of drugs.

Table 8.1– the categories of illegal substances used in top level sport today

type of substance	known ergogenic effects	known health risks
stimulants example: amphetamines	increase alertness, reduce fatigue, increase competitiveness and hostility	can drive competitor beyond safe boundaries can cause lasting tissue and organ damage as well as masking injury are addictive, known to cause death

rHGH
recombinant human growth
hormone cloned through
genetic engineering
	mimics body's naturally occurring hormone
	    HGH produced by the pituitary gland
	    which increases protein synthesis and lean
	    muscle mass
	stimulates bone growth
	increases blood glucose levels
	enhances healing after musculo-skeletal
	    injuries
	used by power athletes such as sprinters,
	    weight lifters, American football players
		muscle joint weaknesses
		acromegaly (giantism) causes bone thickening
		    of hands, feet and jaws
		enlargement of internal organs
		causes glucose intolerance, diabetes,
		    hypertension and heart disease

anabolic steroids
related to naturally occurring
hormone testosterone
example: THG
tetrahydrogestrinone
stanazolol
	increases synthesis of protein within cells
	increases fat free mass, strength and power
	    for aggressive sports such as American
	    football or wrestling
	reduces recovery time between sessions
	increases muscle strength and bulk,
	    promotes aggressiveness
		excessive aggressive behaviour outside the
		    activity
		testicular atrophy in men
		masculinisation in women
		liver damage
		cardiovascular diseases
		causes acne
		causes pituitary failure

blood doping
refers to **any means** by which
a person's total volume of red
blood cells can be increased
often achieved by transfusion
of red blood cells previously
withdrawn from the recipient
 	
rEPO
recombinant erythropoietin
cloned through genetic
engineering **is a form of
blood doping**
	temporarily increases red blood cell count
	    (polycythemia) and hence O_2 carriers,
	    thereby increasing $\dot{V}O_{2max}$ and energy
	    delivery to enhance aerobic performance
	
	mimics body's naturally occurring hormone
	    EPO that stimulates red blood cell
	    production to increase oxygen transport
	    and therefore increases aerobic capacity,
	    hence aids recovery in endurance based
	    activities such as long distance cycling
	    (Tour-de-France) and marathon running
		problem of mismatching can lead to
		    transfusion reaction or allergic reaction
		also runs the risk of hepatitis or HIV pathogen
		
		major risk of thrombosis (blood clot) and
		    heart failure due to increase in blood
		    viscosity
		reduces resting heart rate to dangerously low
		    level during sleep
		
		taking rEPO reduces production of naturally
		    occurring hormone EPO

diuretics
example: bumetanide
	reduce weight quickly (this is a legal use)
	used by gymnast and combat sports where
	    there are bodyweight categories
	reduce concentration of substances by
	    diluting urine (hence increasing urine
	    flow), also used as a masking agent to
	    dilute concentration of illegal substances
	    in urine
		loss of water leads to dehydration and heat
		    loss impairment
		loss of water-soluble vitamins leads to
		    impaired performances

Pain killers

Note that pain killers are legal and may be able to improve training performance because
they can reduce recovery time after a hard session, but they do have negative effects on
body tissues, maybe irreversible effects.

Strategies for elimination of performance-enhancing drugs in sport, WADA

The impact of illegal drug abuse in sport has led to the development of random drug testing programmes under the supervision of WADA (the **World Anti-Doping Agency**), set up in 1998 and tasked with enforcing (figure 8.19) the international regulations on doping or drug taking.

WADA aims to bring together governments, the IOC, international governing bodies and national governing bodies to sort out difficulties by athletes performing on the international stage. WADA is tasked to get all international governing bodies and national governing bodies to adopt and implement its **World Anti-Doping Code**.

Under WADA's World Anti-Doping Code, athletes are required to state 3 months in advance their locations for one hour per day, 7 days a week. This is the time during which random testing could take place. This is called the '**whereabouts rule**' - a system designed to support out-of-competition testing and regarded as a fundamental part of an anti-doping programme.

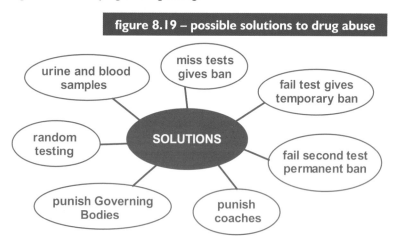

figure 8.19 – possible solutions to drug abuse

- urine and blood samples
- miss tests gives ban
- fail test gives temporary ban
- random testing
- SOLUTIONS
- fail second test permanent ban
- punish Governing Bodies
- punish coaches

This rule has evoked anger from tennis players including Andy Murray, Rafael Nadal and Roger Federer, who feel that the European Union privacy law has been breached.

Random drug testing, (particularly out of season) ensures that athletes are discouraged from cheating the system. This includes missing these random tests under the whereabouts rule. Christine Ohuruogu (Olympic and World 400m track champion) missed three random tests and in 2006 received an automatic one year ban. This was in spite of her passing many other tests during the period when this was happening.

The major problem for WADA is to **police** the globe when some national governing bodies do not do out of season random testing.

In 2016, WADA initiated a major **retesting programme** on global sport. The anti-doping laboratory in Lausanne holds stored urine and blood samples (up to 10 years) that can be retested with improved technology to catch drug cheats who escaped detection at the time. 31 unidentified athletes in six sports have been caught during retests from the 2008 Beijing Olympic Games.

UK Anti-Doping Organisation

UK Anti-Doping (UKAD) is the UK's National Anti-Doping Organisation and is an active participant in the global fight against doping and recognises the need to take an international approach with partners such as WADA.

It is responsible for ensuring sports bodies in the UK comply with the National Anti-Doping Policy. UKAD coordinates the UK's intelligence-led risk based testing programme across more than 40 sports and is responsible for the collection and transportation of samples to a WADA accredited laboratory (figure 8.20).

figure 8.20 – accredited laboratory

In season, testing normally takes place after competitions or matches.

UKAD aims to instil a culture of clean sport by ensuring that all athletes and athlete support personnel understand and practise the **values of clean sport** and the **dangers** of physical, psychological and moral issues associated with illegal drug usage.

Initiatives, such as **100% Me**, educate athletes throughout their careers by providing anti-doping advice and guidance that embrace key values such as hard work, determination, passion, respect and integrity, associated with clean, fair competition.

Drug testing and its pitfalls

figure 8.21 – Diane Modahl

Great care has to be taken when testing takes place. Britain's **Diane Modahl** (figure 8.21) failed a test in 1994 just prior to the Commonwealth Games of that year. It was later discovered that her urine sample had undergone changes while being stored in the testing laboratory and she was cleared of the doping offence. She then sued the British Athletic Federation for their mishandling of the situation. This led to the eventual bankruptcy of BAF and the destruction of Diane's athletic career. Although she was reinstated, she was unable to regain the fitness and excellence needed to compete at elite level.

In the news (in 2017) is the FBIs investigation into Mo Farah's coach, Alberto Salazar, who is alleged to have abused medicines and used prohibited infusions to boost the testosterone levels of his athletes. Mo Farah (double double Olympic Champion) denies breaking anti-doping rules.

There are several **benefits** that come out of law-enforcement involvement:
- It can force people to talk.
- If people don't talk, this can give the impression that they are not a good people.
- It can dig deep into personal information, for example, uncovering illicit bank accounts.

In 2014 Rhys Williams and Gareth Warburton (Welsh International athletes) were sponsored, promoted and took an energy drink that unknowingly contained anabolic steroid metabolites. Both athletes served one year bans and then later were cleared by UKAD.

What are the consequences of drug use?

Currently each case of drug use is considered individually. There are rules and regulations that guide the punishments for drug use, but as in the legal system, each case gets a different consequence depending on the circumstances. Often the consequences include **suspension** or **expulsion** from the sport, **fines** and **stripping** of awards and titles won and **repayment** of earnings.

Limitations of drug testing

The use of drug testing in sport does have limitations in its use, which some people use to debate its place in sport. These include:
- Not all drugs can be tested for. **New drugs** are created all the time, and until they are created, tests cannot be developed for them.
- During testing, the athlete is **exposed** (nudity) before the tester - athletes have to be **observed** where urine samples are taken.
- This stringent procedure was enforced after two male winners in the Athens Olympic Games were found using prosthetic **(false) genitals** and a hidden storage bag for production of their samples.
- **New prohibited lists** are developed each year, which athletes need to know and follow as they are currently held responsible.
- Testing is **expensive**.

Arguments for and against drug taking and testing

The positive and negative implications to the sport and the performer regarding drug taking have been discussed throughout this chapter. Table 8.2 (page 152) summarises the arguments for and against drug taking and drug testing.

Anti-doping rules often lead to complicated and costly administrative and medical follow-ups to ascertain whether drugs taken by athletes are legitimate therapeutic agents or substances which violate the definitive WADA rules and are not allowed.

In the meantime, clean athletes, who are upgraded to podium medal status as result of cheats who have been stripped of their titles, could wait many years before this process is completed.

Table 8.2 - **summary of arguments for and against drug testing and drug taking**

For drug testing and eliminating drug taking	Against drug testing, and allowing drug taking
athletes are role models and young people seek to emulate sports stars	strict more expensive tests have been introduced that may not be affordable for third world countries to use
testing protects athletes reputations and produces positive role models	a strict test returns more false positives (a test result that seems to detect a drug which isn't there)
drugs are not natural	the labelling of some supplements may not be complete or accurate, and some safe supplements may contain traces of prohibited substances athletes can protest that these secondary chemicals may be the products of another bodily process
creates a deterrent for athletes who may consider using drugs to cheat in sport	drug testing does not always catch athletes, and is often having to develop new testing methods for the new drugs being released retesting of stored samples is a very expensive process
anti-doping programmes seek to preserve what is intrinsically valuable about sport (values such as fair play and equity) often referred to as 'the spirit of sport' and the essence of Olympism	the whereabouts rule is time consuming and is perceived as an infringement of human rights
drug taking is illegal, a form of cheating, is unethical and immoral	public respect for all sports professionals suffers if there are frequent drug scandals it becomes harder to believe that all athletes aren't cheats and may cause all victories to be viewed with suspicion
discredits negative role models and reinforces the message to stay clean	false accusations can have an adverse effect on an athlete's career - even if she or he is later proven innocent the loss of earnings is usually significant
promotes health and safety and avoidance of the physical side-effects associated with taking PEDs	drug taking is a short-cut to realising potential, even if athletes risk their health and their athletic careers
the detection methods are accurate and reliable	a stricter test returns more false positives (a test result that seems to detect a drug which isn't there)
TUE certificates protect athletes who suffer from general illnesses/allergies and injury rehabilitation	regulated scientific research in producing safer PEDs, could reduce health risks and recovery it is hard to identify those athletes who are awarded TUE certificates who inadvertently physically benefit from such prescriptions
rewards athletes for their ability, training and efforts, and preserves what is intrinsically valuable about sport	elite athletes gain unfair advantage from training methods such as altitude training and the use of hypobaric chambers, so why not include PEDs?
alternative legal methods can enhance athletic performance, such as altitude training and nutritional supplements, for example, creatine	testing is made more difficult because some drugs are broken down quickly inside the body to produce secondary substrates
public perception could be that PEDs reduce the role of skill and replaces it by chemically induced brute strength and endurance, and as a result may lose interest in the sports in which it is used the harm would be primarily financial	false positives, if leaked to the media, are bad publicity it is sometimes hard to prove one way or another could lead to the demise of professional leagues
drugs are bad for business and commercial organisations do not donate their money out of the goodness of their hearts they do it to attract further business	if everyone took PEDs, spectator entertainment and standards in performance would increase and with it a level playing field and more income

Bribery, bungs, match fixing and betting syndicates

Bribery

Bribery is the act of taking or receiving something with the intention of **influencing** the recipient in some way favourable to the party providing the bribe. Recently there has been alleged corruption, bribery and vote-rigging relevant to the election of FIFA ex-president Sepp Blatter and the organisation's decision to award the 2018 and 2022 World Cups to Russia and Qatar. These allegations have lead to a legal prosecution in the USA and the increased popular cynicism about the fairness and honesty of the whole international process.

Bungs

A **bung** is an unauthorised and **undisclosed payment** to a club manager, or any other decision maker within a club, for example to a scout or club official to 'grease' a deal. In other words, a **secret financial incentive** that makes a transfer happen.

The most common method would be an agent paying a club official, perhaps a manager, a 'backhander', or slice of his own cut, to persuade someone to do a deal. In some cases an agent might work in cahoots with a selling club. For example, a club wants to sell a player and values him at £1m. An agent hawks him around and sells him for £2m. The difference is then split between the agent and whoever he has 'bunged' at the buying club to make it happen.

Match fixing

In organized sports, **match fixing** occurs as a match is played to a completely or partially **pre-determined result**, violating the rules of the game and often the law.

For example, in December 2013, six people in Britain, including Blackburn forward DJ Campbell, were arrested for allegedly fixing football games. The arrests were made by the National Crime Agency after release of a report from FederBet, a Brussels-based gambling watchdog an organization created by the online bookmakers to watch the flow of bets across Europe.

Sports Betting syndicates

figure 8.22 – gambling in sport is big business

Sports betting is the activity of **predicting sports results** and placing a **wager** on the outcome. A sports betting syndicate is a group of bettors that pool the various backgrounds in mathematics, professional gambling, and sport, and produce information, that can be used by the syndicate to select the best betting option. The successful sports-betting syndicates employ a powerful computer that crunches an enormous amount of data to determine the betting between one side and the other. This process is called **simulation**.

Simulation

Simulation is used as a betting methodology that relies on repeated **random sampling** to obtain **numerical outputs** when other mathematical approaches would prove to be too complicated. It takes some programming skills to set it up (though it can be done in a common programme like Excel) but it's a proven way to see what happens when you repeat a set of circumstances over and over again.

The more likely outcomes will occur most frequently, giving you a distribution of probabilities. Knowledge of how frequent the likely and less likely outcomes are to occur is really useful for model bettors. An example of a simulation service is the **Monte Carlo simulation** package.

There are commercially-based corporations whose aim is to make money by encouraging betting habits.

Deviance in the media

Deviance in the media is more prevalent than a generation ago, but this is more than likely due to the **coverage given** to the topic rather than the actual rate of deviant acts committed. The way the media portrays a sporting incident in terms of character assassination can have life-long implications.

For example, the media coverage of Tiger Woods and his alleged mistresses (page 126) became headline news in 2009 and almost destroyed his golfing career.

Sport and the law, responsibilty of IGBs, NGBs and governments

Whilst it would be nice to believe that individuals who participate in sport always adhere to the rules, there are many who try to **gain personal advantage** from the sports they play.

Thus, in recent years, **sporting laws** have become more and more common. Elite sport has become more **commercialised** and more exposed in the **media** so any **inappropriate behaviour** is more likely to attract the attention of law enforcing agencies.

Sport is seen by the law as a special area whereby the law and legal systems does not directly interfere with the specific rules in relation to that particular sport. The **International Governing Body** (IGB) of a particular sport will be the regulator which develops the **laws of the game** of that sport. These will then be expected to be regulated in the various countries by the individual **National Governing Bodies** (NGBs) who regulate the various clubs which play in that particular country.

NGBs are responsible for creating the **rules and regulations** that govern their sport. These are based on a set of principles, policies, and conducts that provide **safety** in equipment and facilities and that support the moral values of **fair play** and **sportsmanship**.

Breaking rules can result in trouble, for example Mike Tyson was famous for his 'ear-biting' behaviour and so was disqualified in the bout against Evander Holyfield in 1997. Whatever Tyson had accomplished prior to this match, he will forever be known for this deviant behaviour.

Behaviour that departs from accepted standards is unwelcome and sports' governing bodies to their best to curb it.

Technology

Modern technologies, such as **instant playback**, assist referees in making the right decisions, such as detecting foul play and confirming the doubt of a successful goal. In rugby this is known as the third (or technical) match official (TMO).

This type of technology helps to **improve player safety** and **reduce frustration** and anger amongst spectators on close umpiring decisions.

Body cameras, worn by the police body, collect a higher quality of evidence that can be used in public prosecutions, in addition to acting as deterrents. **CCTV** cameras also act as **deterrents** as well as recording player and spectator behaviour both inside and outside sports grounds.

Smartphones and **ipads** can be used to record an event.
Modern sports equipment, such as pads and helmets, can offer some protection against on the pitch violence.
Multi-media communications systems, called **Superhighways,** can be used to build up databases quickly and are being used to aid police investigations. This technology can be shared and distributed and so can assist in identifying, for example, soccer hooligans both here and abroad.

Sport legislation and the performer, officials, coaches and spectators

Figure 8.23 outlines the areas in which the law may impact on sport.

figure 8.23 – sport and the law

eliminate discrimination · control violence · player rights · player contracts · SPORT AND THE LAW · spectators · fair competition · players vs officials · coaches

Player's contracts: the **contract to compete** is an unwritten code governing how to strive to play fairly, within the rules. It determines how a player should behave during a game, covering fair play, sportsmanship, respect for rules and officials and trying their best. Acceptance of this contract involves an expectation of how the opposition will play.
Over time, a negative impact has invaded sport involving **gamesmanship**, **win-at-all-costs** attitude and **drug usage**.

Fair competition can be related to teams/player's actions surrounding a game, and it is important that teams start on a level playing field. If this does not occur, the responsible team should be made accountable for their actions.

Professional **player's contracts** are concerned with ever-increasing wages in professional sports.
* Players hire agents to represent them in negotiations of multimillion pound player contracts, trades and promotional deals.
* It is important that players have **legal documents** which ensure wages and sponsorship deals are correctly paid.
* Equally, clubs require such documents in order to ensure players meet the demands laid out within their contracts.
* EU law has played a leading role in the governance of football since the landmark **Bosman ruling** (1995) a decision concerning freedom of movement for workers which banned restrictions on foreign EU players within national leagues.

Players' rights are related to players' contracts. It is now legal for players to leave a professional soccer club for no transfer fee once a player's contract has expired, thereby ensuring employment protection. Players outside the EU need a work permit.

Controlling violence is relevant to actions made both off and on the field of play. For example, players injuring other players with deliberate intent, hooliganism and crowd control. Most violent actions on the field of play are dealt with by the NGB officials who impose penalties such as **red carding**, **yellow carding**, **sin bin**s and **match bans**. When violence in sports is punished, there is a low likelihood of the same violence being repeated.

Sport legislation

In **contact sports**, such as football or rugby, all participants owe a **duty of care** to one another. In order to show a breach of that duty, conduct must be reckless and fall below the standard required of a reasonably skilful and competent professional player. It must be an act that is **more serious** than an error of judgement.

Thereafter, the injury suffered must be foreseeable. For example, it must be the type of injury that one would expect from a foul or tackle.

Given that, the test for **negligence** in the sporting world is a high threshold to meet, since the injured party must gather as much evidence as possible to support his or her case. In some instances, players may also seek compensation from a negligent referee.

Sport legislation

The worrying result of **fiercer professional competition** in the 21st century, particularly in rugby union and football, is an increase in **on-field violence**, the growth of which can be explained by:
*   Pressures exerted by media scrutiny.
*   Obsession with winning brought about by the greater availability of large prizes.
*   Failure of NGBs to develop an adequate framework of regulation and control.

In 1995, Duncan Ferguson was the first British international football player to be jailed for assaulting a fellow professional on the field of play.

Court of Arbitration for Sport

The **Court of Arbitration for Sport** (CAS) was established to settle disputes related to sport through arbitration. See below some examples of their work.

*   In July 2016 the CAS confirmed that the Russian Olympic Committee (ROC) could not enter track and field athletes for the 2016 Rio Olympic Games, with the exception of those cleared by the IAAF under the new competition rules regarding 'neutral athletes'.

*   Dwain Chambers (GB sprinter, figure 8.24) completed a 2-year ban in 2003 for taking tetrahydrogestrinone (THG). He returned to competition and although qualified for the 2008 Beijing Olympics, the British Olympic Committee (BOA) barred him from selection under its bye-law 25 because of the serious nature of his doping offence. CAS overturned the Olympic ban on the grounds that it was not compliant with the WADA code of conduct, and Dwayne did compete in the Olympics.

CAS is able to fine, suspend or ban athletes from their particular sport and resolves disputes ranging from commercial (sponsorship) contracts to appeals against national or sports organisation disciplinary sanctions.

The **elimination** of **discrimination** concerns an extremely important type of law. It is illegal for any club to disallow an individual to become a member of an institution on the grounds of colour or race. Racism in football grounds has been largely stopped as a result of the policy of '**Let's Kick Racism out of football**'.

Spectators

Spectators must act within the law. **Hooliganism** (prevalent in football) is characterised by **unruly, violent and aggressive behaviour by overzealous supporters**. **Video monitoring** has been installed in most football grounds so that police can monitor crowd movement. All manner of legal means and policing tactics have been tried to control hooliganism, including deterrent sentencing, legislation such as the **Football Offences Act (1991)** and the creation of the **Football Intelligence Unit**.

The UK **Crown Prosecution Service** (CPS) has the right to prosecute players and spectators for violence in football grounds as well as outside as witnessed during the European Football Championships held in France in 2016.

Frequently, incidents result in **recriminations** against local police forces, which are accused of targeting, provoking or otherwise mistreating fans. Very occasionally intervening police actions have a disastrous impact on spectator sport.

Hillsborough

For example, the Hillsborough disaster of 1989 was a human crush at Hillsborough football stadium in Sheffield resulting in 96 deaths among spectators. Bereaved families were paid an average of £3,500 each, whilst 16 traumatised policemen received a total of more than £1.5million.

figure 8.25 – Hillsborough

The legislation arising from the Hillsborough disaster is a major example of how responsibility in sport is now answerable to **international law** and no longer contained within the jurisdiction of a specific club or sport.

The **Taylor Report** found that the main reason for the disaster was the failure of police control and not unruly spectator behaviour that initially was thought to have been the cause of this tragedy and initiated the Hillsborough Justice campaign (figure 8.25).

The Taylor Report had a deep impact on **spectator safety standards** for stadia in the UK. Perimeter and lateral fencing were removed and many top stadiums were converted to be all-seated. Most football clubs refurbished or rebuilt (partly and in some cases completely) their stadiums, while others built new stadiums at different locations, and in doing so improved spectator safety.

Coaches

- **Coaches** need to be aware of their legal responsibilities, especially with respect to the advice they give their athletes and the way they manage and supervise participation in sport.
- Coaches should have appropriate insurance that covers both **public liability** and personal accidents.
- Many governing bodies include **insurance** as part of their affiliation fee.
- Coaches have an **ethical and legal** responsibility to educate and protect their athletes from all forms of **abuse** such as drug, emotional and physical abuse.
- In 2017 revelations of historical **child sexual abuse** in premier football academies hit the media. Former football coach Barry Bennell was charged with eight separate offences of sexual assault against an under-16 year old boy.

Officials

Rule enforcement is usually down to the officials who are responsible for ensuring that players abide by the written rules of a sport or game.

- If players fail to do this, then officials have the duty and power to **punish** players as necessary.
- For example, David Beckham was sent off during the 1998 World Cup Argentina game when he deliberately kicked another player.
- Referee responsibilities are no longer in the sole control of governing bodies of sport, but open to an **interpretation by law**.
- The **referee, linesman and camera recordings** interlock to police the game.
- Officials have a **duty of care** towards their players and can be prosecuted if a player is injured through poor referring.
- For example, the case of Smolden v Whitworth (1991), in which a young rugby player was permanently paralysed when a scrum collapsed during a bad-tempered game. It was later ruled that the referee had not acted with competence, and thus was **liable** for the player's injuries.
- In a lot of cases sports injuries can be serious and may result in the victim experiencing a **loss of earnings** or some other **financial losses** in addition to the **physical pain** caused by the injury.

Officials

- **Match fixing**, **bribery** and **conspiracy to bribe** can be prosecuted if found guilty.
- FIFA, football's world governing body, has been engulfed by claims of widespread corruption since summer 2015.
- FIFA's president Sepp Blatter has always denied any wrongdoing, but in September 2015, he too was made the subject of a Swiss criminal investigation, launched alongside the original US inquiry into these allegations.

Despite the **autonomy of sporting rules**, it is clear that they are not exempt from the **scrutiny of the courts** and must currently comply with European law. If legal challenges are brought, it is likely that the governing bodies will seek to justify their rules by reference to the legitimate aims of competitive sport and the continued development of young athletes.

Practice questions

1) Define the terms Gentleman Amateur and Playing Professional.   2 marks

2) The development of rational recreation was very much the result of Britain becoming an industrialised society.

figure 8.26 – the **AAA championships** 1870

   a) Using figure 8.26, explain the characteristics of an AAA Athletics Meeting.   4 marks

   b) Describe amateurism as it concerned Track and Field Athletics towards the end of the 19th century.   4 marks

3) Sportsmanship and gamesmanship are two opposites. Explain the differences between the two in a game of your choice.   6 marks

4) Discuss the potential links between the growth of professional sport and the growth of gamesmanship in sport.   15 marks

5) Using sporting examples, evaluate whether deviance in sport has increased in the 21st century.   15 marks

6) rEPO is an illegal drug taken by endurance athletes such as marathon runners and long distance cyclists.
   a) What is EPO?   2 marks

   b) How does rEPO benefit an endurance athlete?   3 marks

   c) What health dangers might there be in making use of rEPO to improve endurance performance?   2 marks

7) Discuss why sports people might wish to use banned substances. In your answer identify the hazards of taking such substances.   5 marks

8) Discuss some of the current strategies used to eliminate performance-enhancing drugs in sport.   8 marks

Practice questions

9)   a) Provide four arguments for drug testing and the elimination of drug taking. — 4 marks

b) Provide four arguments against drug testing and allowing of drug taking. — 4 marks

10) Discuss the problem of illegal drug-taking in sport.
Focus your answer on one performance-enhancing drug. — 15 marks

11) In 1998, the head of the IOC (Juan Antonio Samaranch) told a newspaper that
'substances that do not harm to an athlete's health should not be banned and should
not be considered as a case of doping'. Discuss this statement. — 15 marks

12) What social issues can encourage a performer to take drugs? — 4 marks

13) Suggest three ways in which national governing bodies are attempting to
discover, punish and prevent the use of performance enhancing drugs. — 3 marks

14) Explain the difference between sport law and national law and discuss
how it has changed. — 6 marks

15) Explain what is meant by 'a contract to compete'.
Describe ways in which gamesmanship breaks this code. — 7 marks

16) Give reasons for spectator violence at professional association football matches. — 5 marks

17) Hooliganism has affected football over the past 40 years.
a) Define the term 'hooliganism' and discuss the reasons why it might occur. — 4 marks

b) What steps have been taken to reduce the incidents of hooliganism in
Premiership football? — 3 marks

18) Explain using one example, how each of the following people interact
with the law in sport.
a) Performers. — 2 marks

b) Officials. — 2 marks

c) Spectators. — 2 marks

19) Discuss the use of modern technologies in combating deviance in sport. — 6 marks

Answers link: http://www.jroscoe.co.uk/downloads/a2_revise_pe_edexcel/EdexcelA2_ch8_answers.pdf

CHAPTER 9: The impact of technology, and talent identification

The impact of technology on the viewing experience

Within the sporting arena there are many examples of technology that have been developed to improve the game and add excitement for the viewing public.

- **Instant replays** are used to help referees make the right call.
- In international rugby, TV replays are available to the television match official (TMO) who can assist in the outcomes of disputed tackles or tries. The TMO is able to advise the central referee on producing fair results.

- **HawkEye** technology has been used in international cricket and tennis and is also being trialled in soccer as part of the goal line assessment.

- The downside to these technologies is that the media can highlight an official's mistakes that could increase in anxiety levels for the officials as the live viewing audience criticise the umpiring decisions.

- **Timing devices** include timing gate systems (for example, as used in alpine skiing), provide real time feedback as the skiers pass through infra red photocells that record splits that can be instantaneously displayed on large public screens. This technology adds to the speed and drama that makes alpine skiing events so popular.

- **Electronic timing devices** are used in sports such as swimming. Touch pads mounted on the wall of each swimmer's lane register instant split and finishing times.

- **Photo finish devices** are high-definition cameras mounted on poles to provide a reliable photo finish system that can provide a rapid and accurate results service for both the media and spectators, either in printed form or by TV screen.

- **Mini cameras**, called action cameras, are associated with outdoor sports, and are often attached to helmets, handlebars and on the front, inside and rear of racing cars, giving the audience a more intimate view of the action.

- **Electronic scoreboards** (figure 9.1) engage the viewing audience with action, statistics, instant replays and results.

figure 9.1 – electronic scoreboards give immediate statistics and replays

In the late 90s, home entertainment was in the form of VHS, to VCD and then DVD.

Such technologies have been a major driving force in the sports entertainment industry and the changes they bring have never remained the same for long.

Table 9.1 - **positive and negative impacts of technology on the audience**

Positive impacts	Negative impacts
sports are a form of entertainment, and providing new technologies such as HawkEye can increase their engagement and knowledge of the game	breaks in play, whilst replays are being judged, slows down the action and increasies the playing time and may lead to spectator frustration
the armchair audience has access to enhanced experience in the home through the use of more cameras/player cam, as a result of miniaturized video cameras	commercial adverts disrupt playing schedules for the armchair spectator
technologies can help to diffuse audience aggression and frustration, when pressure points do not fall prey to with bad umpiring decisions	commercial advertising of sports clothing may be fashion led, as opposed to what is best
a 'miked up' referee further facilitates the involvement of live and armchair fans to engage in real-time play	high tech equipment is expensive to buy for the average spectator/participant
spectator interest and excitement are enhanced by broadcasting and in-stadium replay screens scoreboards that can very quickly communicate results to an audience	some people decry the use of technology to improve sports performance, but in reality it is inevitable
a wider range of sports are accessible and visible through the development of technology, for example, glass walled squash courts	the research and development of sport apparatus and apparel is an industry in itself which creates opportunity for investment and employment

Today, people are more connected than ever before, thanks to the proliferation of communication and entertainment devices. **Smartphones**, **phablets** (the smartphone/tablet hybrid, figure 9.2) and tablets have become tools to accessing video contents online without being limited by location or time.

Contents once limited by linear TV are now accessed by '**consumers on demand**'. Internet has broken all communication barriers and social media has made it even much easier for the public to view and share sports coverage.

The British media is dominated by national outlets, with local media playing a much smaller role.

The role of the BBC
Traditionally the BBC played a dominant role in televising sport, providing extensive high-quality advertisement-free coverage and free publicity in exchange for being granted broadcast rights for low fees.

Today (2017) the BBC showcases key global sport festivals, such as the Wimbledon fortnight (without commercial breaks) making it one of the UK's most prestigious, entertaining and much watched sporting events.

ITV broadcast a smaller portfolio of events, and **Channel 4** broadcast a few events from the 1980s, mainly horse races and so-called minority sports.

The arrival of pay-per-view
In the early 1990s this arrangement was shaken up by the arrival of '**pay-per-view**' in the form of BSkyB. Their dedicated sports channels have since become the only place for some major sports to be seen.

Starting in 2006 the Irish company Setanta Sports emerged as a challenger to Sky Sports' dominance of the British pay-TV sports market. Setanta's UK channel went into bankruptcy administration and off the air in 2009. Between 2009 and 2013 **Entertainment and Sports Programming Network** (ESPN) made an attempt to challenge Sky Sports before its British operations were bought out by Sky's current main competitor.

figure 9.2 – a phablet is the latest hand held computer and phone

Pay-per-view

Pay-per-view (PPV) is a type of pay television service by which a subscriber of a television service provider can purchase events to view via private telecast. The broadcaster shows the event at the same time to everyone ordering it (as opposed to video-on-demand systems, which allow viewers to see recorded broadcasts at any time).

Events can be **purchased** using an on-screen guide, an automated telephone system, or through a live customer service representative.

PPV has been introduced by BT Sport, a subsidiary of the former national telecommunications monopoly BT. Customers pay £5 per month for full coverage of Champions and Europa League matches when they sign up for this TV bundle. Having paid £897m for the rights to all Champions League and Europa League matches over three years, BT will show all 351 games live on a new channel called BT Sport Europe.

With the rise of the internet, the term **internet pay-per-view** (iPPV) has been used to describe pay-per view services accessed online.

PPV is most commonly used to distribute combat sports events, such as boxing, mixed martial arts and professional wrestling.

There is a clear shift from cable TV to direct streaming that is accelerating many industries worldwide. For example, World Wrestling Entertainment (WWE) has partially cut its cable and satellite TV contracts to embrace internet television, and this presents the WWE fans with a cutting edge, subscription-only streaming video service. The smart shift to the live sports pay-per-view business could bring in millions in revenue.

Growth of pay-per-view
The growth of pay-per-view can only go in one direction, as discerning sports fans follow their teams and thus contribute to what is expected to be an increase in growth over the next few years.

Sports TV

There is also a dedicated UK version of Eurosport, called British Eurosport which runs a similar scheme.

Sky Sports Pass lets you watch all seven Sky Sports channels for 24 hours. Sports organisations (federations, leagues and clubs) are pretty enthusiastic about going direct to the consumer for **self-distribution**.

Live sporting events always attract the biggest attention from fans and so enriching the full viewers experience is the main focus point for PPV major broadcasters.

Today sports TV packages are available to suit all your sporting needs and easily filtered using comparative websites.

Table 9.1 - **the advantages and disadvantages of the development of specific media packages**

advantages	disadvantages
there are plenty of choice and deals available, such as a one off payment (pay-per-view) or monthly subscriptions, for the consumer, so the consumer can shop around	not all potential consumers can afford to pay for specific media packages
live global streaming ensures that the armchair spectator has the opportunity of watching key events, such as world boxing championship bouts	installation of specialist equipment could be expensive to install
the armchair spectator is able to access sporting events that would not normally be programmed for terrestrial TV this is particularly the case for European football and boxing matches	specific media packages, such as pay-per-view, could have an impact on gate numbers as more fans watch from home, and so decrease potential ticket revenues for organisers
Manchester United has its own TV network that has global appeal, for a small subscription, the TV channel enables fans to assess all their matches, this club initiative brings in vast amounts of money for the club	the several options offered by specific media packages can be very confusing as prospective customers sift through the choices available to them to get the best deals
pubs are often a magnet for viewing sporting events and so benefit from the footfall	some sports will get a lot of exposure, whilst others get none
specific media packages can offer targeted sponsorship and commercial advertising, for example Bet365	fibre optic broadband is not available throughout the UK and in the home there could be dead sports
	the timing of a global event could be scheduled as a night match/sporting event

Development of elite performers in sport

Excellence is defined as a '**special ability beyond the norm, to which many aspire but few go onto achieve**'. Excellence suggests a specialism of one activity and in sport is judged by international standards. **Talent** is a **natural ability to be good at something, especially without being taught**.

Talent identification is the **recognition** of talent in an individual.

Identification and development of talented individuals

The early identification and development of talented individuals is considered increasingly important. What is needed to become an elite athlete is a rare combination of **nature** (genetic makeup) and **nurture** (the process of socialisation - observing and watching others).

Elite athletes have **talent** in abundance, **work hard** and have the right **psychological** profile.

Identifying attributes that characterise exceptional performers can help talented individuals to progress from **participation** to **elite** level performance.

Personal factors (figure 9.3)

Motivation
Motivated by high competitive drive (i.e. the will to be the best - **intrinsic** motivation).

Elite athletes possess a deep need to always improve, taking their performance to the next level.

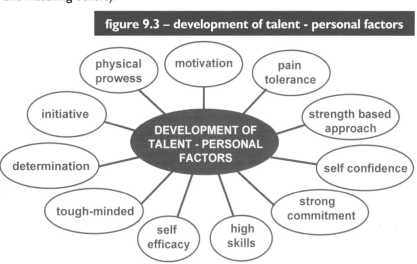

figure 9.3 – development of talent - personal factors

physical prowess · motivation · pain tolerance · initiative · strength based approach · DEVELOPMENT OF TALENT - PERSONAL FACTORS · self confidence · determination · strong commitment · tough-minded · self efficacy · high skills

Initiative

Driven athletes don't wait to be given permission to do something. They are the **leaders** in all they do, setting the standard for excellence.

Determination

All challenges have solutions. Elite athletes are actively looking for the opportunities to help them reach their goal. Failure is not an option.

Tough-Minded

Athletes are expected to do things which stretch them all the time. Tough-minded athletes acknowledge the discomfort, but don't let it stop them.

Taking risks, and pushing through their comfort zone, is part of the champion mindset.

Strength Based Approach

Elite athletes know where they excel and use that to their advantage and are able to find the best approach based upon their strengths and develop the skills necessary to minimize weaknesses.

Strong commitment

This refers to a willingness to give time and energy to something that a person believes in. Instead of viewing obstacles as problems, elite athletes approach them as **challenges** to be overcome. The goal is the primary focus. Even when no one is looking, they continue to push themselves to be the best they can.

Self-efficacy

This is an athlete's self-confidence at his or her specific sport which can affect his or her motivation and ultimate performance, and affects the effort and persistence put into an activity.

Self-confidence

This is a general feeling of trust in one's abilities, qualities, and judgement.

Physical prowess

Physical prowess and natural sporting ability are essential ingredients for elite athletes.

High tolerance to pain

The sportsman should be able to push the body to the limits.

High skill levels

Skills should be consistent.

Social and cultural factors

Figure 9.4 provides a summary of the social and cultural factors that are required to support progressions from talent identification to elite performance.

Family and friends

Primary social groups include parental support and encouragement which is highly related to children's enjoyment, their perceived competence and enthusiasm for physical activity.

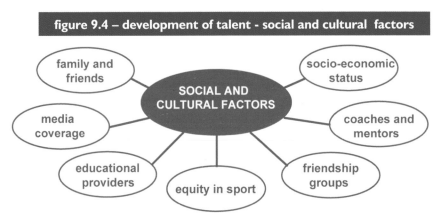

figure 9.4 – development of talent - social and cultural factors

Parents of committed athletes are usually willing and happy to attend their children's training sessions and competitions, in addition to paying for equipment, travel, coaching and medical costs.

Socio-economic status

Socio-economic status (SES) is a critical factor when it comes to opportunities, defined in terms of individual, household and neighbourhood characteristics. All sports are available if you can afford them, but become inaccessible and are not available to those with little money.

Financial support, via **lottery funding** and local grants, is not available until a talented individual has been recognised and so the individual's SES is a key determining factor that influences the progression from talented individual to elite performer.

figure 9.5 – coaches are important

Sports coaches

Coaches assist athletes in developing their full potential, and athlete **mentors** provide **role models** to create aspiration and provide support for young people to achieve their personal best in sport or life.

They give extra motivation and encouragement through their enthusiasm and knowledge for the sport, providing the talented athlete is prepared to accept this guidance and make time to train and compete. Young talented individuals are expected to follow rules and norms dictated by management and coaching staff (figure 9.5).

Friendship groups

The social element of sport is critical to engaging and retaining sports participants. Young talented athletes can be distracted by peers outside of the sporting environment. Team sports foster indentity and friendship, a shared culture of norms and values.

Sport equity

Female athletes have been under-represented in most sport's top flight for most of the twentieth century in most sports and have been prohibited from competing on equal terms with men through sexism and stereotyping (exceptions are in equestrian events). Black and disabled athletes have been largely excluded from many of the key areas of society including sport.

The majority of talented sports individuals are from **middle class** and relatively affluent households, and there are disproportionately few from lower classes and deprived groups and areas.

Sport Equity is about **fairness** in sport, equality of access, recognising inequalities and taking steps to address them. National governing bodies (NGBs) are tasked to address such inequities by increasing participation at all levels. Initiatives such as **This Girl Can** (figure 9.6) and **Street Games** (figure 9.7), could be the starting point where a talented athlete becomes engaged in sport.

figure 9.6 – This Girl Can

Hot and not bothered.

Education providers

Rio Olympics 2016: Where did the Team GB medal winners **go to school**? Overall, just under 70% of the medal-winning athletes were educated at state-maintained schools.

A handful of athletes, including Tom Daley, the diver, were given scholarships to attend independent schools. The interesting statistic here is that **private schools** only educate 7 per cent of pupils and yet are responsible for just over 30% of the medal winning performances.

Grass roots initiatives include creating links between schools and clubs with access to specialist facilities and coaching. This is where a talented individual can progress from **participation** to **performance** level. In addition, school or county sports organisations run trials to select county sports teams, who in turn select their most promising players for regional trials, who in turn recommend players for **national** trials.

figure 9.7 – StreetGames

streetgames.org

Education providers

Structured levels of competitions, such as the **English Schools Track and Field Championships**, provide competition from grass roots participation level to national finals.

Such national competitions have common characteristics of an Olympic Games including opening ceremony with flag bearers, a band and competitors parading around the arena. Talented individuals are often spotted by NGBs at national finals.

figure 9.8 – David Beckham works with youngsters

Structured levels of competitions are reflected within the sporting pyramid model (a process of progression from mass participation to elite level of performance).

Media

The impact of the media is extensive. It gives insight into the effort needed for success at elite level, and a belief in fair play. It can raise the status of a sport and therefore help to promote the sport and inspire young people to participate at all levels.

Role models attract intense media coverage and can inspire future sports stars (figure 9.8).

Development of talent (historic) in East Germany (DDR) and Australia

Over the past few decades, talent identification through to elite performance has been successfully developed in different cultures. Within these cultures, the performance pathways differ, but the progression from foundation, participation, performance, and excellence (the sporting pyramid) is central to their talent development programmes.

Talent development in East Germany

East Germany (DDR or GDR) was one of the first nations to develop a state-run elite sports system.

figure 9.9 – East German sport facility 1969

The total commitment in **East Germany** to produce a world class Olympic team meant that state money was funnelled into their sports development system at the expense of urban re-construction and the general quality of life for the rest of the population. Figure 9.9 shows the sport and congress hall in Scherin, East Germany built in 1969, up to the best standard in the West, and comparable with the UK hub facilities built in 2006.

State-of-the-art facilities included swimming flumes and hypoxic chambers.

Figure 9.10, page 167, shows the elite sports pathway used by the East Germans to develop their talent streams.

Primary school ID programme

Pupils were **screened** by specialist PE teachers, coaches and medical staff that created a potential sporting talent.

Child and youth sport boarding schools

Potential sporting talent would be sent one of the country's 25 child and **youth sports schools**. The athletes were in effect **full-time** sportspeople whose every physical need was met. They were given free accommodation, food, recreational opportunities, education, and of course the best coaching and training in the world.

Annual Spartakiad

The Spartakiad, adopted from the Soviet Union, was modelled as a mini-Olympics, and its purpose was to the drive of the East German sports machine. District competitions were held annually, national competitions every two years and a National Sports Festival every four years. The Spartakiad replicated the pressures experienced at global sports competitions.

State-run sports clubs

All sports schools were linked to state-run sports clubs. They provided the opportunity for sportsmen and women to train full-time without jeopardising their amateur status.

National sports institutes

Elite athletes then moved on to National sports institutes which had state-of-the-art facilities as illustrated in figure 9.9, page 166. Within these institutes, the foundation for the East German National squads developed, and they provided a closed environment for the final preparations in the run-up to major global competitions.

Each institute employed medical teams that could monitor the levels of PEDs fed to all athletes, which meant that they were clean before leaving the DDR for competitions, and could reap the benefits of hard training and doping.

East German National squads

The fulfilling of the TID programme lead to the national squads from which teams were selected to represent the country in international competitions.

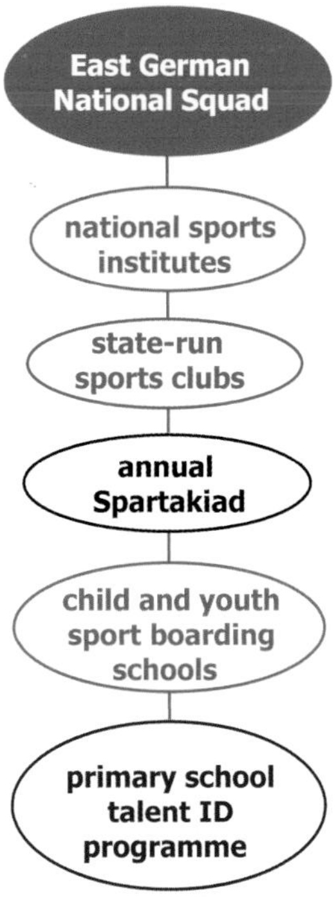

The effect of this process was that East Germany was able to win most of the gold medals in female track and field events at the Munich Olympic Games. East Germany was second to the USSR in the overall medal count in Montreal (1976) and Moscow (1980). Two of the world records set by DDR female athletes in this era still stand (400m and discus throw).

Final preparation for the Olympics was the German College of Physical Culture in Leipzig – home to most of the 'supportive medicine'.

The whole system was **scientifically-based** in terms of training, diet and sports medicine. Those who succeeded were given material benefits way above that of the average citizen.

figure 9.10 – diagram of East German TID system

- East German National Squad
- national sports institutes
- state-run sports clubs
- annual Spartakiad
- child and youth sport boarding schools
- primary school talent ID programme

Talent development in Australia

After winning eight gold, seven silver and two bronze medals at the Munich Olympic Games in 1972, the Montreal Games of 1976 did not produce one Australian winner. This was a stark warning to the Australians, with a great history in competitive sport, that the world had moved on. Unlike many countries, they decided to do something about it. There was clearly a need for better coaching, improved facilities (figure 9.11), pre-games international competition and the freedom, both financial and in terms of providing the time for training, to train as hard as the Europeans.
Here they really meant the East Germans.
The old philosophy 'to do your best' was no longer enough.

figure 9.11 – the AIS at Canberra

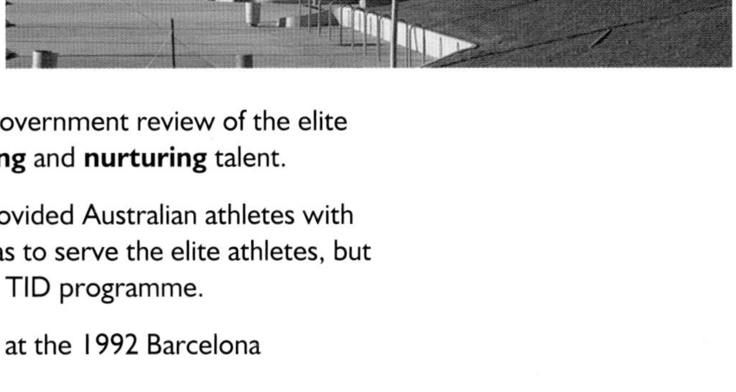

Talent ID in Australia was similar to the East German model. A government review of the elite sports system identified the need for a central focus for **identifying** and **nurturing** talent.

The **Australian Institute of Sport** (AIS) opened in 1981 and provided Australian athletes with world class training facilities. The mission statement of the AIS was to serve the elite athletes, but not miss out on the grass roots, as was reflected in the Australian TID programme.

The success of the AIS programme can be judged by the fact that at the 1992 Barcelona Olympics, Australia won 27 medals, including seven gold medals.

TID model Australia

Figure 9.12 shows the elite sports pathway used by the Australians to develop their talent streams.

Modified sports programme

Each Australian sport developed a junior version that developed basic skills for that sport, for example, Netta netball.

School programmes were updated with various competitive sports awards, and a stringently applied testing system was used to identify young talent. This would lead on to early selection for state and/or national squads and top class coaching.

Talent ID programmes

The Australian sports commission (ASC), based in Camberra, set up a national talent and development programme that aimed to identify potential athletes. Screening included a bank of fitness and basic body measurements to identify a best fit sport for individuals. These athletes were fast tracked into sport-specific programmes at regional and state level.

Sports clubs and regional zones

Athletes progressed into club sport, which provided a tiered system of ability. At this point athletes had the opportunity to represent their region.

State-level sport

Most sports in Australia had state-level teams, which gave the talent pool the opportunity of competing in the 'state of origin' competitions.

National Sports institutes – Australian Institute of Sport (AIS)

The state institutes were non-residential, centrally located for coaches, athletes, sport science and medical teams. In addition to the performance pathway from the modified sports programme to state level sport, the AIS provided another opportunity for potential talent to be identified.

Australian National Squad

This squad provided the elements of the Australian National teams for major events, such as the Olympic games or the Commonwealth games. Since 1998, the AIS has branched out from the central model at Canberra, to state-run facilities so that athletes can stay locally. This was led by the need to reduce funding for sport in a new world economic situation.

The AIS TID model has provided a **world best-practice** for elite athlete development and was used as a model for the development of UK talent.

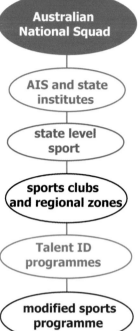

figure 9.12 – diagram of Australian TID system

Australian National Squad

AIS and state institutes

state level sport

sports clubs and regional zones

Talent ID programmes

modified sports programme

Talent development and support services in the UK

The original Talent Identification and Development programme which operated in the UK began in 1998 following the start of **lottery funding** of which sport was a 20% part. Prior to this point, there were two years of zero exchequer funding (from central taxation) and near or total bankruptcy of several sports which relied on this funding for their NGB activity.

Some of these sports based their future model on the East German and Australian models as already explained. These new UK models included:
*   Grass roots **searches for talent** at ages 12 to 14 within major cities.
*   Development of **facilities** 'within reach of one million people at 30 minutes travel'.
*   Such facilities were centred around existing facilities where possible.
*   Usage of the 2002 Manchester Commonwealth games facilities then being planned.
*   Provision of **coaching** and advice for selected groups.
*   Channeling of the selected young people into **local clubs** where it was assumed that coaching and competition could continue.
*   Development of a **UK Sports Institute** covering the scientific elements of sports training.

The embryonic UK TID model (figure 9.13)

For example, the 1998 track and field athletics system involved up to eleven hubs based in Cardiff, Bath, Birmingham, Sheffield, Manchester, Loughborough, London (Lee Valley), London (Crystal Palace), Gateshead, Belfast, Edinburgh.

Funding (from the lottery) then became available to build facilities around which the hub provision was centred. Medical support and screening, and strength and conditioning support were provided at each hub.

The main philosophy of provision was for people within **National teams** and **podium potential**. This provided the top level of the performance pyramid with the world class training environment required by the Government who were officially monitoring the whole process.

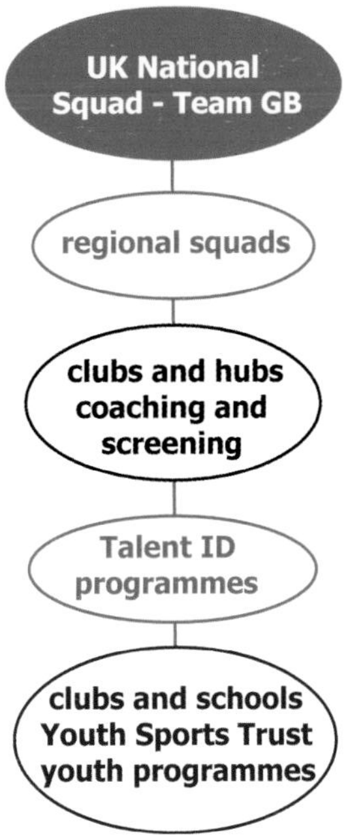

Clubs and schools

Since all children go to school, interested school staff recommended perceived talent to attend clubs, where slightly more focused activity (than in school PE lessons) occurred. Here the ideas behind training were given and hopefully received.

The **Youth Sports Trust** (YST) began to establish Sports Colleges (which were the titles given to ordinary schools which had a reputation for sporting excellence and good sports facilities) which attracted small grants for coaching. The Trust also promoted links with local clubs and coordinated use of facilities.

The target was for 2 hours per week of PE or sport for every child, and pupils within the scheme became the base of the sporting pyramid.

Talent ID programmes

The original TID programmes relied on recommendations from clubs or schools, and groups of youngsters attended hubs where available. These young people were then screened down to a manageable group who then undertook 2 years of coaching and training in World Class facilities.

For example, the Manchester Track and Field Athletics TID programme attracted 69 young people aged between 12 and 16, who undertook physical tests which screened down to 24 for the main programme. The programme included a structured **conditioning** regime and **medical** support (physiotherapy), sport **psychology** and **nutritional** advice.

Clubs and hubs

The programme relied on clubs to provide technical advice and support. Clubs (and the regional sports bodies) provided the competitive structure up to national level.

The hubs were being built and extended during this period, so that the basis of world class facilities which eventually provided the environment within which Team GB athletes could evolve.

Regional squads

Regional squads were in existence at the start of the TID programame, and the top young people were selected to attend training groups led by experienced coaches.

National squads

National squads became based at various **hubs** (using the superb facilities) depending on the sport, led by coaches employed by NGBs. Regular **residential get-togethers** provided coaching, medical screening and support services, plus psychological-behavioural assessments and nutritional advice. These national squads were exposed to **international competitions** (for example, the annual throws meeting at Halle in Germany) and were fed into UK teams with opportunities of competing in major global sporting events.

figure 9.13 – diagram of UK embryonic TID model

UK National Squad - Team GB

regional squads

clubs and hubs coaching and screening

Talent ID programmes

clubs and schools Youth Sports Trust youth programmes

The private sector - soccer and scouts academies

In soccer a strong scouting network works throughout the country looking for football talent. Their main priority is to recruit young players with a technical aptitude, movement and mental skills and temperament. Very few of these young players will make it through the academies and achieve professional contracts (page 175 for further notes).

2017 development routes from TID through to elite performance

National sporting organisations, such as **UK Sport**, have increasingly recognised the limitations with traditional TID approaches which mainly emphasised 'genetic' determinants of talent and focus on age-group success rather than senior success.

More **contemporary developmental routes** to elite performance are highly structured with multi-dimensional approaches that take into account all the variables across all disciplines that are needed by elite performers.

Figure 9.14 traces the talent pathway that most NGBs use in 2017.

Perhaps the most important element is **lottery funding**, and as long as it lasts, it should sustain UK Sport programmes. Recently (2017), the sale of lottery tickets has fallen, resulting in decreased budgets for home countries.

The provision of funding (overseen by Sport England and the other home country Sports Councils) depends on the performance of a sport in the latest Olympic Games or World Championships according to the formula set out in the **Whole Sport Plans** proposed by the NGBs of the individual sports (page 174).

In the case of athletics, the gradual fall off of funding has led to the reduction of hubs to one centralised facility based at Loughborough University (figure 9.15) which is almost exclusively only available to those athletes in the National Squad who have achieved the top status.

At Loughborough, **medical** back-up, sport **psychology** advice, and **accomodation** and **life-style** support are provided to the athletes, as well as professional **coaching** and access to the best **training facilities** in the country.

The remaining 7 English hubs still exist and are mostly available to **regional** and club groups for training. The Welsh, Scottish and Northern Irish hubs continue to support athletes who are at elite **Commonwealth Games** level.

UK Sport and the respective home countries have far greater financial control over NGBs than in the past. Lottery funding is the mainstay in the development routes of the Performance Pathways, and as a result of Whole Sport Plans and NGBs (page 174), **Talent and Performance Pathways** have become far more uniform in structure and centralised in control.

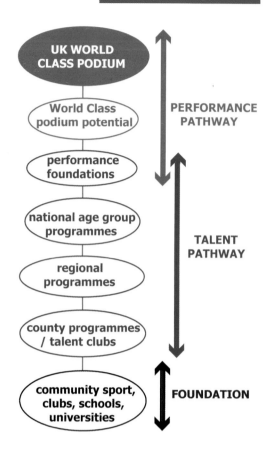

figure 9.14 – UK sport talent pathway 2017

figure 9.15 – Loughborough University HIPAC

Organisations providing support and progression from talent identification to elite performance

The providers of excellence in sport are mainly:
- The Government **Department for Culture, Media and Sport.**
- **UK Sport**.
- **Sport England**.
- **British Olympic Association**.
- **Disability Sport England**.
- **British Paralympic Association**.

Organisations providing support

Figure 9.16 depicts the organisations involved in UK Sport.

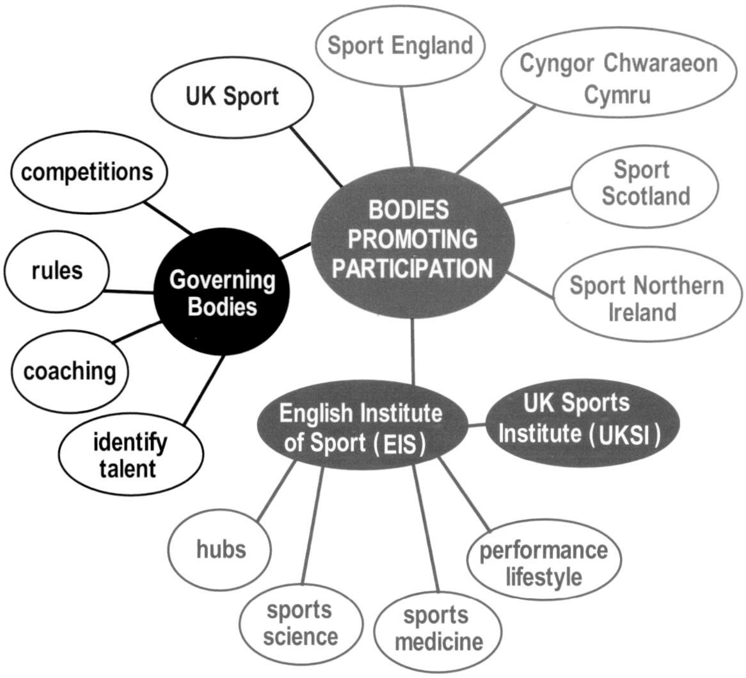

UK Sport

- UK Sport is an agency that operates under **government** direction.
- The primary role of UK Sport is to strategically invest **National Lottery** and **Exchequer** income to maximise the **performance** of UK athletes in the Olympic and Paralympic Games and the **global events** which precede them.
- Decisions are made on a **four year basis** wherever possible to cover a complete Olympic or Paralympic cycle but are focussed on an **eight year performance development mode**l.
- Success is measured by the **medals won**, the number of medallists developed, and the quality of the systems and processes in place to find and support the nation's most promising **future champions**.

To achieve this UK Sport invests around 70 per cent of its income through two channels:
- **Central funding** for sporting **National Governing Bodies** (NGBs), enabling them to operate a **World Class Programme** (WCP – more detail on page 172 onwards).
- Ensuring athletes have access to outstanding support personnel and training environments to prepare them to compete against the best in the world.
- Funding is in the shape of an **Athlete Performance Award** (APA). This award, funded by National Lottery income, is paid directly to the athletes and contributes to their living and sporting costs.
- UK Sport also runs a number of world leading centralised **strategic** support services including the development of **world class coaches** and **talent identification** campaigns to fast track future medallists in to the right sports.

- The **UK Sport coaching team** seeks to ensure the delivery of quality coaching to athletes on **UK Sport's World Class Performance Pathway**, a system devised to identify, develop and refine talented British athletes.
- To achieve this, the **UK Sport World Class Coaching Strategy** must deliver targeted and innovative programmes specific to the needs of world class coaches.
- Coaching (figure 9.17) is one of a number of key elements of the high performance system, and alongside other key performance support services such as **Sports Medicine** and **Sports Science**, **Performance Lifestyle** and **Research** and **Innovation**, plays acrucial role in ensuring the ongoing success of British athletes.

figure 9.16 – bodies promoting participation

Sport England

Cyngor Chwaraeon Cymru

UK Sport

competitions

Sport Scotland

BODIES PROMOTING PARTICIPATION

rules

Governing Bodies

Sport Northern Ireland

coaching

identify talent

English Institute of Sport (EIS)

UK Sports Institute (UKSI)

hubs

sports science

sports medicine

performance lifestyle

figure 9.17 – sports coach UK

sports coach UK
The National Coaching Foundation

Great Coaches...Great Sport

UK Sport

- UK Sport works in conjunction with partners, such as the English Institute of Sport (EIS), by providing trained and accredited **Performance Lifestyle** practitioners to work with athletes to develop the necessary skills needed to cope with the unique demands of being an elite performer.

- **Lifestyle Support** is designed to support, advise and mentor talented athletes in managing their personal development and lifestyle.
- **Performance Lifestyle** aims to help the individual to develop skills to effectively manage all their commitments including sport (training and competition) and non-sport (family, education and employment).

UK Sports Institute (UKSI)

UKSI provides world class facilities and coordinated support services. For example, the National Sports Centre at Bisham Abbey, where GB women's hockey (figure 9.18) is based.

Its **Athlete Medical Scheme** provides the UK's top Olympic and Paralympic athletes with **free medical care**. It also organises and sponsors world class coaching conferences, which present the UK's top coaches with opportunities to gain new insights and skills to develop future World, Olympic and Paralympic Champions.

UK Sport and UKSI devolve their regional responsibilities into the Home Country Institutes, for example, the **English Institute of Sport** (EIS).

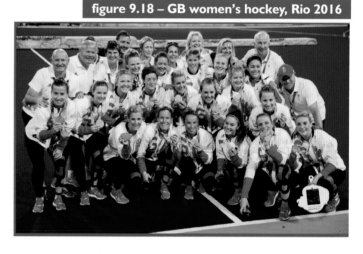

figure 9.18 – GB women's hockey, Rio 2016

National Institutes of Sport - English Institute of Sport (EIS)

The EIS aims to develop and produce performers at the **elite level** of the sport development pyramid, and who will therefore become part of the lottery funded **World Class Programme** (figure 9.19).

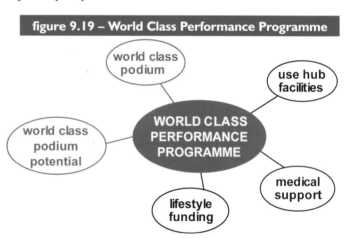

figure 9.19 – World Class Performance Programme

World Class Performance Programme (WCPP)

Funded by the National Lottery through UK Sport, the WCPP selection is based upon the potential to win medals at an Olympic or Paralympic Games and has two distinct levels:

World Class Podium (WCP)

WCP supports sports and athletes with realistic medal capabilities at global events.
This group of elite athletes should be standing on the medal podium at the next world or global games for their sport.

World Class Podium Potential (WCPP)

WCPP supports sports and athletes at the stage of the pathway immediately beneath WCP, who have demonstrated realistic medal winning capabilities for future Olympic or Paralympic Games. Athletes at WCPP level are typically four to six years away from the podium.

Membership of a WCP group or National Squad carries great intrinsic and extrinsic esteem (in terms of adulation from the press and people who follow the sport) and ensures high **motivation** to succeed.

EIS has a network of world class services that support athletes on the WCP.

Regional multi-sport hub sites

- The 'hubs' (multi-sports High Performance Centres) provided by the Institutes of Sport for elite sportspeople, are intended to be located within 1 hour travel time of a million people, and 30 minutes travel time for 250,000.
- What is happening is that Governing Bodies are insisting that members of the World Class Performance groups locate themselves near to a hub, so that coaching and medical support can also be provided simply and at less cost.
- For example, UK Athletics have created their national hub for elite athletes at Loughborough University (figure 9.15, page 170).
- An evolving network of **satellite centres**.

Lifestyle funding

- The **Performance Lifestyle Programme** which provides supplementary career and education advice.
- The EIS's talent development work aims to identify, recruit and progress the most promising young athletes and put in place the systems, pathways and support to facilitate their transition from **talented junior** to **elite international performer**.

Sports science and medical support systems.

- Top quality support by **strength and conditioning** specialists, medical support teams such as **physiotherapist** and **sports massage** personnel (figure 9.20).
- **Sports science** specialists, and sport psychology experts assist and advise on most situations facing the aspiring talented performer.

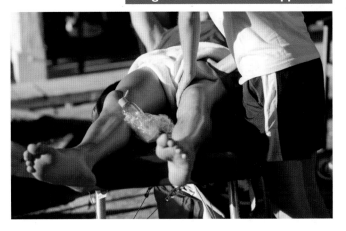

figure 9.20 – medical support

The main point of this activity is to provide a **worry-free environment** for the sportsperson to train for up to **6 hours per day for 6 days of the week** (allowing for some rest and recovery time).

In terms of sporting excellence, pre-supposing an individual has the talent to achieve excellence, then he or she must have the **opportunity** provided by facility **provision** near enough to be feasible for regular **travel**.

National Governing Bodies of Sport

NGBs are tasked with **overseeing** their sport and **organising** their existing and future direction.
These bodies are responsible for:
- Establishing the **rules**.
- Organising **national competitions**.
- **Coaching** within each individual sport.
- Selecting individuals for **funding**.
- Picking **teams** for **international** competition.

NGBs, together with local partners, are working together to create a new **satellite club** on each school setting, linked to an existing community 'hub' club, and run by coaches and volunteers from that hub club.

By being located on a school site, the satellite club is within easy reach of young people, but is distinct from school physical education as it is run by community volunteers.

Sports clubs

Sports clubs **affiliate** to NGBs and provide opportunities for young talent to gain **competitive experience** in leagues and national competitions.

Most sports clubs nurture their talent, offer financial concessions, provide quality **coaching** and services to develop their young athletes. For example, athletics' clubs charge as little as £2.00 to use a **stadium facility**, **equipment** plus **coaching**. In contrast other sport clubs, such as tennis and golf, charge for coaching and often make it financially inaccessible for the many who do not have enough disposable income. NGBs operate within the **international governing body** umbrella, for example, the **IAAF** for athletics, and **FIFA** for soccer.

Whole Sport Plans and NGBs

Whole Sport Plans are the delivery contract between **Sport England** and each of the 46 funded **National Governing Bodies** for Sport (NGBs). Each NGB is required to produce a whole sport plan which should include everything relating to its particular sport, through the full range of abilities from **participation** at the basic level, to **elite** level.

The plan must state how that sport will achieve Sport England's '**start, stay and succeed**' objectives, and use 60% of NGB **funding** on the **14-25 year old age group**. The intention is to create a sporting habit for life.

To be eligible for Whole Sport Plan funding, NGBs must also meet high standards of **governance** and **financial control**. Sport England has invested £493m into 46 sports between 2013 and 2017. Payment is by results, with withdrawal of funding to governing bodies that fail to deliver agreed objectives.

Of the £22 million received by UK Athletics, Sport England allocated £8.8 million of the total investment for UK Athletics to get more people involved in informal running. **Park run** is an example of a successful grassroots scheme which satisfied this criteria.

figure 9.21 – Dina Asher-Smith

UK Athletics wants to increase the number of talented athletes who could go on to elite and world class level (figure 9.21 of **Dina Asher-Smith** who went from bag carrier in London 2012, to fifth in the Rio Olympics 2016) by focusing on increasing and enhancing **coaching**, as well as improving the domestic competition opportunities for talented **disabled** athletes.

Talent development and support services

Investment in elite sport within Britain has increased considerably since 1996. If such investment is to have a positive impact on British sport, it is apparent that some of it must be targeted towards athletes that have the greatest potential of producing successful performances at major international events.

There are two predominant methods that broadly capture athletes who are currently identified within sport:

- **Natural selection** is aimed at identifying talented individuals that are already participating within a sport due to the recognition of performance or scouting.

- **Scientific selection** is a more proactive procedure by which identification of the talented occurs as a result of testing individuals on values that are associated with expertise within a certain sport.
    - For example, the physical, physiological and psychological attributes that affect performers within sprinting or weightlifting.
    - By using scientific research to identify the optimum environment for nurturing these criteria, resources can be targeted at those individuals that have the greatest potential of becoming outstanding performers.

Working in partnership, UK Sport, National Institutes of Sport and NGBs are tasked with **identifying** and **developing** sporting talent.

Talent identification programmes (TIPs)

- **TIP UK** is part of the World Class Programme and promotes competitions such as the British School Games with its competitive environment.
- Access to **Talented Athletic Scholarship Scheme** (TASS, government funded to support athletes on academic courses) and **Advance Apprenticeship in Sporting Excellence** (AASE) provide a structured training and development route across a number of sports for talented young athletes (aged 16-19), who have a real chance of excelling in their sport, either by competing on the world stage or securing a professional contract.

Talent Identification and development

Talent identification programmes usually **examine**, **judge** and **assess** a performer from watching them compete in a competitive situation. If the player is deemed 'good enough' they are invited to an academy for a trial period.

Academies are special training centres set up by clubs to help them develop young players.

The TID system used by **professional football clubs** involves the use of **scouts** who work for or are attached to the clubs monitoring competitive matches. The criterion typically used assesses players on their techniques, balance, personality and speed.

Once recruits have entered the club system, clubs can build up a sustainable system that enables talent transfer within an aligned pathway vision (delivering tailored solutions to build sustainable programmes) that will **develop talent** from novice to elite performers.

This process can be supported by pathway analytics as explained above, such as the **Pathway Health Check** (PHC, page 176) devised by Sport England, which reviews the athlete's progress, fitness levels achieved and whether the athlete is transitioning well between junior and senior levels.

In contrast to soccer TID, some sports aim to identify **raw talent** as a starting point, providing **physical attributes** are met. For example, the **British Rowing TID programme** identify, recruit and develop individuals with no prior experience, to become Olympic rowers through their Start programme.

Rowing and Start
There are a number of **Start centres** around the UK that are hosted by the local rowing club and provide a training base for athletes. Each Start centre employs a full time professional coach who is responsible for the recruitment and development of athletes. As part of this development all Start rowers attend regular **training** and **testing** camps to monitor their **progression**.

Potential candidates need to match the **physical criteria** required for rowing: **females** need to be 5'10 and taller and aged between 14-22 years old, and **males** 6'2 and taller aged between 14-20 years old.

Graduates of Start, including Helen Glover, Alex Gregory and Heather Stanning have gone on to win Olympic, World and European medals.

England pathway for netball – an academy development
Satellite academies (figure 9.22): County Netball Associations (on behalf of England Netball) manage and deliver about 15 sessions per year. Young netballers to learn how to train on their own, and to understand, experience and practice some of the different components required in a training programme.

County academies: County Netball Associations manage and deliver the training programmes set by England Netball (15-30 sessions per year) providing athletes with the support and skill set they need to progress to the next level of the pathway, the Regional Academy.

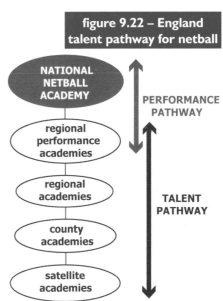

figure 9.22 – England talent pathway for netball

England pathway for netball – an academy development

Regional Academies: are located across the country and operate year round individualised training environments for athletes, delivering between 3-4 hours per week of coaching. There will be up to 20 athletes in each of the Regional Academies, some of whom will also attend National Academy training and may be part of the U19/U17 England Squads.

Regional Performance Academies: are located across the country and operate year round individualised training environments for athletes, delivering between 5-7 hours per week of coaching. There will be up to 20 athletes in each of the Regional Performance Academies, some of whom will also attend National Academy training and may be part of the U19/U17 England Squads.

The **National Academy** operates via centralised and weekend camps, bringing together the best U17 and U19 players in England for extra coaching and training. It also provides athletes with an opportunity to access similar support services that are available to senior athletes, for example, individualised strength and conditioning programmes, on-site physiotherapy, performance lifestyle and medical services.

Prior to tours and Netball Europe, U19 and U17 squads will be selected from the National Academy.

Long-Term Athlete Development (LTAD)

LTAD is a model used by majority of NGBs in the UK that was developed by Istvan Balyi in 2001. For example, figure 9.23 outlines the six stages of the late specialisation model. The philosophy of this LTAD model is as follows:
*   It aims to **retain** athletes for life as well as develop them.
*   It hopes to match desire and talent of a performer to an appropriate training environment.
*   In turn, this should lead to increased **retention** and increased **success**.
*   It hopes to establish a **clear development pathway** for athletes.

The effectiveness of TIPs

*   Recruiting talented athletes on such schemes increases the chances of producing **more medals** on the world stage.
*   Gives talented athletes considerable material benefits, **financial support**, including time to train, access to **professional coaches** who provide highly structured training programmes, and the use of top **facilities**.
*   Assess to high tech sports science and **sports medicine therapies**.
*   Promotes the use of a system which is **scientifically** based in terms of screening, training, diet and sports medicine.
*   Talented youngsters are directed towards sports that most suit their **strengths**.
*   Selection is based on **natural talent** and not socio-economic background, thus ensuring equal opportunities to the talent pool.

Disadvantages of using TIPs

*   Selectors/scouts need to be able to look beyond the immediate success and characteristics, and look at the components such as age-related speed and balance, which are better predictors of potential performance.
*   There is the possibility that **late developers** are not spotted.
*   Early versus late specialisation needs to be considered on an individual basis.
*   Talented athletes have **no guarantee** of realising their potential. They could get injured on the way.
*   Identifying future potential is difficult, as predictions are being made regarding how well an athlete may develop, rather than just assessing their current ability.
*   **Growth** and **maturation** have a marked effect on an athlete's ability at a given time, and need to be taken into consideration.

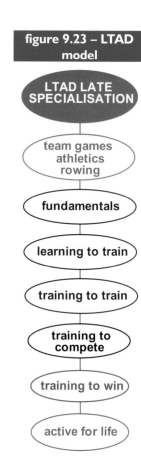

figure 9.23 – LTAD model

Disadvantages of using TIPs

- Talented individuals that are effective at a young age will not necessarily be the same ones that are effective in future years.
- For example, **Michael Jordan** (figure 9.24), was dropped from his junior high school team and went on to become one of the greatest players of all time.
- Towards the end of adolescence, late developers often surpass and become better athletes than early developers.
- A sports person's **attitudes** and **psycho-behavioural** characteristics are difficult to detect in a trial situation, and so these characteristics should be monitored from within the development programme.
- From recruiting many talented athletes, statistics show that only a few athletes reach elite performance level.
- Such TID programmes are **expensive** to run and are very inefficient in terms of creating global successes.
- There are only a **finite number of talented individuals** and the more popular sports may attract the best from this talent pool.
- For example, UK rugby has an established high profile that attracts tall strong players that could be good throwers.

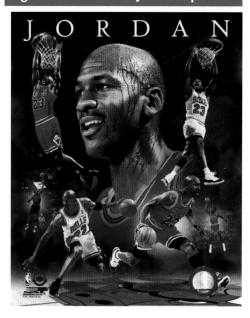
figure 9.24 – Michael Jordan superstar

EIS Performance Pathways

Performance Pathways build and sustain highly effective systems for talented athletes to ensure success at future Olympic and Paralympic Games.

The EIS Performance Pathways work in partnership with UK Sport World Class Programmes to identify and develop talented athletes and to construct the underpinning support systems through the following four work areas:

- **Pathway Frontline Technical Solutions**: delivery of tailored solutions to identify and develop talented athletes that meets the needs of each individual sport such as talent recruitment, talent transfer and development of curriculums.

- **Pathway Education**: provision of educational opportunities for development of coaches and managers covering topics unique to the elite developing athlete.

- **Pathway Analytics**: the use of diagnostic tools that robustly measure and benchmark the effectiveness of their performance pathway. This includes the **Performance Pathway Health Check** (PHC) which provides a support system that provides a set of procedures that can be used to review current systems and practices which support the development of world class athletes and future medal winners.

- **Pathway Strategy**: assists individual sports to develop and implement an aligned pathway vision and strategies from foundations level to elite podium level.

EIS initiative

An example of an EIS initiative is the **Army Elite Sports Programme** (AESP) - a joint collaboration with the British Army and UK Sport. Launched in 2014 ASEP aims to identify future Olympic medallists for the Tokyo 2020 Olympics and beyond (figure 9.25). The AESP is funded by a £1.4m donation the British Army received for providing some of the security at the London 2012 Olympic and Paralympic Games.

figure 9.25 – soldiers practise shooting

In terms of impact, the EIS Performance Pathways have worked in partnership with 20 Olympic and Paralympic sports, over 100 world class coaches, run 12 national athlete recruitment campaigns and assessed over 7000 athletes.

The UK is keen to promote **sport participation** for many reasons: **health** benefits, **societal** benefits and as a feeder to sporting **excellence**.

Practice questions

1) Comment on how the future of sport may be affected by the developments in technology. — 6 marks

2) Sports are a form of entertainment. How have contemporary technologies enhanced the entertainment value for both live and armchair spectators? — 5 marks

3) a) What is meant by the term 'pay-per-view? — 1 mark

   b) Briefly describe how pay-per-view has grown over the past decade. — 3 marks

   c) Discuss the advantages and disadvantages of the development of specific sports media packages. — 6 marks

4) a) Differentiate between excellence and talent. — 2 marks

   b) Describe some of the personal factors needed for the development of sporting talent. — 4 marks

5) a) What is talent identification and what strategies are currently in place to develop it in the UK. — 6 marks

   b) Discuss the effectiveness of talent identification programmes within the UK. — 6 marks

6) Which organisations are concerned with developing excellence in the United Kingdom? — 4 marks

7) What are the core elements of the World Class Programme and what are the main aims of each one? — 6 marks

8) What is meant by Sports Science and what contribution can it make to the development of excellence in sport? — 4 marks

9) Describe the developments in either East Germany **or** Australia which led to their success in subsequent Olympic Games. — 5 marks

10) Describe a talent identification programme implemented by a UK governing body of a sport. — 5 marks

11) Explain how the structure of sporting organisation in the UK is able to develop talent. — 5 marks

12) There are two methods of talent identification: natural selection and scientific selection. Define and explain positive and negative aspects for each method. — 6 marks

13) Describe the administrative system (institutes of sport) underpinning elite sport in the UK and account for its structure. — 6 marks

Practice questions

14) Briefly identify and describe what you think UK Sport is doing to satisfy the needs of elite British performers.   4 marks

15) a) One of the key roles of National Governing Bodies is to produce a Whole Sport Plan. Outline the key features of a Whole Sport Plan.   3 marks

    b) Select a sport and explain how this NGB has implemented a Whole Sport Plan.   3 marks

16) Early identification of talented individuals is considered increasingly important. Discuss the personal factors required to support progression from talent identification to elite performance.   15 marks.

17) What does TASS stand for and how does it help to develop sporting talent?   3 marks

18) Discuss the role of National Agencies in the development of an elite performer.   8 marks

19) The English Institute of Sport (EIS) aims to develop and produce performers at the elite level of the sport development pyramid. How does the EIS achieve these aims?   8 marks

20) The UK World Class Programme that supports elite athletes, relies on the services of the three main areas of sport science, namely physiology, sport psychology and biomechanics. Discuss the ways in which an elite athlete can use these services to improve his or her sporting performance?   15 marks

21) Models of an athlete development programmes, such as the Long-term Athlete Development (LTAD), were developed by Istvan Balyi in 2001. What is the philosophy behind such models?   3 marks

Answers link: http://www.jroscoe.co.uk/downloads/a2_revise_pe_edexcel/EdexcelA2_ch9_answers.pdf

Edexcel A Level Physical Education Examination Paper

The A level examination structure consists of:

- Two papers, one of 2 hr 30 min (component 1), the second 2 hours (component 2).
- Component 1 paper is worth 140 marks, and component 2 paper is worth 100 marks.
- Each paper includes short and 15 mark extended questions.

Component 1, Scientific Principles of Physical Education (9PE0/01)
- Topic 1: Applied Anatomy and Physiology.
- Topic 2: Exercise Physiology and Applied Movement Analysis.
Biomechanics is embedded within the content of Topics 1 and 2.

Component 2, Psychological and Social Principles of Physical Education (9PE0/02)
- Topic 3: Skill Acquisition.
- Topic 4: Sport Psychology.
- Topic 5: Sport and Society.

Our answers to short and extended practice questions (located at download link www.jroscoe.co.uk/downloads/a2_revise_pe_edexcel/) have been presented in bullet format to enable clear identification of the point being made.

Bullet point responses can be used when command words 'state', 'name', 'identify' and 'list' have been used. Otherwise, you must write your answers in continuous prose and paragraphs.

It is advisable to sketch out a short plan (such as a spider diagram) for the extended questions.

Edexcel Assessment objectives for A Level Edexcel Physical Education are included in the introduction to the questions and answers electronic file at www.jroscoe.co.uk/downloads/a2_revise_pe_edexcel/

It is important that you use correct terminology, accurate knowledge and its application, supported by relevant examples in sufficient detail, when answering a question.

Key command words used in examination papers

Your first task when answering a question is to understand what the question is actually asking. Underline the key command words (within the question) and its interpretation, to maintain focus in your answer.

Advantages and disadvantages
Clear statement of why one condition is better that another. Would normally need justification and/or qualification relevant to the question.

Analyse
Break down into component parts and identify their characteristics.

Apply
Using the information provided, link it directly to practical and relevant situations within sport.

Assess
Judge the relevance and accuracy of information provided.

Calculate
Be able to enumerate and evaluate data in numerical form.

Characteristics
Common, agreed factors for a situation, structure or process.

Comment
Present a written evaluation of the worth of a situation in the context of sport or physical education.

Compare
Identify similarities and or differences between two or more situations.

Consider
Look at the information given and give an opinion as to its worth in its context.

Contrast
Identify differences and draw attention to the significance of these differences.

Define/What is meant by....?
Formal and precise description frequently of a technical term/less formal by definition.

Describe
Use of quantitative or qualitative information to explain a statement or a relationship between factors. This term is maybe qualified as 'briefly describe'. Examples are frequently used.

Differences
A comparison between two states in the question. You should be precise and not be tempted to wander.

Discuss
Presentation of both sides of an argument, seeking an opinion based on knowledge and analysis with a justified conclusion.

Evaluate
Estimate the worth of something either qualitatively or numerically quantitatively.

Explain
Justification beyond simple statement or descriptions required (the why). Will frequently require examples, sometimes qualified as explain briefly. Consider number of marks allocated.

Give
Provide an answer from recall.

Identify and explain
Linking of cause/problem and effect/solution. Marks awarded only if links are made.

Interpret
To explain and translate information into a simpler form.

Justify
To explain based on evidence or detailed examples, the accuracy of a statement or opinion. The more detail the better.

List
A number of points or features, frequently only a single word. No description required.

Name
No explanation required or credited. Will normally require use of a degree of technical language. One or two words.

Outline
Briefly state a plan of a situation.

Plot, Sketch and Label
Used for graphical presentation. For a sketch, graph paper is not required. Important factors are correct labelling of axes and shape of graph. Plotting requires the use of appropriate scales on axes and accurate plotting points.

Principle
Theoretical concept underpinning a practical example.

State
Express clearly and briefly.

Suggest
More than one option available which require a justification linked to a question. Not to be answered from pure recall.

INDEX

INDEX